SELF-ACTUALIZATION
AND
SPIRITUAL SELF-REGENERATION

Other Theosophy Trust Books

- The Bhagavad-Gita and Notes on the Gita
by WQ Judge, Robert Crosbie, Raghavan Iyer, HP Blavatsky

- Theosophy ~ The Wisdom Religion
by the Editorial Board of Theosophy Trust

- Mahatma Gandhi and Buddha's Path to Enlightenment
- The Yoga Sutras of Patanjali
- Meditation and Self-Study
- Wisdom in Action
- The Dawning of Wisdom
by Raghavan Iyer

- The Origins of Self-Consciousness
in *The Secret Doctrine*
- The Secret Doctrine, Vols. I and II
- The Key to Theosophy
- The Voice of the Silence
- Evolution and Intelligent Design
in *The Secret Doctrine*
by H.P. Blavatsky

- The Ocean of Theosophy
by William Q. Judge

- Teachers of the Eternal Doctrine
by Elton Hall

- Symbols of the Eternal Doctrine
by Helen Valborg

SELF-ACTUALIZATION
AND
SPIRITUAL SELF-REGENERATION

BY

RAGHAVAN IYER

THEOSOPHY TRUST BOOKS

NORFOLK, VA

Self-Actualization and
Spiritual Self-Regeneration

Theosophy Trust books may be ordered through Amazon.com, CreateSpace.com, and other retail outlets, or by visiting:

http://www.theosophytrust.org/online_books.php

ISBN-13: 978-0-9992382-0-2
ISBN-10: 0-9992382-0-5

Library of Congress Control Number: 2017950339

Printed in the United States of America

O nations undivided,
O single people and free,
We dreamers, we derided,
We mad blind men that see,
We bear you witness ere ye come that ye shall be.

. . .

Rise, ere the dawn be risen;
Come, and be all souls fed;
From field and street and prison
Come, for the feast is spread;
Live, for the truth is living; wake, for night is dead.

Algernon Charles Swinburne

The future, philosophers tell us, will never resemble the past. The future is indeed much larger than the past. If one takes man's age for about twenty million years and puts it into a twenty-four hour scale, six thousand years of recorded history do not amount to half a minute. Who is entitled, on the basis of what we already know about the age of man, to set limits on the future? When people set limits on the future, history is finished for them, but not for others. There are many people today who are willing to cooperate with the future, who are not threatened by the universal extension of the logic of the American Dream to the whole of humanity, and who are also willing, despite past mistakes, to persist and to continue to make experiments in the use of space and time and energy. One day, maybe even in our lifetime, perhaps around the year 2000, there might well be those who, remembering these trying times of subtle pioneering in the surrounding gloom, could say without smugness:

> We dreamers, we derided
> We mad, blind men who see
> We bear ye witness ere ye come
> That ye shall be.

Lobero Theatre, Santa Barbara
October 20, 1975
Raghavan Iyer

CONTENTS

INTRODUCTION

The feeling that something is vaguely wrong with contemporary life and society is no secret for many people. The physicist Steven Weinberg famously remarked that the more we learn of the universe, the more meaningless it seems to be. Most people find this view philosophically and psychologically unacceptable, since human lives are saturated with value, and they seek meaning in those lives. Weinberg's view was given sharp focus by the Existentialists of the mid-twentieth century, exemplified by Albert Camus and Jean-Paul Sartre, wherein the world is absurd and we are left to invent meaning without any support from nature. Yet the cognitive dissonance between an allegedly meaningless universe and humanity's quest for meaning and value cannot be satisfied or dispelled by such a perspective. The void left by such a perspective results in distressed mental, moral and physical conditions. At the turn of the millennium, a best-selling book was titled *Plato Not Prozac*, reflecting a suspicion that human life cannot be made meaningful by the right psychiatric chemical cocktail aimed to reconcile one to an empty conformity, and that some degree of philosophical reflection is needed for a fulfilling life. Deep within each human being is the conviction that there is value and meaning in the ways we choose to live, and thoughtful people are justified in the quest to find them.

For those who were present at the Lobero Theatre in Santa Barbara, California on October 20, 1975, Professor Iyer's lecture on "Self-Actualization" – from which the first essay in this book, "The Self-Actualizing Man" was produced – profoundly echoed a similar talk he gave in 1952 as President of the Oxford Union at Oxford University. "Self-actualization" represents a concept derived from Humanistic psychological theory, especially from the theory championed by Abraham Maslow that self-actualization represents the growth of an individual toward fulfillment of the highest need in human life, that of meaning. Maslow, an American psychologist of the mid-twentieth century best known for his theory of psychological health, recognized that the quest for meaning in life is innate in human beings—that we are "hardwired" for self-actualization - and that we must fulfill our human needs in a rough order of priority, culminating in self-actualization. Without setting a hard-and-fast definition of "self-actualization", Maslow circumscribed the concept by listing the 12 most important characteristics of the self-actualizing person, which Prof. Iyer brilliantly re-states in his essay. Ever the regenerator and synthesizer of ancient, classical wisdom with contemporary knowledge, Professor Iyer spoke to the hearts of all, rekindling that hidden flame that inspires the listener to step outside of oneself to grasp the timeless teaching of the dignity of being human.

In these articles, Raghavan Iyer boldly addresses this quest for human meaning. Between 1975 and 1989, he printed the Theosophical journal *Hermes* (published in Santa Barbara, CA), which explored the psychological, philosophical and mystical traditions of West and East; each of the essays in this book are drawn from that journal. These essays cover many topics, and often they round on the malaise of our times, bringing clarity and insight to the issues of self and relationships with others and the world. In doing so, he invites us to rethink our culturally indoctrinated and limited concepts of who and what we are, what the 'I' is, and what we are capable of becoming. His message is that we are, in reality, more than we assume we are and that realizing that truth involves critical renewal in thought, feeling and action. These essays present a radical revision of what we are as humans—individually, together, and as part of the whole universe—from many perspectives, drawing on ancient and modern sources of understanding and in the light of Theosophy.

These essays contain the profound possibilities of human nature and life within a global and universal context, yet they equally contain practical steps for the exploration of oneself and for growth toward richer being and greater understanding. The pervasive sense of inadequacy that infects a narrow, fearful, ego-centered consciousness is neither the fate of each human being nor an excuse for not taking tentative, practical steps toward self-actualization, toward becoming what we can be and, in truth, ultimately are.

Though presenting a vision of what we are and can come to practically embody, these articles do not demand or expect blind acceptance or belief. Rather we are given suggestions for taking a journey of discovery that promises to regenerate our sense of self and transform our experience of living and of the world. Drawing on philosophy and psychology, they show that humanity has always had ways of both discovering value and determining meaning in life. The isolating sense of separation from one another and from the larger world can abolished even while one's autonomy and self-sufficiency are strengthened. But this regeneration cannot be done without clearly thinking about the self and what it is. To do that requires critical distance from what we assume ourselves to be and reflection on what our experience actually tell us when stripped of mental preconceptions and culturally accepted presuppositions.

This book invites us to undertake that self-initiated journey. And it shows that the journey is rich with possibility at every step, turning away from the past and looking to the future for each individual and for humanity as a whole.

Prof. Elton Hall

Ithaca, NY September 2017

****

NOTE: All of the articles and readings in this work can be found in their original forms on the Theosophy Trust website at https://www.theosophytrust.org/. Editor, Theosophy Trust

THE SELF-ACTUALIZING MAN

The contemporary image of the self-actualizing man arose in the context of the broader concern among humanistic psychologists with a bold new departure from the pathological emphasis of a great deal of psychoanalytic literature since Freud. It is only when we see this model from a philosophical, and not merely from a psychological, standpoint that its affinities with classical antecedents become clearer. The distinction between the philosophical and psychological standpoints is important and must be grasped at the very outset.

The philosophical standpoint is concerned explicitly with the clarification of ideas and the removal of muddles. It seeks to restore a more direct and lucid awareness of elements in reality or in our statements about reality or in what initially seems to be a mixed bundle of confused opinions about the world. It is by sorting out the inessential and irrelevant that we are able to notice what is all too often overlooked. The philosopher is willing to upset familiar notions that constitute the stock-in-trade of our observations and opinions about the world. By upsetting these notions he hopes to gain more insight into the object of investigation, independent of the inertia that enters into our use of language and our ways of thinking about the world. By giving himself the shock of shattering the mind's immediate and conventional and uncritical reactions, the philosopher seeks to become clearer about what can be said and what cannot even be formulated.

Most of our statements are intelligible and meaningful to the extent to which we presuppose certain distinctions that are basic to all thinking, to all knowledge, and to all our language. Although these distinctions are basic because they involve the logical status of different kinds of utterance, their implications are a matter for disagreement among philosophers. By discriminating finer points and nuances that are obscured by the conceptual boxes with which we view a vast world of particulars, the philosopher alters our notion of what is necessary to the structure of language, if not of reality. However, as Cornford pointed out in "The Unwritten Philosophy," all philosophers are inescapably influenced by deep-rooted presuppositions of their own, of which they are unaware or which they are unwilling to make explicit. The philosopher makes novel discriminations for the sake of dissolving conventional distinctions. And yet, what he does not formulate – what he ultimately assumes but cannot demonstrate within his own framework – is more crucial than is generally recognised. Whether it be at the starting point of his thinking or at the terminus, the unformulated basis is that by which he lives in a state of philosophical wonderment or puzzlement about the world.

Our statement of the philosophical standpoint refers to knowledge as the object of thought but also to the mind as the knower, the being that experiences the act of cognition, the mode of awareness that accompanies the process of thinking. It is the mind that gets into grooves, that has uncriticised reactions to the world in the form of a bundle of borrowed ideas and compulsive responses. At the same time, it is the mind in which clarification and resolution are to be sought; and in the very attempt to seek clarification through new discriminations, it comes to a point where it empties itself or cannot proceed any farther. It might also experience some sort of joyous release out of the very recognition of the fullness of an enterprise that necessarily leads to a limiting frontier.

Philosophical activity, at its best, might be characterized as a patient inching of one's way. It requires a repeated redrawing of a mental map, moving very slowly, step by step. It is most effectively pursued through a continuing dialogue among a few who respect themselves and each other enough to be able to say, "You"re a fool," occasionally and to have it said of oneself. Such men must become impersonal by refusing to hold on to any limiting view of the self and by refraining from playing the games of personalities caught in the emotional experiences of victories and defeats. It is only by becoming impersonal in the best sense that a man is ready to enjoy a collective exploration in which there are many points of view representing relative truths, in which all formulations are inconclusive, and in which the activity itself is continually absorbing and worthwhile.

Whereas the philosophical standpoint is concerned with knowledge and perception, with clarity and comprehension, the psychological standpoint requires us to talk in terms of freedom and fulfillment, of release and of integration. Psychologically speaking, a man's feeling that he is freer than he was before is very important to him. This condition involves a sense of being more fulfilled than he expected to be in the present in relation to his memories of the past and also in relation to his anticipations about the future. Since the experience of feeling freer is meaningful to a man in a context that is bound up with his self-image, the psychological standpoint must always preserve an element of self-reference. A man's false reactions or wrong ideas are important to him psychologically in a way that they would not be philosophically. Regardless of whether they are true or false, good or bad, a man's reactions to the world are a part of himself in a very real sense. If he were to surrender them lightly, he would be engaged in some sort of pretense; he might be conniving at some kind of distortion or truncation of his personality.

It may sound odd to plead in this way for the psychological importance of our self-image, because we tend to think we are crippled by a self-image that is generated by an awareness of our defects and limitations. Still, we know from our intimate relationships that to think of a person close to us in an idealized manner that excludes all his weaknesses and failings is an evasion of authenticity and may even be a form of self-love. No mental projection on a love object can be as enriching as a vibrant if disturbing encounter with a living human being. To be human is to be involved in a complex and painful but necessary awareness of limitations and defects, of muddles, of borrowed and distorting preconceptions, of antithetical and ambiguous reactions, and of much else. If we are to recognise and live with such an awareness, we cannot afford to surrender our sense of self – even if intellectually we could notice the falsity in many elements in our perceptions of ourselves and of others.

The distinction between the philosophical and the psychological standpoints may be put in this way. Whereas a philosopher is committed to an exacting and elusive conception of truth, the psychologist is concerned with the maximum measure of honesty in the existing context. Of course, one cannot maintain honesty without some standard of truth, some stable reference point from which we derive criteria applicable at any given time. On the other hand, one cannot be really sincere and determined in the pursuit of philosophical truth without being honest in one's adherence to chosen methods and agreed procedures of analysis. Clearly, philosophy and psychology are interconnected. In the earliest Eastern and Pythagorean traditions, the pursuit of wisdom and self-knowledge were merely two aspects of a single quest. Since the seventeenth century, the impact of experimental science and the obsession with objectivity and certainty have sharpened the separation between impersonal knowledge about the external world and the subjective experiences of self-awareness; and the latter have been excluded in the psychologist's concern with the constants and common variables in human behavior. Nonetheless, the psychologist has not been able to ignore the individual's need for security and his feeling of self-esteem. And certainly, in the psychoanalytic concern with honesty, the element of feeling is extremely important, independent of any cognitive criteria. To feel authenticity, to feel honesty, to feel fulfillment, each is integral to the psychological standpoint. To dispense with such personal feelings and to see with the utmost intellectual objectivity are crucial to the philosophical enterprise, although the very term "philosopher" as originally coined by Pythagoras, contained, and even to this day retains, an impersonal element of *eros*.

We must now proceed to characterize our contemporary condition both from the philosophical and the psychological standpoints. We can see immediately that, in terms of the elevating concept of the philosophical enterprise presented so far, modern man is singularly ill-suited for it. Most men do not have the time, the energy, the level of capacity, or even the will to think for themselves, let alone to think through a problem to its fundamentals. Even professional philosophers are not immune to our common afflictions – the appalling lack of time for leisurely reflection, the pace and pressures of living, the overpowering rush of sensory stimuli. In our own affluent society, the struggle for existence is so intense that (as in Looking-Glass Land) it takes all the running we can do to keep in the same place. One's nerves, our raw sense of selfhood, are constantly exposed to the tensions and frustrations of other people, and one's state of being is continually threatened by this exposure because one finds one's identity at stake. In these circumstances, it is not surprising to find that most thinking is adaptive and instrumental. The activity of the mind is largely preoccupied with the promotion of material ends or the consolidation of social status, or the gaining of some token, external, symbolic sense of achievement that is readily communicable among men. A great deal of our thinking, even the most professionally impressive, is a kind of get-by thinking.

What is the chief consequence of so much shallow thinking? For those few who are willing to question everything, take nothing for granted, and who want to think through an idea to its logical limits, it is truly difficult to function in an environment in which the emphasis is on what seems safe because it is widely acceptable. The pressure to think acceptable thoughts is double barrelled, for our thoughts may be deemed acceptable in terms of standards that are already allowed as exclusively acceptable. Acceptability is the decisive hallmark of much of the thinking of our society. Most of the time we are so anxious about how we appear to others when we think aloud our responses to any problem that we cannot even imagine what it is like to experience the intensity of *dianoia*, of thinking things through in the classical mode. To take nothing for granted, to think a problem through with no holds barred, regardless of how we come out or of our "image," requires a courage that is today conspicuous by its absence.

One might say, philosophically, that thinking things through, as demanded by the Platonic-Socratic dialectic, is bound up with that form of fearlessness which is decisively tested by one's attitude to death. We are all haunted by a feeling of pervasive futility, an acute sense of mortality, an awful fear that looms larger and paralyzes us though with no recognizable object – a fear of being nothing, a fear of annihilation, a fear of loss of identity, a perpetual proneness to breakdown and disintegration. Thus, it is enormously difficult for us to give credibility in our minds to, let alone to recognise at a distance, authenticity in any possible approximation to a state of fearlessness which dissolves our sense of time and makes a mockery of mortality. And yet this remote possibility was itself grounded by classical philosophers in the capacity of the mind to think through an idea or problem in any direction and at the same time to value the activity of thinking so much that in relation to it death and all that pertains to our sense of finality and incompleteness becomes irrelevant.

Our contemporary culture is marked not merely by a shrinking of the individual sense of having some control over one's life and one's environment but also by an increasing loss of allegiance to the collectivist notions of control transmitted by the political and social philosophies of the eighteenth and nineteenth centuries. Psychologically, we could characterize our age as the historical culmination of man's progressive inability to take refuge from his own sense of vulnerability in some compensatory form of collectivist identity. If a person in our society really feels that he cannot take hold of his life, that he has no sense of direction, that he has not enough time for looking back and looking ahead, and that all around him is rather meaningless, then it is small comfort for him to be told that as an American or as a member of the human race he can exult in the collective conquest over natural resources. The repeated ideological efforts to reinforce such a sense of vicarious satisfaction are more and more self-defeating

From a philosophical standpoint, we live in an age impoverished by the inability of men to find the conditions in which autonomous and fundamental thinking can take place. From a psychological standpoint, our social situation facilitates rather than hinders the widespread fragmentation of consciousness. In our daily lives, the flux of fleeting sensations is so overpowering that we are often forced to cope with it by reducing the intensity of our involvement with sensory data. All our senses become relatively dulled. The fact that we do seem to manage at some level may simply confirm the extraordinarily adaptive nature of the human organism. The key to our survival at a more self-conscious level may be the development of a new cunning and resilience in our capacity for selection. Although we do not notice most things while driving on the freeway, we do seem to display a timely awareness of that which threatens us. Our consciousness, though fragmented, may be sharpened in ways that are necessary for sheer survival. The really serious consequence of this is in regard to interpersonal encounters and relationships.

As early as the seventeenth century, John Locke observed that in a modern atomistic society, where large numbers of men are held together chiefly by impersonal bonds of allegiance to central authority, other men do not exist for any one man except when they threaten him or when they appear to him as persons who could be of advantage to him. In present-day society, we can see all too clearly how very difficult it is for even the most conscientious to retain a full awareness of their fellow citizens as individual agents, as persons who suffer pain and are caught up in unique sets of complexities. How much more difficult to see others even if strangers as persons with capacities and inner moral struggles that go beyond visible manifestations, as individuals who are more than the sum of all their external reactions and roles. We enter into most of our relationships on the basis of role specialization; and we are thereby driven, more than we wish, in our most primary affective encounters, by calculations of advantage or by fears of invasion and attack. A psychoanalyst from Beverly Hills has suggested recently that a marital relationship is becoming increasingly difficult to sustain because of the cumulative pressure of collective tension. Even though a loving couple may live together on the basis of shared memories and commitments and of close intimacy, their relationship may be unable to carry the burden of a host of social frustrations and milling anxieties that come from outside but that they cannot help turning against each other.

Given the sad predicament of the individual in contemporary society, it is hardly surprising to find various earnest-minded men vying with each other to diagnose our prevailing sickness, thereby adding to the collective gloom. Many of these diagnoses are identified with psychological and psychoanalytic approaches that are colored by a preoccupation with the pathological. In the context of this majoritarian pessimism, which goes back to Freud himself, it required a large measure of cool courage for a small band of humanistic psychologists to initiate an alternative mode of viewing the human situation. They have not evaded any of the stark facts of our present malaise, and at the same time they have dared to provide a democratized, plebianized version of a model that is humanistic and optimistic. In place of earlier concepts of the well-adjusted man, we now have the model of a man who, although (and rightly) not adjusted to existing conditions, is capable of exemplifying, releasing, living out, and acting out what is truly important to him as an individual.

Even though humanistic psychology has been launched in this country with the fanfare of a revolutionary movement, it has actually filled a vacuum created by the fatigue of monotony attendant on much of the so-called scientific psychology. Whatever else may be said about the behavioristic, reductionist, and mechanistic models of man, they are undeniably and invariably dull and unexciting. The boredom is pervasive. If one is so unfortunate as to surrender wholly to these current versions of secular fundamentalism, life loses its savour and lustre. As one critic has suggested, the worst thing about these depressing models of human behavior is not that they claim to be true but that they might become true.

It is highly significant that a crucial point of departure for the humanistic approach came from a man, Viktor Frankl, who was not merely reacting against current orthodoxy on intellectualist grounds. The necessity of a new way of looking at the human condition came to Frankl out of the depths of authentic suffering – out of the intense pain and mental anguish he experienced in a Nazi concentration camp. Indeed, many of the existentialist and phenomenological modes of thought fashionable in our society originated in postwar Europe. Frankl's is the uncommon case of a therapist who can write with compelling conviction about man's search for meaning. Faced with the most meaningless and unbearable forms of suffering, Frankl saw the profound significance for some prisoners of a deliberate defiance in their minds of the absurdity of their condition and the dignity of an individual restoration of meaning as a means of psychological survival. Frankl was, therefore, able to see after the war why many of his patients were unwilling to be treated as malfunctioning machines or as anxiety-driven bundles of inhibitions and neuroses. It was much more important for them to engage in the supremely private and uniquely individual act of assigning meaning to their own condition.

Frankl then took the unorthodox step of reinforcing his discovery by making a pointed reference to the classical tradition. The emphasis on the noetic (from *nous*) in man is fundamental to what has come to be called logotherapy. The classical concept of noetic insight could be explained in a variety of ways. A simple and very relevant rendering of the Platonic concept of insight is that it enables one man to learn from one experience what another man will not learn from a lifetime of similar experiences. In their capacity to extract meaning and significance out of a pattern or a medley of recurrent experiences, human beings are markedly different from each other. Such differences between men are acutely apparent at a time when "experience for its own sake" has become the slogan of an entire generation. The refusal to evaluate experiences by reference to any and all criteria is the sign of a deep-seated form of decadence. The rejection by the young of the imposed and restrictive criteria offered to them by their parents and professors is understandable, but unfortunately it leads many to surrender to the mind-annihilating dictum of "experience for its own sake."

In the classical tradition, the notion of noetic insight was exemplified in an aristocratic form. The wise and truly free man was one who had so fully mastered the meaning-experience equation that he had wholly overcome the fear of death and thereby gained a conscious awareness of his immortality. His comprehension of the whole of nature, of society, and of his own self in terms of their essential meanings placed him in a lofty position of freedom from the categories of time, space, and causality. As employed by contemporary humanistic psychologists like Frankl, the notion of insight is democratized into a basic need for survival – into a desperate and ubiquitous concern on the part of struggling human beings to grapple somehow with their chaotic and painful experiences so as to extract a minimal amount of meaning.

In the writings of Abraham Maslow we are provided a portrait of the self-actualizing man in a manner that is accessible to all and yet reminiscent of the classical models of perfection. He investigated the attitudes of a fair sample of people who displayed common characteristics in relation to the way they regarded the world and themselves, despite their differences in regard to age, sex, social status, profession, and other external conditions. From his empirical observations, he tried to derive the identifying marks of a self-actualizing man. He hazards the tentative conclusion that only about one per cent of any sample out of the population of contemporary Americans are examples of self-actualizing men. This is not to suggest that in our contemporary culture only one per cent is *capable* of becoming self-actualizing men. Presumably, the proportion of such men would increase with a greater awareness of what is involved in becoming a self-actualizing man. As a matter of fact, the figure of one per cent is ten times higher than Thoreau's figure of the one in a thousand who is a real man.

Maslow makes a simple but crucial distinction between deficiency needs and being needs. Human beings function a great deal of the time out of a sense of inadequacy. They seek to supply what they think they lack from the external world. This sense of incompleteness will be intensified by the experience of frustration in repeated attempts to repair the initial feeling of deficiency. But there is also in all men a sense of having something within them which seeks to express itself, which is fulfilled when it finds appropriate articulation. One of the important features of this distinction between deficiency needs and being needs is that the same need could function at different times as an expression of a sense of deficiency or of a sense of being. It is in his manner of coping with both his sense of deficiency and his sense of being that a self-actualizing man reveals his enormous capacity for self-dependence. Maslow tries to give an exhaustive list of characteristics of the self-actualizing man. We shall mention only a few, those that seem particularly significant in the context of our consideration of the subject.

An essential mark of the self-actualizing man is his capacity for acceptance. He accepts himself and the world. Although he may reject certain elements of the world around him, he has sufficient reasons for accepting the world with its unacceptable elements. The world he accepts includes the world of society and extends into the world of nature. It includes an acceptance of particular persons. This wide-ranging acceptance of the world is possible for a self-actualizing man because he has accepted himself. His knowledge of himself may be incomplete, and there may be elements in himself which he dislikes or wishes to discard. And yet there is meaning to a fundamental act of acceptance of oneself with all one's limitations. If the act of acceptance is real, it will be strong enough to withstand all the threats from the external world. The self-actualizing man is aware of particular and partial rejections from external sources, but he can never give up on himself or on others. His essential acceptance enables him to see reality more clearly. He sees human nature as it is, not as he would prefer it to be. He will not shut out portions of the world that are unpleasant to him or that are not consonant with his own preferences and predilections. He is willing to see those aspects of reality that remain hidden to other men to the extent to which they conflict with their own prejudices. His fundamental act of acceptance also involves negation. He negates the distortion implicit in our immediate sensory responses to the world and in the exaggerated inferences derived from such immediate responses.

A second characteristic of the self-actualizing man is his spontaneity. Having made his fundamental act of acceptance, he is simple and direct and spontaneous in his responses. He is not burdened by the anxiety of calculation or by the fatigue of tortuous rationalization. He can make an appropriate yet spontaneous response in many a context, not all the time but often enough to see beyond conventionalities. In everyday human encounters, many opportunities are forfeited because of the habit of mutual suspicion. The self-actualizing man is able to negate conventional signs and symbols because he is not obsessed with social acceptance. He is not trapped by the totemistic worship of token gestures that restrict meaningful involvement. He is thereby less vulnerable to collective modes of manipulation. Consequently, he loses his sense of striving. He continues to grow through his mistakes and failures, but he grows without anxiety and without an oppressive awareness of the opinions of others or the crude criteria of success and failure. A real sense of freedom is released by his fundamental act of acceptance and by the spontaneity of his responses to the world.

A third characteristic of the self-actualizing man is his transcendence of self-concern. He centers his attention on non-personal issues that cannot be grasped at the level of egotistic encounters. He is aware of the needs that must be met in the lives of others, in interpersonal relations and in society. He does not view the problems of human beings in terms of the mere interaction of egotistic wills. He is not exempt from the tendency to ego assertion, but he refuses to participate in the collective reinforcement of ego sickness. This form of sickness arises when the ever-lengthening shadow of the ego provides a substitute world of wish fulfillment, leaving a man with no sense of the breadth or depth of reality or of having a grip on the suprapersonal core of human problems. By seeing beyond personal egos, the self-actualizing man gives himself opportunities to extend his mental horizon and re-create his picture of the world. He can move freely between larger and more limited perspectives, thereby attaining a clearer perception in relation to any problem of what is essential and what is not.

With an enlarged perspective there emerges a capacity for cool detachment and an enjoyment of privacy. A man cannot attain to true freedom if he is incapable of enjoying his own company. Many people today have become cringingly dependent on the need to interact with others, to the point of psychic exhaustion. Men are so involved in their projections of themselves in familiar surroundings that they are unable to stand back and view their activities free of egocentricism. The self-actualizing man appreciates the need for self-examination. He knows that in order to meet this need he must provide space within his time for solitude, privacy, and quiet reflection. He thus enhances his sense of self-respect and maintains it even when he finds himself in undignified surroundings or in demeaning conditions. He places his valuation of being human in a fundamental ground of being that goes beyond the levels at which he interacts with others.

The attaining of a high level of authentic impersonality strengthens in a man his independence of culture and environment. A fourth characteristic of the self-actualizing man is his very real enjoyment of a sense of autonomy. The notion of autonomy is a part of our inheritance from the Socratic concept of the individual, and it has been transmitted since the seventeenth century in modern presuppositions concerning man as a rational moral agent. But although this notion is embedded in the vocabulary of liberal, democratic theory, it has been considerably undermined by the prevailing tendency to see men as intersubstitutable, to view most acts as predictable, and to explain most human responses mechanistically in terms of instinctual drives or the functioning of systems and subsystems. It is therefore against very great odds that the self-actualizing man gives existential authenticity to the abstract notion of individual autonomy as an agent, a knower, and an actor.

He fully enjoys the activity of being a spectator, a knower, an actor, and a moral agent.

He has a sharp sense of his own individuality and of the boundaries of himself. Having boundaries is essential to the notion of self-actualization, but these boundaries will not coincide with the contours of selfhood reflected in the totality of culture-bound responses. The self-actualizing man may choose to express his individuality in the language and symbols provided by his cultural and social context, but these modes of expression will not obscure his sense of transcendence of his environment. This sense of inner space enables him to recognize more alternatives than appear on the surface and to feel himself capable of choosing meaningfully among them. He is aware of an open texture within his mind and his personality that helps him to be open to the world outside him. This awareness will take the form of a freshness that he brings to bear on his appreciation of persons and situations and of particular moments. This quality of freshness is all too rare in our everyday encounters. Particularly in our highly individualistic and competitive society, men are starved from a lack of authentic and generous appreciation of each other. The self-actualizing man would distinguish himself by his constant readiness to give unqualified appreciation and praise to other people. This does not mean that he is not capable of discrimination. The more he discovers some new and subtle facet of life that draws out his rich and free-ranging appreciation, the more he is able to bring freshness and joy to every situation. The enthusiasm that goes with freshness generates a sense of self-expansion that goes with what Freud called the oceanic feeling and what Maslow calls a peak experience. It is a sense of losing oneself in the vastness and richness of the world around us.

The self-actualizing man is, paradoxically, so secure in his efforts to find himself that he is also able to forget himself. He becomes a universal man who emancipates himself from the prison house of his personality and enters into the kingdom of mankind. The more he actualizes himself, the more he can transcend himself. In place of the sense of being "acculturated" in the stifling way associated with the localization of one's allegiances, the self-actualizing man experiences the exhilaration, the grandeur, and the nobility of being truly human. He embodies the spirit captured by Whitman in his poem "Song of the Open Road." He becomes an "encloser of continents." This will have a profound bearing on all his relationships. He will be able to relate to many different types of persons and react to a wide variety of situations with humour and compassion. He will show a shrewd perception of the relation between means and ends. His creativity will enable him to recognize opportunities for growth where other men see only limitations. He is so absorbed in what has yet to be tried and yet to be accomplished that he will have no time to brood over his past achievements and failures. He lives in that dimension of the present which points to the future.

All of this may seem rather Utopian and irrelevant to our contemporary situation, although we can see little increments of the qualities of a self-actualizing man in certain moments in our lives, and we know only too well the effects of the opposite kinds of attitudes in our daily experience.

Given this portrait or model of the self-actualizing man, we might ask how this contemporary concept differs from the classical ideal of the man who has attained to the fullness of self-knowledge. In Platonic thought, the attainment of this ideal involved a deliberate mastery of the dialectic. In the classical Indian tradition, the ideal of spiritual freedom cannot be reached without a deliberate voiding of all limited identifications and allegiances, a persistent endeavour to recapture the self-sustaining activity of an unconditioned consciousness. For the mystical quest, this means the recovery of an inward center which is full of creative potential but around which there are fluctuating boundaries. Such a rebirth is impossible without a preliminary process of dying, a dissolution of the sense of false identity, and the gaining of confidence in a new mode of awareness. The distinction between being a separate knower and having an external world to be known is gradually weakened, without sinking back into a state of mindless passivity.

It would be appropriate here to take two statements of the classical ideal. The stoic philosopher Marcus Aurelius wrote:

> This, then, remains: Remember to retire into this little territory of thy own, and above all do not distract or strain thyself, but be free, and look at things as a man, as a human being, as a citizen, as a mortal. But among the things readiest to thy hand to which thou shalt turn, let there be these, which are two. One is that things do not touch the soul, for they are external and remain immovable; but our perturbations come only from the opinion which is within. The other is that all these things which thou seest change immediately and will no longer be; and constantly bear in mind how many of these changes thou hast already witnessed. The universe is transformation: life is opinion.

In the classic Indian text on self-knowledge, *Atmabodh*, the true nature of the Self is depicted by Shankara in the following way: "I am without attributes and action, eternal and pure, free from stain and desire, changeless and formless, and always free.... I fill all things, inside and out, like the ether. Changeless and the same in all, I am pure, unattached, stainless and immutable."

Clearly, the concept of self-sufficiency given by Marcus Aurelius presupposes a particular theory about the mental processes through which the eternal transformations of the universe are reduced to static opinions. This theory is bound up with a certain view of the relation between the distorting mind and the indwelling soul, both of which are consubstantial with different dimensions of cosmic reality. Without deliberate reflection on such premises, a man cannot become a true philosopher or attain a fundamental equanimity of soul. On the other hand, our contemporary humanistic psychologists do not concern themselves with presuppositions about human nature. They do not hold any definite or formulated concepts about human essence and human potentiality or the processes involved in attaining any stated goal of human perfectibility. Instead, it is assumed that human beings act out what they think they are and thereby find out more about themselves.

Similarly, we can readily sense the vast difference in conceptual content between the contemporary model of the self-actualizing man and the classical formulation in *Atmabodh* of supreme self-affirmation. There are several complex and abstract presuppositions implicit in building a mental framework which enables a man to feel that he is essentially attributeless and beyond all conditions, while he is also partially embodied in attributes and conditions. If the contemporary model of the self-actualizing man seems to be conceptually less demanding, this is merely because it is assimilated to our everyday picture of psychological health as the absence of known forms of pathology. Humanistic psychologists like Maslow do not wish to pronounce about how the process of self-actualization takes place, partly because it could happen in many more ways than could be put in a paradigmatic scheme. It is important in its way to protect this diversity of paths and to maintain the greatest possible tolerance in regard to processes of human growth that we can hardly claim to understand. We must preserve a necessary agnosticism here.

The model of the self-actualizing man should not be seen as a static, textbook typology with which we can readily identify, thereby gaining some form of vicarious satisfaction – some form of compensatory consolation in our own current preoccupations with the varieties of human sickness. Nor should we mistake it for a model that could be elaborated by more empirical research. There is, in fact, no substitute either for the philosophical task of confronting alternative presuppositions or for the practical endeavour of singling out visible examples of maturity in the quest for self-awareness. The former is needed to stimulate our intellectual imagination, and the latter is indispensable in stirring our emotions and canalizing them in a worthwhile direction. The two functions are interrelated to a greater extent than we may suppose. By daring to unravel our presuppositions and to confront them with those derived from the classical philosophical and mystical traditions, we are in a better position to find an underpinning for that continuity of consciousness which, at some level or the other, is essential to the exemplification of a critical distance in our day-to-day encounters with the world around us.

In our attempts to move away from the treadmill of conformity and from much that is unnatural in our contemporary society, the model of the self-actualizing man could be a valuable starting point in formulating a feasible ideal for ourselves. The self-actualizing man seeks to know what to do now, and at the same time to see sufficiently beyond the present to enjoy a wider sweep, a larger perspective than what we constantly use in our competing concerns. If most pathological cases are persons with either a fixed stare or a wandering gaze, then a man who uses both eyes steadily is, by contrast, wholesome and healthy. The sense in which the self-actualizing man is using both his eyes is best understood in the context of an old tradition. The *Theologia Germanica*, for example, refers to the eye of time and the eye of eternity. It is no small thing to find any man in our society who is willing to use both these eyes "to see life steadily and as a whole."

There is indeed an even more distant yet inspiring ideal in the classical traditions of East and West. Many a mystical text refers to "the mysterious eye of the soul," which is capable of a synthesizing vision that enables the fully awakened man to use the eye of time and the eye of eternity without becoming dependent either on the ideal or on what seems real here and now. For such a man, as for the poet, "the Ideal is only Truth at a distance," but he is not infatuated with his image of the ideal to such an extent that he loses contact with the concerns of other men who need, in some sense, the illusions to which they cling at any given time.

We could honor the classical ideal without devaluing the contemporary model of the self-actualizing man. Is the difference between them simply a matter of belief, or a variation of technique, or a question of successive levels and processes of awareness? Without proposing to answer these questions, it is in the hope that the model of a self-actualizing man will not become yet another modish fad that it has here been put in the broader perspective of a hoary tradition that we have still to recover. We are perhaps now in the early stages of a long exploration that, fortunately, cannot be charted at present. What is surely more important is that as many of us as possible should share in the excitement of taking the first step, of commencing the journey inward so that we may enrich each other and respond with sympathy to those who seek our support.

Hermes, January 1976
Raghavan Iyer

THE SENSE OF SELF

Feeling, while going about, that be is a wave of the ocean of self; while sitting, that he is a bead strung on the thread of universal consciousness: while perceiving objects of sense, that he is realizing himself by perceiving the self: and, while sleeping, that he is drowned in the ocean of bliss; – he who, inwardly constant, spends his whole life thus is, among all men, the real seeker of liberation.

Shankaracharya

All the varied vestures of the incarnated human being are distinct sheaths on adjoining planes of consciousness, each with its own rates of vibration, all participating in the potency of ideation and mirroring archetypal relations. What is implied in the Vedantin association of the lower vestures with unwisdom is the false sense of separateness, the illusory stability and entitative existence that we ascribe to a form. What is the significance of the seven orifices in the human face and the thirty-three vertebrae of the spine? What is to be understood from the varying textures of the different layers of skin? Is the physical body to be analysed in terms of its constituent elements, or is it to be viewed in relation to the pulsating rhythmic movement in the heart? Such questions are rarely asked. Most human beings take for granted a haphazardly acquired and habitually retained assemblage of sensory perceptions and residues identified with a name and form which is really a static mind-image of the body. Individuals deny themselves the possibility of direct experience without the mediation of routinized anticipations or of frozen images projected upon objects. Anyone may learn to discern and comprehend the recurring patterns, resistances and responses of the body. Even more, a person may come to view the body, as the *Gita* depicts, as a nine-gated city. A person can learn to use the body as a musician wields a musical instrument, self-consciously impressing energy upon its myriad life-atoms caught up in chains of interconnected intelligence.

The body is a vast and complex matrix of interdependent centres of energy, each of which puts a human being in touch potentially, and therefore in many cases unconsciously, with everything else that exists on the physical plane. The body exists at a certain level of material density, with a biological entropy built into it, as well as a degree of homeostatic resistance to the atmosphere around. This level of resistance in the physical body enables it to maintain itself and is the basis of physical survival. Those who truly reflect upon this could make a significant difference by the deliberate and creative interaction of their own ideas and feelings. For example, while eating food, a person's thoughts, emotional states, magnetic field and inward reverence to the invisible elements of food can make a fundamental difference to the qualitative osmosis of energies transmitted to the organism. The body can be seen as a sacred instrument in rethinking one's entire relationship with the world. There is reflective intelligence at the lunar level and the astral and physical vestures are subject to various cycles and different rates of motion. These cycles are mathematical equations and patterns at the cellular level. The mathematics of the complex system that is the physical body, with all its cycles, corresponds closely to the mathematics of the galaxies and the vast cosmos. One could come to learn from the natural cycles and then from the particular bent given to them by one's own emanations, thus gaining some grasp of one's dominant anticipations and typical responses. Whoever engages in daily self-study could come to discern the distinct ways in which the body affects the mind during different portions of the day and the week, as well as the succeeding phases of the lunar month.

Shankaracharya lived at a time when ritualistic practices were widely prevalent, and many had become blindly dependent upon detailed and complex knowledge of what to do, when, during each of the many subdivisions of the day. All of this knowledge would not enable a person to get to the core of the causal body – the delusive identification through an 'I' with limiting conceptions of space and time, together with the persisting notion of oneself as the actor. Shankara taught that one must get to the root of the 'I-making' tendency – the illusory sense in which one is separate from the world which is supposed to exist as clay material for one's purpose. This false conception of selfhood becomes deeply rooted because it is pleasurable, owing to passive identification with those sensations that have pleasing responses in different parts of the body. It is reinforced in the language and the milieu of those valuations of segmented aspects of conduct which tend to routinize, making a person take experience totally for granted, just as the physical senses can lead an unthinking person to take for granted that the more solid a thing seems to the tactile sense, the more it is solid in reality. There is a radical failure to understand that the whole visible world is like a screen, hiding a vast mathematical activity, and that for all its bewildering complexity, this phenomenal realm may be reduced to certain primary relationships that archetypally correspond to the numbers between zero and ten.

By rethinking much of what one took for granted before, one could come to conceive of an exalted state such as Shankara conveyed in *The Crest Jewel of Wisdom*. In this serene state an individual would be devoid of all sense of psychological involvement in any of the desires and aims, any of the obsessions, passions, infatuations and concerns of the world, in any of the criteria of success and failure or pseudo-valuations of people generally. Furthermore, having no sense of tightness, of excessive, anxious-ridden involvement in the activities of the body, such a person begins to experience a tremendous exhilaration, a rhythmic breathing and a profound peace. It is like seeing a part of oneself carry out its natural functions, and yet remaining totally outside every kind of manifestation in which any single portion of oneself is involved. A person who reaches this stage can combine with this detachment a deep gratitude, a joyous affirmation that there is a certain value to the body as a pristine vesture. At the causal level – in what is called the *karana sarira* or causal body – fundamental ideas prevail which are often hidden to most human beings but which, if they were examined, would wipe out whole chains of thinking, complex patterns of activity over many years. They would all be eradicated by getting to the core of a fundamental idea. A person who steadily works on the plane of ideation so renovates the thought-body that it becomes possible to release self-consciously the inexhaustible potentiality of divine energy. The entry points between the causal body and the astral vesture are made more porous and, in time, the physical body may reflect and transmit the radiant joy of universal ideation.

A person may learn to live in attunement to the plane of those enlightened free men who are not captive even to the vast conceptions of space and time associated with the universe as a whole. Such a person will be ever engaged in intense meditation upon the Unmanifest, which increasingly becomes the only reality. A person who begins to see through the eyes and with the help of the illumination of the *Guru* finds that the physical body is only a dim reflector of light-energy and also provides a means of shielding the divine radiance. By extending the possibilities of human excellence to the uttermost heights of control, purification, refinement and plasticity that can be brought about by the deliberate impact of disciplined thought upon gross matter, one can revolutionize one's conception of matter. Einstein pointed out in the twenties that a lot of what is called matter simply dissolves into a prior, primordial notion of space. The body can become an architectonic pattern in space which has within its own intricate symmetry an inherent intelligence that is not transparent at the level of image and form. It has the capacity of holding, releasing and reflecting the highest elemental associations that accompany the profoundest thoughts. Nature is the great magician and alchemist. The wise man is an effortless master of lunar forces, correlations, patterns and potencies.

The critical fact for any human being as a self-conscious agent is the capacity of objectivizing, of putting upon a mental screen as an object of reflection anything, in principle, that one wishes. A human being recognizes the range of self-consciousness through a process of progressive abstraction. This includes familiarization with what looks initially like mental blankness – like pitch-black night, where there are no conventional signs, no contours or landmarks, no north or south, east or west. A person who begins to sense the depths of subtle matter will discover that what seems to be a void or darkness is in fact a rich, pulsating light-substance that is porous to the profoundest thought. Then one realizes what initially was simply a bald fact about human beings – taken for granted and therefore forgotten – that all things are mutually and vitally interrelated. Human beings are generally so conditioned by mechanical responses to the ordinary calendar and clock-time that they can hardly apprehend the immensity of the doctrine of relationality, which presupposes that the visible world is a vast psychological field of awareness. The universe exists because there are minds capable of generating conceptions that have points of common contact and thereby an outwardness and extension sustaining an entire field of consciousness. As one cannot set any limit in advance to the range and development, the possibility and the power of all the minds that exist, one cannot readily imagine what it is like to negate everything that exists, to stand totally outside it.

Initially, it is extremely difficult to imagine all of this, so the whole world is at first apprehended as so unfathomably mysterious as to engender a feeling of alienation and fear. But why should moving into more expanded states of consciousness make one afraid? Who is afraid, and afraid for what? At any given time there is a film or shadowy image that is one's false self between one's inherent capacity to make a vaster state of consciousness come alive and one's captivity to the familiar array of objects and opinions. One is like the fabled monkey which, in trying to collect nuts from a jar, held onto them so tightly that he was not able to open his hands and get any. There is an impersonal, impartial sweep to the mental vision of a Man of Meditation that simply cannot correlate and connect with, or take at face value, the common concerns of the world. It is necessary to grasp the strength and richness of viewing the universe as an interior object of intense thought which could be expanded indefinitely, eliminating self-imposed and narrow notions of identity and embracing vaster conceptions of the Self. The significance of this standpoint lies in that continuity is upheld but not formulated. Herein is the basis of indefinite expansion, of growth without hindrance. Existing frontiers of knowledge cannot provide the basis of judgement of the potential realm of the knowable. What is now known is meagre in relation to the immensity of the unknown. It is meaningful to relinquish the delusive sense of certainty to which so many people cling at the expense of an ever-deepening apprehension of relationality.

In general, human beings seem to need the illusions that sustain them. There is something self-protective in relation to all illusions. At least people are thereby helped from becoming fixated on obsessional delusions. There is even something enigmatic about why particular persons are going through whatever they endure. A great deal of human frustration, pain and anxiety, fear and uncertainty, arises from the desperate attempt to keep alive a puny sense of self in an alien world. Individuality arises only through the act of making oneself responsible for the consequences of choices, of seeing the world as capable of being affected by one's attitudes and, above all, as an opportunity for knowing and rejoicing in wisdom and for rising to the levels of awareness of higher beings. The plane of consciousness on which such beings exist is accessible to all those who are willing to stretch themselves, patiently persist in going through the abyss of gloom, and endure all trials. Infallibly, they can enter those exalted planes and experience a strong sense of fellowship with beings who at one time would have seemed inaccessible. This ancient teaching is worthy of deep reflection. Its abstract meaning pertains to the elastic relation between subject and object, subjectivity and objectivity, and their mutual relativity as illustrated in one's daily experience. A vast freedom is implicit in this no-ownership theory of selfhood. It is helpful to break up one's life into periods and patterns, to note one's most persistent ideas, ambitions and illusions, as well as those points on which one's greatest personal sensitivity lies, and to make of these an object of calm and dispassionate study, to be able to see by questioning and tracing back what would be the assumptions which would have to be true for all of these to exist. To do this is to engage in what Plato calls *dianoia*, 'thinking things through', whereby in one day a person could wipe out what otherwise would hang like a fog over many lives. There is a fusion of philosophical penetration and oceanic devotion which is characteristic of high states of consciousness. There is no separation between thought and feeling – between *Manas* and *Buddhi* – such as is ordinarily experienced.

At one time a natural reverence existed in all cultures in ritual forms which eventually became empty of significance or could no longer be made meaningful when languages were lost or philosophical conceptions were neglected. Individuals today cannot force themselves to be able to feel any of the traditional emotional responses to any single system of ritual. Human beings should creatively find their own ways of making sacred whatever it is that comes naturally to them. What is sacred as an external object to one person need not be to another. The forms of ritualization have all become less important than they were, and that is not only due to the rapid pace of change but also because of the volatile mixture of concepts and of peoples all over the world, together with a growing awareness of the psychological dimension of seemingly objective conceptions of reality. But even though there is a pervasive desacralization of outward forms, the deepest feelings of souls are unsullied by doubt. It is only by arousing the profoundest heart-feelings that one can open the door to active spiritual consciousness. There is in the heart of every person the light of true devotion, the spontaneous capacity to show true recognition and reverence. To do this demands a greater effort for some people than for others. When human beings come to understand the law of interdependence that governs all states of consciousness, their impersonal reason as well as their intense feelings will point in the same direction. It is only this single-minded and whole-hearted mode of devotion which will endure, but its focus must be upon universal well-being.

> It is not the individual and determined purpose of attaining Nirvana – the culmination of all Knowledge and wisdom, which is after all only an exalted and glorious selfishness – but the self-sacrificing pursuit of the best means to lead on the right path our neighbour, to cause to benefit by it as many of our fellow creatures as we possibly can, which constitutes the true Theosophist.

Hermes, February 1979
Raghavan Iyer

NOETIC SELF-DETERMINATION

If the general law of the conservation of energy leads modern science to the conclusion that psychic activity only represents a special form of motion this same law, guiding the Occultists, leads then also to the same conviction – and to something else besides, which psychophysiology leaves entirely out of all consideration. If the latter has discovered only in this century that psychic (we say even spiritual) action is subject to the same general and immutable laws of motion as any other phenomenon manifested in the objective realm of Kosmos, and that in both the organic and the inorganic (?) worlds every manifestation, whether conscious or unconscious, represents but the result of a collectivity of causes, then in Occult philosophy this represents merely the ABC of its science. . . .

But Occultism says more than this. While making of motion on the material plane and of the conservation of energy two fundamental laws, or rather two aspects of the same omnipresent law – Swara *– it denies point blank that these have anything to do with the free will of man which belongs to quite a different plane.*

Psychic and Noetic Action
H. P. Blavatsky

Gupta Vidya, the philosophy of perfectibility, is based upon the divine dialectic, which proceeds through progressive universalization, profound synthesis and payful integration. These primary principles are inseparably rooted in the cosmogonic archetypes and patterns of universal unity and causation. They are in sharp contrast to the expedient and evasive methodology of much contemporary thought which all too often proceeds on the basis of Aristotelian classification, statistical analysis and a sterile suspicion of intuitive insight. Whatever the karmic factors in the ancient feud between these divergent streams of thought, it is poignantly evident that their polar contrast becomes insuperable when it comes to understanding human nature. *Gupta Vidya* views the human situation in the light of the central conception of an immortal individuality capable of infinite perfectibility in its use of opaque and transitory vestures. The greater the degree of understanding attained of Man and Nature, the greater the effective realization of spiritual freedom and self-mastery. In the methodology of modern thought, however, the more sharply its conceptions are formulated, the more inexorably it is driven to a harsh dilemma: it must either secure the comprehension of Nature at the cost of a deterministic conception of Man, or it must surrender the notions of order and causality in favour of a statistical indeterminacy and randomness in Nature, thereby voiding all human action of meaning. *Gupta Vidya* not only dispels this dilemma, but it also explains the propensity to fall prey to it, through the arcane conception of two fundamental modes of mental activity. These were set forth by H.P. Blavatsky as "psychic" and "noetic" action. They refer to much more than "action" in any ordinary sense, and really represent two distinct, though related, modes of self-conscious existence. They provide the prism through which the perceptive philosopher can view the complex and enigmatic relationship between human freedom and universal causality.

All creative change and all dynamic activity in the universe are understood, in the perennial philosophy of *Gupta Vidya*, as spontaneous expressions of one abstract, pre-cosmic source symbolized as the Great Breath. In its highest ranges this is Spirit, and beneath that, it encompasses every mode of motion down to and including action on the physical plane.

> Motion as the GREAT BREATH (vide "*Secret Doctrine*", vol. i, *sub voce*) – *ergo* "sound" at the same time – is the substratum of Kosmic-Motion. It is beginningless and endless, the one eternal life, the basis and genesis of the subjective and the objective universe; for LIFE (or Be-ness) is the *fons et origo* of existence or being. But molecular motion is the lowest and most material of its finite manifestations.

Psychic and Noetic Action

Several important consequences follow from this single origin of both subjective and objective reality. For example, the strict unity and universal causality implied by the conception of absolute abstract Motion entail the basic principle transmitted from ancient knowledge into modern science as the law of the conservation of energy. In a world of finite manifestations, such as that of molecular motion, this law has immense importance. The conception of entropy is an allied principle equally crucial in understanding the particularized motions and relationships between objects having specific kinds of energy in the world as we know it. Yet this does not really reveal much about the deeper sense in which there is collection and concentration of energy, from the highest *laya* state down through the physical plane of manifestation. There is a sense in which enormous energy is held waiting to be released from higher to lower planes. Potential energy, related to the higher aspects of the ceaseless motion of the One Life, transcends all empirical conceptions based upon observable phenomena.

This virtually inconceivable scale of modes of subtle manifestation of the Great Breath has immediate and evident implications in regard to cosmogony. But it is also highly significant when applied to the subjective side of conscious existence. Whilst the laws of physical motion and energy are natural modes of manifestation of that divine Breath, no merely objective description of them can do justice to the *subjective* side of purely physical events, much less to deeper layers of human consciousness and noumenal reality. Every plane or octave of manifest existence has both its subjective and objective side, even as every plane has its own dual aspect of activity that may variously be seen as more gross or more subtle, more concrete or more abstract. This vertical dimension of existence is often spoken of as the distinction between the subjective and the objective, though this is quite a different sense of these terms from the lateral distinction applied to any particular plane. The tendency to confuse or conflate these two senses of the subjective-objective distinction is in direct proportion to the grossness or concreteness of an individual's state of consciousness. Insofar as an individual's range of consciousness is limited to constellations of objects, persons and events, it will not be capable of comprehending the notions of metaphysical subjectivity or objectivity, or of metaphysical depth.

This is crucial when considering the seemingly abrupt transition from medieval to modern thought accompanying the movement away from a vastly inflated, but exceedingly particularized, conception of the subjective realm towards an almost obsessive concern with physical objectivity. As the capricious happenings and hearsay of the "age of miracles" were gradually replaced by a rigid conception of external and mechanical order, it increasingly came to be understood that the inner life of man must also conform to universal laws. In what was a marked advance upon earlier notions of both physics and psychology, there emerged, in the nineteenth century, the explosive recognition that everything in the psychological realm is also subject to causality. This was powerfully put forward as part of a grandiose ethical scheme by George Godwin, the philosophical anarchist. Late in the nineteenth century several social scientists argued that if causality is to be applied to all phenomenal events and processes, it must also apply in some way to the world of what may be called psychic action. It must, in short, be applicable to all the states of mind experienced by human beings in bodies with brains.

It thus becomes vitally important to draw a clear-cut distinction between the mind and the brain, taking account of the subjective and objective aspects of both. In general, contemporary science has been either unwilling or unable to do this. Without this essential distinction, however, it is impossible to generate any firm basis for the notions of autonomy, self-determination, individuality, free thinking and potent ideation. Arcane philosophy begins at that precise point where an abyss has been discovered between the mind and brain. It is indeed a glaring gap, for though causality applies to both, it is difficult to discern clearly what the relationship could be between them, let alone to find exact correlates between the two parts of the distinction in terms of specific centres and elements. Without the assured ability to distinguish decisively between them, the temptation is great to deny free will altogether and succumb to a reductionistic and mechanistic view of human nature. This the occultist and theurgist must deny, in theory and in practice.

> The actual fact of man's psychic (we say manasic or noetic) individuality is a sufficient warrant against the assumption; for in the case of this conclusion being correct, or being indeed . . . the collective hallucination of the whole mankind throughout the ages, there would be an end also to psychic individuality. Now by "psychic" individuality we mean that self-determining power which enables man to override circumstances.

Psychic and Noetic Action

All human beings have some experience not only of a persisting sense of individuality, but also of an ineradicable sense of being able to separate themselves from an observable objective field They have a deep sense of being able to affect it consciously, and indeed even to control it. To dismiss so vital and universal an experience would be to betray a narrow, pseudo-philosophical prejudice towards mechanistic determinism. Not even all animals have precisely the same stimuli or reactions. Certainly, human beings in very similar environments respond quite differently to external stimuli. One cannot deny, then, that a human being can make a vital difference to his environment through his calm appraisal of it, or even through simply comparing or sharply contrasting it with something else. Either through the fugitive sense of memory or through the fervent thrill of anticipation, based upon a relaxed sense of identity projected into the past and the future, or even through heightened perceptions of the unsuspected relations between one's own circumstances and those of other beings, individuals make decisive choices among newly discovered alternatives. So long as they can ask probing questions about the degree to which they can possibly alter their mental outlook, they can truly determine for themselves, through these subtle changes of attitudes, their untapped ability to alter these circumstances. In general, such attitudes may be rather passive or defiantly resistant to circumstances. But they may also include an intelligent acceptance of circumstances rooted in a capacity for conscious cooperation with necessity. One may completely transform one's environment through rearranging elements in it, through constructive dialogue with other agents and, above all, through an inner life of daily meditation and effortless self-transcendence. Thus free will can function, and so unfolds a unitary consciousness coolly capable of deft self-determination.

Having understood all this, the main challenge is to come to a clear comprehension of the self-determining power in man and, more specifically, to understand the delicate operation of the diverse faculties of the mind in the compelling context of universal causality. In this regard, the shrewd argument of George T. Ladd concerning mental faculties is crucial. Having contended that the phenomena of human consciousness must require a subject in the form of a real being, manifested immediately to itself in the phenomena of consciousness, he proceeded to consider how that real being perceives its relationship to the activity of consciousness.

> To it the mental phenomena are to be attributed as showing what it is by what it does. The so-called mental "faculties" are only the modes of the behaviour in consciousness of this real being. We actually find, by the only method available, that this real being called Mind believes in certain perpetually recurring modes: therefore, we attribute to it certain faculties. . . . Mental faculties are not entities that have an existence of themselves. . . . They are the modes of the behaviour in consciousness of the mind.

Psychic and Noetic Action

In other words, Ladd denied that one can comprehend the real being, or unit consciousness, exclusively through those recurring modes that are associated with certain "faculties". Just as one would find the idea of a unit being, in this metaphysical monadology, incompatible with crude physical behaviourism, it is also incompatible with psycho-physical and psychological behaviourism. Put another way, the inherent power of manasic "I-am-I" consciousness transcends all patterns such as those which inhere in the volatile *skandhas.* The human being can consciously transcend all behaviour patterns. He can readily transform anything through tapping his inherent powers of volition and ideation. Ladd then concluded:

> The subject of all the states of consciousness is a real unit-being, called Mind; which is of non-material nature, and acts and develops according to laws of its own, but is specially correlated with certain material molecules and masses forming the substance of the Brain.

Psychic and Noetic Action

Full understanding of these laws, mastery over action and the capacity to coordinate the mind and brain can come only from a strong intention to attain these ends, together with a purgation of one's entire field. One cannot work with incompatible mixtures, which are inevitably explosive. One cannot infuse the potency of the noetic mind into the polluted *psyche.* One must purge and purify the *psyche* before it can absorb the higher current of transformation which is alchemical and fundamentally noetic.

The question then becomes how, in practice, one can readily recognize the subtle difference between an illusory sense of freedom and a real and valid sense of self-determination. Insofar as people are misled by everyday language and by fleeting sense-perceptions, and insofar as they have an associationist picture of mixed memories and indelible images, rendering them essentially passive in relation to mental and emotional states, they may totally fail to see that all these familiar states fall under laws of causality. They may also be unable to make significant noetic connections. For E.M. Forster in *Howards End,* "Only connect!" was the great *mantra* for those who would become wise and free. Based upon luminous perceptions of noetic connections, one must learn to see their causal chains and calmly project possible consequences of persisting patterns tomorrow, next year and in the future. One must then take full responsibility for the future consequences of participation in connected patterns. The moment one recognizes and perceives significant connections, one will see that at different times one could have made a distinct difference by the way in which one reacted, by the degree of sensitivity one showed, and by the degree of self-criticism one applied to these states. The moment a human being begins to ask "why", he demands meaning from experience and rejects uncritical acceptance or mere passivity towards anything in life, including the recognizable sequence in which mental phenomena manifest.

Through this noetic capacity to question the association and the succession of events, one can decisively alter patterns. One can thus move from an initial level of passivity to a degree of free will whilst, in the act of seeing connections and making correlations, raising questions and altering patterns. Given the Buddhist doctrine of *skandhas*, or the Hindu doctrine of *sanskaras*, each personality collects, over a lifetime, persisting associated tendencies. These persisting tendencies of thought and character are reinforced by appropriate emotions, desires and habits. Hence, the mere making of sporadic alterations in the inherited pattern of tendencies will be a poor example of free will, since over a longer period of time the pattern itself is conditioned by certain basic assumptions.

To take a simple example, as long as the will to live is strong and persistent, there is a sense in which free will is illusory. One lacks the fundamental capacity to make significant changes in one's *skandhas* or personality. This is an expression of *prarabdha* karma, the karma with which one has begun life. It is already reflected in one's particular body, one's mind, one's emotions, character and personality – and, indeed, in one's established relationship to a specific heredity and environment. This is part of the karma one cannot alter easily from within. Though these ideas go far beyond anything that is conceived in ordinary behaviouristic psychology, it is vital that the complex notion of free will be raised to a higher level, making greater demands and requiring more fundamental changes in one's way of life and outlook. It is precisely at this point that the distinction between psychic and noetic action becomes crucial. One must understand the locus in consciousness of the incipient power of free will, and then distinguish this from the fundamental source of will which lies entirely outside the sphere of the personality and the field of *prarabdha* karma, *skandhas* and *samskaras*. Speaking of Ladd's conception of mind as the real unit being that is the subject of all states of consciousness, H.P. Blavatsky commented:

> This "Mind" is manas, or rather its lower reflection, which whenever it disconnects itself, for the time being, with karma, becomes the guide of the highest mental faculties, and is the organ of the free will in physical man.

Psychic and Noetic Action

Whereas *manas* itself is noetic, and signifies what could be called the spiritual individuality, there is also that which may be called the psychic individuality – this same *manas* in association with *kama*, or desire. This projected ray of *manas* itself has a capacity, though intermittent, for a kind of free will. Consider a human being who is. completely caught up in chaotic desires and who is extremely uncritical in relation to his experiences, his tastes, his likes – in short, to his self-image. Even that kind of person will have moments of disengagement from emotion and a relative freedom from desire. In such moments of limited objectivity the person may see what is otherwise invisible. He may see alternatives, recognize degrees, glimpse similarities and differences from other human beings in similar situations; gradually, he may sense the potential for sell-determination. Even lower *manas*, when it is disconnected from *kama*, can exercise free will, giving guidance to the mental faculties that make up the personality. This limited application of free will, however, is obviously quite different from full self-determination. The projected ray of *manas* is the basis of the *psychic* nature and potentially the organ of free will in physical man. *Manas* itself is the basis of the higher self-conscious will, which has no special organ, but is capable, independent of the brain and personality, of functioning on its own. This noetic individuality is distinct from the projected ray of lower *manas,* which is its organ, and distinct too from the physical brain and body, which are the organs of the *psychic* lower *manas.* This source of spiritual will is characterized in the *Bhagavad Gita* as the *kshetrajna,* higher *manas,* the silent Spectator, which is the voluntary sacrificial victim of all the mistakes and misperceptions of its projected ray.

The contrast between the silent Spectator and the despotic lower *manas* explains the difference between the psychic and the noetic. Wherever there is an assertion of the egotistic will, there is an exaggeration of the astral shadow and an intensification of *kamamanas.* When the projected "my" of *manas* becomes hard and cold, it tends to become parasitic upon others, taking without returning, claiming without thanking, continuously scheming without scruples. Ultimately, this not only produces a powerful *kamarupa,* but also puts one on the path towards becoming an apprentice *dugpa* or black magician. *The dugpa* or sorcerer works through coercive imposition of combative will. It accommodates nothing compassionate or sacrificial, no hint or suggestion of the supreme state of calm. This suggests a practical test in one's self-study. If one is becoming more wilful, one is becoming more and more caught up in lower psychic action. One's astral body is becoming inflamed, fattened and polluted, and one is losing one's flickering connection with the divine and silent Spectator. This is a poor way of living and ageing, a pathetic condition. If, on the other hand, one is becoming humbler and more responsive to others, more non-violent, less assertive and more open to entering into the relative reality of other beings, loosening and letting go the sense of separateness, one is becoming a true apprentice upon the path of renunciation, the path of white magic. The benevolent use of noetic wisdom, true theurgy, is the teaching of *Gupta Vidya.*

The silent Spectator is capable of thinking and ideating on its own. It is capable of disengaging altogether from lower *manas,* just as lower *manas* can disengage from *kama.* This skilful process of disengagement is similar to what Plato conveys through Socrates in *Phaedo* and also in the *Apology.* It is a process of consciously dying, which the philosopher practises every moment, every day. By dying unto this world, one can increasingly disengage from the will to live, the *tanha* of the astral and physical body. It is possible by conscious spiritual exercises for the individual progressively to free higher *manas* from its lower manasic limitations, projections, excuses, evasions and habits. It can come into its own, realizing in its higher states what Patanjali calls the state of a Spectator without a spectacle. This requires repeated entry into the Void. Even to those who have not deeply meditated upon it, the idea of supreme Voidness *(shunyata)* is challenging; it appeals to an intrinsic sense of sovereign spiritual freedom that exists in every human soul as a manasic being. As a thinking, self-conscious agent and spectator, every individual is, in principle, capable of appreciating and understanding, at some preliminary level, the possibility of universalizing self-consciousness. But actually to expand consciousness and gain emancipation from all fetters requires a life of deep and regular meditation.

This majestic movement in consciousness towards metaphysical subjectivity is directly connected with the capacity to contact in consciousness the noetic and noumenal realm behind the proscenium of objective physical existence. It is evident, for example, that the solar system is a complex causal realm involving planetary rotation around the sun according to definite laws. From the standpoint of *Gupta Vidya,* everything is sevenfold. This is as true of planets and constellations as of human beings. The solar system also involves seven planes, and each of its planets has seven globes. The physical sun is, then, the centre of revolutionary motion by the planets on the physical plane. This regulated activity is no different from anything else seen on the phenomenal plane in the manifested world. It is a representation in physical space of invisible principles. All such physical entities have correlates on the invisible plane, both subjective and objective.

Starting with the fundamental principle of universal unity and radical identity of all motion and activity in the Great Breath, there are close connections between the metaphysical aspects of all beings. Hence, there are metaphysical correlations between the subtle principles in human nature and the subtle principles of the sun and planets. Thus, there are invisible aspects of the moon which correspond to the lower principles in man, the psychic nature of the human being. There are also higher principles which correspond to *Atma-Buddhi* and to the noetic capacity of higher *manas.* Depending upon whether a human being is mired in psychic consciousness or rises to the noetic realm, he or she will have more or less self-conscious affinities with these different aspects of the solar system. When they look to the sky at night, their responses will differ not only on the physical plane but also on these invisible planes. One person may simply be impressed by the brightness of Venus in relation to the moon, being entranced by the physical beauty of the phenomenon. Another person might be interested to think in terms of the recondite activities and functions known even to contemporary astronomy. Still another, who is deeply rooted in the philosophy of *Gupta Vidya,* and a practitioner of regular meditation, would see something quite different in the heavens.

It is a common observation that different people see different things and derive different meanings from the same phenomena. Different people embody different degrees and balances of psychic perception and noetic apprehension of psycho-physical phenomena. To be able to see noetically one must begin by focussing upon the Spiritual Sun. This means that one must embark upon a programme of meditation and mental discipline directed to making conscious and consistent a secure sense of immortality. True immortality belongs to the *Atma-Buddhi-Manas,* the noetic individuality, and must be made real as an active principle of selection in reference to the lower principles. A person who does this will be able, like the Vedic *hotri,* to draw upon the highest aspects of the lunar hierarchies around the full moon and also the sublime energies and hidden potencies of the Spiritual Sun.

To perceive and connect the noetic in oneself with the noetic in the cosmos requires a synthetic and serene understanding. Such understanding is the crystalline reflection of the ineffable light of

Buddhi into the focussing field of higher *manas. Buddhi,* seen from its own subjective side, is inseparable from the motion of the Great Breath, whilst its objective side is the radiant light of higher understanding. noetic understanding is, therefore, rooted in universal unity. Its modes are markedly different from the analytical method of the lower reason, which tends to break up wholes into parts, losing all sight of integrity and meaning. No matter what the object of one's understanding, the fundamental distinction between psychic and noetic implies a subtle and vital difference between the set of properties that belongs to an assemblage of parts and the set of properties that belongs only to the whole, which is greater than the sum of its parts.

If one is going to use an analytic method, one must begin by recognizing that there are different levels of analysis requiring different categories and concepts. Merely by breaking up a phenomenon, one may not necessarily understand it. The *yogin,* according to Patanjali, does the opposite. He meditates upon each object of concentration as a whole, becomes one with it, apprehending the *Atma-Buddhi* of that phenomenon through his own *Atma-Buddhi.* He draws meanings and produces effects that would never be accessible to the analytic methods of lower *manas.* Others, for example, may decompose sound into its component elements of vibration, yet fail to hear in them any harmony or special melody; they may talk glibly about motion and vibration, yet be deaf to the harmony produced through vibrations. A musically tone-deaf physicist may know quite a lot about the theory of sound and yet may lack the experience or ability to enjoy the experience of masters of music. Conversely, those who are masters of music, and who may know something about the analytic theory of sound, may know nothing about what the *yogin* knows who has gone beyond all audible sounds to the metaphysical meaning of vibrations.

Thus there are levels upon levels of harmony within the cosmos spanning the great octave of Spirit-Matter. *Gupta Vidya,* which is always concerned with vibration and harmony, provides the only secure basis for acquiring the freedom to move from plane to plane of subjective and objective existence. The arcane standpoint is integrative, and always sees the One in the many. It develops the intuitive faculty which detects what is in common to a class of objects, and at the same time, in the light of that commonality, it enjoys what is unique to each object. It is this powerful faculty that the theurgist perfects. Through it, he quickly moves away from the phenomenal and even from manifest notions of harmony. And through noetic understanding he can experience the inaudible harmony and intangible resonances that exist in all manifestation. A person attentive to the great tone throughout Nature will readily appreciate the music of the spheres. Such a person can hear the sound produced by breath, not only in animals and human beings, but also in stars and planets. Such a hierophant becomes a Walker of the Skies, a Master of Compassion, in whom the power of the Great Breath has become liberated. All ordered Nature resonates and responds to the Word and Voice of such a hierophant, who lives and breathes in That which breathes beyond the cosmos, breathless.

Hermes, January 1987
Raghavan Iyer

CONTINUITY, CREATIVITY
AND CHOICE

Suffering arises out of exaggerated involvement in a world of colour, forms and objects, maintained by a false sense of personal identity. As long as people persist in this pseudo-continuum of existence, they necessarily forfeit the exercise of their inner creative capacities and cannot fully seize the opportunities of self-conscious evolution. Human beings produce a false sense of self out of a series of intense particularizations of will, thought and feeling, all of which become the tokens of selfhood. As a result, in the very process of fragmenting oneself into a diversity of desires and conflicting and colliding aims, or of limiting oneself by conceptions which must be concretized in some narrow programme in space and time, suffering is built into one's life. All exaggerations of the void and illusory ego, all failures to recognize the over-arching One, all attempts to live as if one were the centre of the world and without any self-conscious awareness of the beyond, mean that one can only gain happiness, pleasure or fulfilment at a cost. An obscuring shadow follows all pleasure – a compulsive feedback, a necessary negation, an unavoidable depression. When people do not detach themselves and negate excessive involvement in advance of every thought, the negation must come from outside, and after a point people lose their hold over the central thread of unifying or synthesizing awareness.

Suffering is the obscuration of the light of universal understanding. As long as we live in terms of narrow conceptions of ourselves, shrunken conceptions of space and of time, and with an exaggerated intensity that will necessarily be followed by an external negation, suffering is built into our life. It is coeval with that ignorance of the real which makes what we call human life possible. Human life is a passing shadow-play in which human beings identify with roles and, like candles, are eventually snuffed out, It is a play with a brief intensity focussed upon a paltry role and based upon identifications with name and form. One who experiences great suffering, or who reflects deeply upon the relationships at the very root of this process, may come to see that the world and oneself are not apart.

The world is at least partly of one's own making but it is also made by the limiting conceptions of other human beings. They have become involved in the creation of a world in which limitation is a necessary part, and they too have forgotten what they innately knew. All human beings begin life by sounding the OM. They all have a cool awareness of the ineffable when they are little children, before they begin to lisp and to speak. In the youth of their sense-organs they experience wonder in relation to the whole of life. In the process of growing up, however, they take on the illusions of others – of parents, elders, teachers, and a variety of people around them – and then they become forgetful of what they already knew. We may reawaken awareness only by self-conscious self-renewal. Awareness is like a colourless universal light for which there are as many focussing media as there are metaphysical points in abstract space. Each human being is a ray of that light. To the extent to which that ray projects out into a world of differentiated light and shade, and limitations of form and colour, it is tinctured by the colouring that comes to it from a mental environment. Philosophically, the mental environment is far more important than the external physical environment.

When one sees this process archetypally, one recognizes that there is no separation between oneself and the world except in language, reactive gestures, and in certain uncriticized assumptions. Most importantly, there is no separation of oneself from other human beings as centres of consciousness. The notions of "mine" and "thine", attached to pleasure and pain, to joy and suffering, are arbitrary and false. Is that which gives one great joy exclusively one's own? And, on what grounds do we assume that the suffering of human beings in numerous states of acute self-limitation is purely theirs? Does each one have his own exclusive property rights in collective human suffering and thereby have nothing to do with us? Suffering is intrinsic to the universal stream of conditioned existence. Most living is a kind of pseudo-participation in what seem to be events, but which are merely arbitrary constructions of space-time, and are largely non-events. When a human being comes to see that involvement of a single universal consciousness in a single homogeneous material medium, the very notion of the individual "I" has dissolved.

We are all aware when we go to the dentist and submit ourselves to something that seems physically painful, through our very awareness of what is happening and our deliberate attempt to think away from our identified involvement with the part of the physical body which is suffering, we can control our sensations to some extent rather than being wholly controlled by them. If this insight could be extended, we might see that the stream of universal consciousness is like an ever-flowing river – in which all conceptions of "I" and "you" and "this" and "that" are mere superimpositions – and then we could begin to stand consciously at some remove from the process of life. Suppose a person came to listen to a discourse of the Buddha with petty expectations, because somebody said it would be quite good, or worth hearing, or fairly interesting. Someone else might have come with a deeper idea because he or she was awake as a soul and had the thought that it is a tremendous privilege to be in the magnanimous presence of a *Mahatma*, and hence he or she might be lit up. If one is truly lit up, one's wakefulness makes the greatest difference to the whole of one's life. It could be gathered up self-consciously at the moment of death. But even a person who comes with so profound a thought into a collective orbit where there are many souls in states of only relative wakefulness and caught up in residual illusions, may forget the original moment.

The suffering of human life is a jolt which the whole gives the part, the individual ray, to reawaken in it a memory and awareness of the original moment. Here we can see the significance of certain meditations undertaken by Bhikshus. In Buddhist philosophy there are references to meditations on the moment of birth. Yet how are we to meditate on it when it is an event that has no sense of reality for us? It is simply a certain date on the calendar. The mystery of individuality lies in the privilege and the possibility of making one's own connections within what otherwise would be a vast, fragmented chaos of events. One could make these connections simply by habit, in terms of one's first thoughts, or in terms of the reactions of the world and the opinions of others. Or one could make them self-consciously from the standpoint of the whole. This, of course, is very difficult to experience immediately, but every human being can begin to grow in this direction. A fearless and dispassionate examination of the past shows that a lot of what once seemed extremely important was utterly insignificant and a lot of what looked impossible to go through was relatively easy. One could take stock of one's awareness independent of external events and focus it upon intense periods in the past which seemed to be especially painful, meaningless, or terrifying, but which one came through. Then one can ask whether, just as one now feels a kind of remoteness from past events, so too at the very moment of birth, did one feel a kind of remoteness from future events? Was one really involved, or only involved in one part of oneself? Then one can shift to the moment of death and raise the difficult question whether one can see oneself dying. Can one actually see a certain moment where there is an abandonment of a corpse which, through the natural processes of life, must decay and disintegrate and, while seeing this, still hold to an immense awareness of the whole? A person who is able to imagine what it would have been like to stand at a distance from the foetus that became the baby boy or girl can also imagine being at a distance from the corpse which is being discarded. He or she can also see that there is a thread that links these moments, and that the succession is no more arbitrary than the pattern of a necklace when seen from the standpoint of the whole.

The One Life comes into a world of differentiation through prismatically differentiated rays. We can sense in the gentle quality of dawn light something that does not participate in the opalescent colours of the day, something removed from what we call heat and light, cold and shade – a quality of virginal light that is a reminder of states of matter appropriate to states of consciousness which are created and held as potential by beings in general. Then we can begin to see that the whole point of human suffering in its collective meaning is to overcome pain and the false sense of separation. This is the point in consciousness where human beings as individuals could maintain a noetic and complete wakefulness – *turiya,* a profound awareness from a standpoint which transcends the greatest magnitudes of space-time. It goes beyond solar systems and intimates that the depths of space represent in the very core of apparently nothing, a subtle creative gestation of matter. If one can see the whole world in terms of its plastic potency, as radiant material for a single universal spiritual sun, then one gains the dignity and the divinity of being a self-conscious individuating instrument of the universal Logos.

This is the sacred teaching of all Initiates. It is the teaching of Jesus in the *Gospel According to John,* the teaching of the Buddha in the *Heart Sutra,* and the teaching of Krishna in the *Bhagavad Gita* and in the *Shrimad Bhagavatam.* These beings, fully awake, see that all human life, including human suffering, is a projection of a false involvement in a false sense of self. They bear witness to the reality of universal consciousness, not as something potential but as that which can be used as plastic material for new forms of spiritual creation. Creative imagination is not an abstract immaterial force, but the most rarefied and subtle form of material energy that exists. It can be tapped by concentration. By repeated and regular attempts at concentration upon this conception of the One, negating the false sense of the self, one builds and gives coherence to one's subtler vehicles, shaping what is now chaotic matter and forming a temple, a worthy vesture for a self-conscious being aware of the divinity of all beings and capable of maintaining that awareness through waking, dreaming and deep sleep. Having entered into the void, having entered into the light beyond these states of consciousness, the awakened soul remains in it by choice, while giving the impetus to other human beings to make the same attempt. Suffering and ignorance are collective; enlightenment and spiritual creativity are universal. This is the great hope of the timeless teaching concerning true continuity of consciousness.

Within the limits of time, however, which is an illusion produced by the succession of states of consciousness, there is only a before and an after, and no full scope for creativity. Consider, for example, a moment of love. Suppose you suddenly come into contact with someone of whom you could say, like the poet Yeats, "I loved the pilgrim-soul in you." There is a magical, intense flow between two pairs of eyes, and in one instant, a taste of eternity. If two individuals later tried to understand this in terms of what was there the day before and what was there the day after, they would have simply slipped onto another plane. If two people who have such a golden moment of co-awareness later on forget it or identify it with passing and contemporary illusions, then of course they might see it simply as a date in a calendar to be remembered by ceremonial tokens. That is not the same as re-enactment, because the essential quality of that moment was the absence of before and after, or any noticeable succession of states of consciousness. It was not as if they met calculatingly with anticipations and fears, and it was not as though soon after they thought of it as a memory of an event. They simply experienced in a moment of fusion of consciousness a freedom from the false division of eternal duration into a past, a present and a future. It was as if they stood not in one city, not in one street, not in one place, but in eternal space. This is an experience which by its very nature is so profound and beautiful that many people desperately look for it. This may be where the critical mistake is made. In the very attempt to look for it, one might overlook opportunities and arenas where it is more likely to happen. The very notion of seeking it, or wanting it, of manoeuvring it, is stifling.

Our experience of time involves craving and memory. Time is bound up with fragmented consciousness in a universe of change and a constantly moving world of process. At best, it is a deceptive device of convenience for gaining a sense of control in eternal duration, to serve purposes arising from the standpoint of the narrow needs of some particularized self in relation to other particularized selves, where it is useful to talk in terms of a before and an after. Consider a good physician who has seen you at different times and to whom you are more than a file. When receiving an examination, it is as if you are both friends looking together at a common medium which is the physical body you inhabit and which has certain cycles and a history. Two minds looking together at the same body can suddenly see connections between before and after. Patterns emerge. A serial view of time has practical convenience.

We have, however, another view of time which allows us to discover other types of patterns and connections. If all patterns and connections had to be discovered exclusively by individual human beings, then the human predicament would be even more grave than it now seems. Because many patterns are already given, it is a case of looking for them with a deep detachment, so that one does not cut up and fragment the process. Suddenly one may see that there is a certain moment here and another point, tendency or characteristic there with which it connects. E.M. Forster employed this idea in his novels and expressed it as a mantram – "Let us connect." To him, in pre-1914 England, the whole difference between human beings moving from the sheltered world of 1914 into the increasingly stormy and socially disordered world of Europe after the First World War, was in the extent to which they could survive the collapse of inherited identities and self-consciously create their own connections. Either human beings forge their own connections or connections will be made for them, but then they will sound arbitrary or malignant, suggesting that some dark, hostile Fate as in Thomas Hardy's novels, is causing everything. When human beings can self-consciously make these connections, they begin to live with an increasing sense of freedom from time. Time may be seen in terms of eternal duration, which is prior to it, and hence there are golden moments. Time may also be seen in terms of mere convenience, according to a calendar, to help facilitate a limited involvement between human beings, in limited roles and contexts, to take place in a reliable manner. This mode of time may even be made to approximate some broader concept of distributive justice. Time must be seen as an illusion, must be seen for what it is, if a person is to gain the real continuity of consciousness connected with true creativity.

Today there are various fascinating studies of creativity, which cite examples such as Kekule's dream that was critical in biology. Kekule dreamt one night of a serpent eating its tail and when he woke up, he got a flashing insight into the circular rather than linear nature of certain processes of growth which are fundamental in molecular biology. The more one looks at such cases, the more one comes to see that truly creative beings cannot be programmed. Even in a society fearfully hostile to creativity, creative minds can still use available resources compassionately. Typically, creativity is difficult to attain because there is too much desire to have it programmed and delivered according to a schedule set by personal consciousness. This comes out in capitalist society in its most extreme form when people feel that there must be a kind of pre-established, controlled, and mechanistic way in which one could have creativity by numbers. By emphasizing substitutability and measurability, by regarding human beings as labour-units who are convertible terms, one can evolve an aggregated view of output and product which is truly dead for the creative artist. A great potter has no sense of excitement in looking at a pot. It is already dead. What was alive was the process of visualization and the process of taking that mental image, while the potter's wheel was moving, and seeing the shape emerging. The magical moment of emergence is real. Most people, of course, want the result so that they will be able to say in a drawing-room, "Oh, this is a pot made by so-and-so." Human beings in general have a parasitic attachment to the products of creativity but the vital process of creativity eludes them because it defies ordinary modes of division of time.

Here, then, is the most critical point, both in relation to continuity of consciousness and in relation to the Demiurge. The Demiurge in the old myths and in many a rustic Hindu painting, is like Vishnu asleep, from whose navel a lotus emerges which is the universe. Mahavishnu is floating upon the great blue waters of space. Around the serpent on which this Great Being rests there is a circle within which a whitish milky curdling is taking place. Intense activity surrounds the periphery of the great wheel of eternity, on which is resting in a state of supreme, pure inactivity, the divine Demiurge, itself only an aspect of the Logos. The great Rig Vedic hymn states, "The One breathed breathless." It was alone and there was no second. Alone it breathed breathless. There is a transcending sense of boundless space, in relation to which all the notions of space that we have – of an expanding universe, of a closed universe, of solar systems, and galaxies – all of these are like maps and diagrams relating points that are already conceptually separated out and which have boundaries, but are merely partial representations or surface appearances upon the depths of a space which has no boundaries or contours, and which is never delineated in diagrams.

If continuity of consciousness is to be seen not as something individual but rather universal, embedded in the very process of the manifestation of the One in and through the many, then it is necessary to think away from conceptions of time that are arbitrary and to a view of space which is boundless. Metaphysically, the reason why the Demiurge can both be involved in space fashioning many systems, and also witness all of these like bubbles upon a surface, is because space is not empty. After three hundred years of thought and experiment, modern science is catching up with ancient wisdom and is beginning to see that there is no such thing as empty space, that the content of space is not dependent on other categories of measurement or upon other standpoints of perception. What looks like pitch-black darkness could in fact be enormously full from another and more profound understanding. In one of the great passages in the early part of *The Secret Doctrine*, the commentary upon the *Stanzas of Dzyan* says that what to the Initiate is full is very different from what appears full to the ordinary man. The more human beings self-consciously expand awareness, the more they can free their deeply felt conceptions of the world, of reality, and of themselves from the notions of part and limit, from future anticipations and a present cut up into separate particular events, and the more they can bring a conscious sense of reality to their own mental awareness of space as a void – what the Buddha called *Sunyata,* Emptiness – and the more they can replace the ordinary conception of form by the Platonic, which is not bound up with anything fixed.

Archetypal forms are like flashes of light. We may represent them by external coatings or by geometrical figures, but that is to imply that they are fixed, whereas in fact they are in a ceaseless, fluid interconnection. A constant transformation is taking place in the Divine Mind from one into another appearance of a geometrical form. There is a profound statement of this conception, which has great application to the individual who wishes to meditate upon it and use it in daily life: "The world is a living arithmetic in its development and a realized geometry in its repose." Every human being is involved in that arithmetic, and therefore growth is possible for the individual. Further, beyond and above that which changes, grows and develops, each is also consubstantial with the One that breathes breathless. Therefore, for the deeper Self, the whole universe is a realized geometry in repose.

If one went to sleep with a self-conscious awareness, using such profound images to extend the conception of the very reality of the world that one will enter into when going to sleep, and if on waking up one could greet the world in terms of these great divine images, then the whole world would become a vast playground for creativity and the freely created expression of a dancing intelligence that is involved in everything. One can suddenly find immense joy, a kind of *eros* or love, surging within. Then of course one would not identify love with a deficiency need. Creativity has nothing to do with a sense of incompletion, except in the sense in which the whole of manifestation is necessarily incomplete. It has to do with a sense of something tremendous welling up from within. There is a necessarily unprogrammed, unpredictable nature to the creative artist in every man. A human being could look towards every context and situation, and self-consciously greet the world as a creative being, but to do this requires the courage to break with one's sniggering, supercilious, paranoid self. One must wake up and be unafraid of the divine inheritance that belongs to every man. This, however, can never be done collectively. Individuals can only do this by choosing to strike out on their own. We have an excellent definition given in the very first essay of H.P. Blavatsky on "What is Theosophy?": The true Theosophist is one who independently strikes out and godward finds a path. All create their own paths back to the original source, based upon original inspirations, unique and priceless opportunities out of each one's particular stock of experience of making reason come alive as the embodiment of beneficent forces, the eternal verities, the quintessential truths of all history.

Even though such decisions cannot be made collectively, none the less the whole of humanity is now coming closer to what is called the moment of choice, the time where consciousness must either move forward or vacate vehicles because it cannot maintain the patterns of the past. This follows directly from the principle that the whole universe is continuously implicated in involution and evolution. In a universe of ceaseless motion there is a breathing in and a breathing out: one universal homogeneous spirit breaks into rays just as at dawn rays emerge out of the light. They get involved in what become in time separate forms of differentiated matter. Having become involved, they must eventually reach a point where matter has descended to the level of maximum differentiation. Then spirit is withdrawn from its involvement in the most heterogeneous matter back into its original source. This is what is symbolized in the serpent eating its tail. It led to Hegel's metaphysical theory of evolution, because it makes of every man's journey an integral part, while at the same time only a partial and to some extent apparently separate expression of one collective universal process. How can we move from this scheme to the concepts of choosing and a moment of choice, which are bound up with the notion of individual responsibility?

We may, as some have done, compare the earlier systems of philosophy to the developing states of consciousness of a child. After birth every baby resides in a state of awareness that is so bound up with the mother that it has no sense of being separate. There follows a second stage when an awareness of particularity, detail and multiplicity emerge together with a sense of being not separate but simply someone who is resting, so to speak, in the bosom of the mother, of the whole, of space. Then comes a third stage when the little child becomes enormously fascinated with its conception of itself, a kind of solipsistic or even narcissistic stage where it becomes very interested in its own feelings. It gives a kind of definition and clarity to its own desires, taking hold of itself in terms of its own wants and needs. A point surely does come, without tracing the whole process in detail, where a person begins to experience something of the joy and the thrill of having to make a decision, of taking a stand, of having to choose.

By analogy and correspondence what seems thrilling at the time of puberty – being able to choose – may be applied on the plane of the mind to being able to choose an idea, a system of ideas, or a philosophical system. This is not merely selecting a series of particularizations, but choosing a whole way of thinking out and giving shape, direction and authentic continuity to one's mental development. All of this has become difficult to understand because of the operation of an evolutionary paradox: the necessary homogenization of the *psyche* is accompanied by the increasing necessity for responsible choice free of psychic influence. This may be the historical destiny of America – to foster a hazardous jelling of people from all parts of the world, producing a huge, homogenized, psychic amorphism. Everything is kept in a fluidic state so that as wise beings enter into it, they will, in taking on this plastic material and using the enormous power released by mixing and mingling, give that energy an ennobling sense of direction. This means a moment of choice is emerging for a whole race or a nation. Many people are aware of this in America today. There was a time when glamour was attached to being decadent, but much of that nonsense has been swept away. Today the pre-packaged tins of glamour have become so boringly or pathologically familiar that there is no novelty anymore attached to them. It is as if human consciousness has drained the last drop of false involvement in all of these soulless dregs of matter that are being spewed forth. This is happening because there is a complex convergence of forces and Karma is working very fast in giving people their precise allocations. There is a tremendous opportunity also for those who can work with the Promethean solar forces of the future, which at this time are extremely subtle, imperceptible yet causally crucial.

We are at a new point in history where persons cannot, as in older days, merely go by labels. Individuals have become much more sophisticated and a significant increase in self-consciousness, in regard to the eclecticism of the human mind, has emerged. The moment of choice takes a variety of forms, but in the end all the choices come back to one basic choice: living in terms of a false conception of psychic identity caught passively in a series of events happening to oneself, or living self-consciously with awareness as a noetic being. Put in a starkly simple way, one is either going to be a psychic being and behave more childishly as one grows older, or one is going to be noetic and actually grow up. To behave noetically is to reawaken something of the pristine, beautiful awareness of a baby but while one is grown up. One may be in one s forties or fifties and still have self-consciously something of the thrill found in a baby's face looking out on the world with eyes of complete truth, accepting the wonder of life.

This must be deliberately and individually chosen. The insidious legacy of vicarious atonement makes people think that this can happen to them without their having to do anything, simply by being on the side of the correct doctrine or on the side of God. The Buddha came to destroy the false idea that simply by making one dramatic and tearful choice, all the rest will automatically happen. No doubt there is much wisdom in what Jesus said: "Seek ye first the kingdom of God and all else will be added unto you", but to seek the kingdom of God is to seize the critical moment of choice. "Whom choose ye this day, God or Mammon?" This formulation by itself is too narrow because its interpretations limit the magnitude of the choice to the sphere of the false self. In the presence of the light one either has to build in and for the light or one has to live like a vampire in fear of the light. Human beings have to become self-conscious, creative beings who can continuously release creativity, the light of understanding, and true sympathy, and who can thereby gain contentment and joy in a more collective sense of human welfare and a more universal sense of progress. Otherwise, they must lapse back into their habits and then, lacking responsibility, they cannot help plunging into a pattern which is one of vampirization or mere mechanical, automaton-like living.

There is a stern logic to this choice because it is not taken at any one point of time alone. Once we grasp the choice in its full sense, it is one that is taking place at every moment in time. Hence the Buddha said that no moment of carelessness in relation to continuity of consciousness is possible. Eternal vigilance is the price, not only of political liberty, but even more of spiritual freedom. This is because eventually human beings who understand the logic of this choice and have made a critical choice, accept the consequences, connecting in turn to other choices, thereby creating a cumulative cycle. They also connect that cycle of ascent to various tokens of memory, objects in their lives, friends, or their contact with the Lodge where they rekindle regularly their spiritual impulses. Eventually they reach a point where they can understand the inexplicable joy, as well as the burden, of choosing a thought. Functionally, the definition of an enlightened being, of an Initiate, is a being who chooses every thought. Things do not happen to Initiates; thoughts do not come to them. They choose them. To be able to get to the ultimate capacity not only to choose every thought but to make it a living reality by mastering the power of *Kriyashakti,* totally purified creative imagination, is an exalted ideal truly inspiring and relevant to every human being. By renewing one's sense of the reality of this ideal, one can reach a point where one can give up altogether the false notion of personal or individual spiritual progress. It is replaced by a beautiful awareness that whatever happens is a kind of resignation to the universal flow of light working through one self-consciously. It is like swimming on the ocean. We appreciate that the collective pull of the ocean is divine harmony, in terms of which one cannot lose.

If good karma is that which is pleasing to the real man, to the *Ishwara*, the divine within, then good karma is universal harmony. None can lose if they really are unafraid of anything coming to them in terms of universal divine harmony. Fear arises only for those who would somehow like everything programmed and arranged for them, so that if things go wrong, they can blame it on the people who arranged it, and if things go right, they could forget to say thanks and take the credit. Fortunately, this small-minded view of the world cannot be supported any longer. We have reached a point where it is really the same for all. It is a matter of choosing consciously the divine harmony and saying that whatever eventually comes is not merely what I deserve but what I desire. We must come to that point in life where we are ready for everything and anything, and see the whole of life as being on the side of that in us which alone is capable of surviving. Then we shall be happy to let go that which cannot be supported by a living person who is willing self-consciously to die. At the same time we shall be assured, in a cool, relaxed and totally conscious way, of the universal currents of divine harmony within us. Then we could say that we are human beings who have chosen rightly and fundamentally. This is not once-and-for-all. We shall have to reinforce and renew it many times a day, not in the old sense of ritual but simply by becoming aware of our thinking processes. One day it could have meaning for us to say that we actually choose our thoughts and life-atoms, that we have not one reaction which is not submitted by us to the process of deliberation. Then many more shall be worthy of the most sacred of all titles in collective evolution, of being what Emerson called Man Thinking, a *manasaputra*, a trustee of the sacred fire of individual and universal self-consciousness, with "the priceless boon of learning truth, the right perception of existing things, the knowledge of the non-existent."

Hermes, October 1977
Raghavan Iyer

RELATIONSHIP AND SOLITUDE

True Love in this differs from gold and clay,
That to divide is not to take away.
Love is like understanding that grows bright
Gazing on many truths; "tis like thy light,
Imagination! which, from earth and sky,
And from the depths of human fantasy,
As from a thousand prisms and mirrors, fills
The Universe with glorious beams, and kills
Error, the worm, with many a sun-like arrow
Of its reverberated lightning.

Percy Bysshe Shelley

The principle that all human beings should be treated as ends in themselves and not as means constitutes the core of Kantian morality. It rests upon an older conception of the world as a coherent structure intelligible to the pure reason of man. This world is a moral order precisely because human beings are an integral part of it. The human mind, by an act of pure, universal, impersonal reason, is able to discern the ethical order within the natural order. Each human being is a self-determining agent within a universe which itself may be seen as a kingdom of ends. Every human being as a responsible agent can become a monarch within his or her own modest kingdom by living in terms of ends that are self-chosen. We rule ourselves by making those ends meaningful in our lives.

For the practical realization of this possibility, we must assume that every human being is inherently capable of acting spontaneously without interfering with other human beings. We know that this noble mode of action is not achieved because reason is clouded by irrational passion. Pure universal affirmation is distorted, dissolved and even destroyed in the midst of the blinding partialities of confused human beings captive to conflicting impulses, aims, motives and desires. Suppose, however, that these self-chosen ends were intrinsically compatible, and that each person, in willing an end, asked the question, "If everyone wills this end, is it compatible for all human beings individually to pursue it without mutual interference?" At one level, a general answer would only yield a formal criterion of action. Is there a practical way, however, in which we could readily recognize in ourselves any fall from the autonomous state of a self-determining, rational being? We must identify any desire to interfere with others as springing from a part of ourselves which cannot be underwritten by the moral order and which the universe cannot protect.

Although theoretical formulations have a certain value, nonetheless, in the familiar but treacherous territory of tortuous rationalization and sinuous self-deception, as well as the psychological pessimism of our time, they only communicate negatively. And yet, while we may not fully know what it means to pursue our own ends without interfering with other individuals, we can surely recognize instances where one human being is crudely using another. We recognize this in its extreme form in politics, but the idea that any government could have total control over the human mind is self-contradictory if human beings are intrinsically self-determining agents. This also applies to any theory of continuous interference through conditioning, any supposedly benevolent, massive manipulation such as "Skinnerism."

The crucial challenge is whether we can, long before we are confronted by extreme cases, apply to all contexts a truly philosophical framework of indefinite growth in human relationships. Can we recognize not only the obvious ways in which we use other people, but also the pure ideal wherein we determine a chosen end without ever treating anyone else as a means? Can we understand the complexities of lower *Manas* solely through the desire for universal affirmation? We need a more complex view of human nature and especially a subtler understanding of the mind. It is not enough to see human beings merely in terms of use and misuse, least of all in the Benthamite language of self-interest, because people generally do not really know what is to their advantage over a long period of time in every context. All utilitarian formulations eventually tend to break down. It may even be better to think away altogether, in human relationships, from the ends-means dichotomy because it has been tainted by narrow and short-sighted perspectives.

Is there a nobler way by which we can come to understand what it is for two human beings to help each other, to share with each other, and not to use each other? Even though the sacred idea of love is degraded every day, there is no human being who does not understand what love means at some level. The counterfeit of love is false romantic idealization which soon becomes empty and irrelevant. True love involves the many complexities of human beings, the manifest weaknesses and also the hidden poignancy in the archetypal relationships between father and child, husband and wife, teacher and pupil, and between two friends. If two people can sense something beyond themselves, can they also see how the direction of their relationship could be meaningful? Even though in their weakest moments there is a tendency for either to take advantage of the other unconsciously or in the name of the good, is there still a feasible possibility of self-correction? Must relationships tend to become prisons or can they evolve in the direction of liberation? In the everyday contexts of human relationships, the critical question is whether we are becoming more tyrannical in relation to others or are allowing our closest encounters to enhance the joys of individuation.

These fundamental inquiries hurt because any pertinent discovery of the subtle forms by which the tyrannical will masquerades as love destroys our delusive relationships. Mere intellectual awareness does not help, and this is the point we have reached in contemporary culture. People know so much about all abuses of trust that they are terrified of any irrevocable commitment. They are afraid to spend time with their relatives; afraid to assume burdens of responsibility in relation to children;

afraid of intimacy with others and most of all afraid of deep introspection and meditative solitude. Relationships have broken down because many have become painfully aware of all the ambiguities, perversions and tyrannical elements in the human *psyche*. The atmosphere is so polluted that we almost dare not breathe. Therefore, the most simple, natural analogies, let alone idyllic models of archetypal relationships, do not speak to the disillusioned. They need a fundamental solution and not only an acute awareness of human failings. There is no total solution in the empirical realm that is compatible with the sum-total of goodness in the universe, but a fundamental solution can emerge when individuals are willing to rethink their conceptions of themselves.

The therapeutic counsel of the great healers of souls is as relevant now as it was in the days of the Buddha and the Christ. There are those whom the immemorial teaching does not transform, even though they spend a lifetime with it. There are those who are afraid it is going to alter them and therefore never enter the stream. There are those who progressively find it affecting them, and are able by an unspoken trust to use it and be benefitted by it. And then there are those very few who are deeply grateful for the supreme privilege of witnessing the presence of this timeless teaching. They are constantly focussed upon the eternal example nobly re-enacted by *Avatars* who portray the magnificent capacity to maintain, with beautiful balance and ceaseless rhythm, the awesome heights of cosmic detachment and boundless love. These mighty men of meditation are also illustrious exemplars of the art of living and masterly archers in the arena of action. They cannot be understood in terms of external marks or signs. It is only through their inner light that individuals can come into closer contact with the inner lives of beings so much wiser and nobler than themselves. Those who cherish this truth may find the inner light within their own silent sanctuary through deep meditation, in their incommunicable experience of poignant emotions, in response to soul-stirring music, or in their ethical endeavours through honesty and self-examination.

Human beings willing to take their lives into their own hands can acknowledge when they have used a person as a means to their own end, and see this as unworthy. Highly evolved souls who fall into such abuses will go into a period of penance. They will engage in a chosen discipline of thought and action so as to atone for their past misuse. Penance is not to be understood in terms of externals. True *tapas* touches the core of one's inward integrity. It fosters a calm reliance upon the great law of universal unity and ethical causation. It is rooted in the wisdom that protects right relationships. The tragedy of the human condition is that when we make moral discoveries we cannot readily go back to those we have wronged and rectify matters. Either it would be too painful or the individuals involved are not accessible. But we can correct our relationships at a higher level of integrity. We could prepare ourselves, in a practical way, to come out of the old and smaller circles of loyalty. We could authentically enter into the family of man and become members of that brotherhood of human beings who do their utmost, in the depths of solitude and self-examination as well as in the gamut of their relationships in daily life, to re-enact in simple situations what at an exalted level is effortlessly exemplified by the Brotherhood of *Bodhisattvas*.

Those who make this heroic effort become pioneers who point to the civilization of the future. They gestate new modes in the realm of pure ideation and bring them down into the region of the visible, laying foundations for a more joyous age in which there will be less defensiveness, fear and strain in the fit between theory and practice. Some want to get there straightaway, but they have never really asked themselves whether they have paid off their debts, or even faced up to the consequences of what they did before. This is a common error, but nonetheless it is insupportable in a cosmos that is a moral order. We cannot erase what went before, though we can make every new beginning count and insert it into a broader context. The great opportunity that the Aquarian Age offers is to gain a sense of proportion in relation to oneself, entering into an invisible brotherhood of comrades who are making similar attempts. Their mutual bonds come alive through their inmost reverence for their teachers, who exemplify in an ideal mode what their disciples strive to make real in their lives through sincere emulation to the best of their knowledge.

We need to function freely in the invisible realm of growth where all formulations can only be initial points of departure, and all interactions may serve as tentative embodiments of ideals. We know today, even in terms of the inverted insights of the lunar psychology now so widely disseminated, that our responses to others are in part truths about ourselves. We are aware that weak people are going to see weakness everywhere, or are going to be threatened by stronger people who remind them only more acutely of their own weakness. In the worst cases, the weak either try to pull down the stronger through image-crippling or try to live off them vampirically. On the opposite side, there are divine equivalents to these demoniac extremes, because evil is merely a privation of the good. Evil is only a shadow cast by a good which is not static: the more we seek it, the more it moves through degrees of relative manifestation extending into the unmanifest realm and beyond into that which cannot be called "good" or "true" or "beautiful" or anything, because it is beyond all appellations and attributes.

There is then a process that is the opposite of vampirization. Instead of subtracting from someone else for our own benefit every time we see something that is strong or admirable, we could try to be silent learners. This is not easy. Very great souls, wherever they are born, reveal themselves as archetypal learners. By learning all the time they readily assimilate the best from those they encounter, and thus rapidly learn in every direction. *Light on the Path* gives the most comprehensive and precise instruction: "No man is your enemy: no man is your friend. All alike are your teachers." This mode of learning is a way of drawing from others which enriches all. The archetypal mode is so basic that it cannot remotely resemble institutionalized, routinized, inherited conceptions of learning. One can enact a whole manvantara within a single night if one is serious about learning, simply by sitting quietly in a restaurant and watching people coming and going, working and conversing. Learning is ceaselessly going on everywhere but it can become truly self-conscious only if one is sufficiently humble. It is absurd to insist that there is no alternative to manipulation in human relationships. What makes vampirization possible is a kind of perverted strength, a determined persistence in weakness. An Initiate will see in such sad cases not a weakling, but an old sorcerer playing sick games behind a weak exterior, using the guise of weakness for the sake of sordid traffic in human vulnerability. There is present a reflected ray of the divine, but its strength shows itself demoniacally, inverted through a perverse determination which can only push the person along the inclined slope that culminates in the irreversible utter loneliness, annihilation, and extinction of the vital connection with the *Atman*. We need to meditate deeply on the opposite to see to the very core of what is happening. We can only do this if we can witness what we see with a commensurate compassion. The self-destructive sorcery of vampirization and manipulation must be met by a tremendous love, such as that of Krishna, Buddha, or Christ, for the faint spark of moral perception in that unfortunate human being desperately needs to be fanned before it is wholly extinguished.

Meditation upon the nature of good and evil also points to a process that is the opposite of the demoniac tendency, through extreme insecurity, of breaking down the images of stronger people. True learners, in contrast to fickle sycophants, are skilled in the enjoyment of excellence. They are willing to worship the imprint of impersonal truths about human nature in the acts and utterances of noble souls, wherever they may be discerned. Diverse individuals may find kinship with exemplars of human excellence in ancient myths, in recorded history, and in the secret fraternity of living sages. If we sit down and calmly reflect upon the best persons we have ever known, upon those we most respect, we may come to see the finer qualities hidden in the creative depths of these beings. Continuous effort generates strength. If we love enough we will readily recognize that we are initially not worthy enough to appreciate all the excellences of higher beings. We need knowledge, self-study, and the companionship of those who are our comrades in the quest for wisdom. Then we become intuitively capable of drawing to that orbit wherein we sense without profanation a sacred dissemination and steady diffusion of ideals that may be incarnated by degrees. This is the only possible strength compatible with a spiritual cosmogony and an emanationist conception of human evolution. Strength is truly that which is compatible with further growth. This is no static notion of strength and there can be no external measure of it. Human beings are the greatest cowards when they will not admit a mistake and when they will not face themselves. The greatest heroes are the ones who show the courage needed for constant self-correction. True strength has nothing to do with indices of power in the visible realm. It shows itself in the inner life of man, in psychological struggles, and in the moral sphere. As we begin to gain a little of this inward strength, we prepare ourselves for more. Then it becomes natural and spontaneous to rejoice in the existence of those stronger than ourselves.

It is possible even now to recover something of that faded memory of the joys which were once experienced in families where one could insert one's whole conception of oneself into a larger fellowship. We can no longer do this mechanically in *Kali Yuga*, least of all in a competitive society, and in relation to the family as defined merely in terms of blood ties and physical heredity. We have to re-discover and re-create the small family before we can join the greater family of man. We need to think about humanity as a whole, the human situation, human needs, human sufferings, and the glaring gap between the human predicament and all the expertise in the corridors of power. But we should not presume that we know enough about such matters. It would be better to seek to become effective servants of Those who alone have the wisdom needed to enlighten and elevate the whole of the human race, but who cannot do so without the help of companions. Drawn out of different cultures, they are the global forerunners who are willing to serve as "Fortune's favoured soldiers" in the *Army of the Voice*.

These companions realize that true solitude is not loneliness, but the experience of a more intense fellowship that goes beyond the human kingdom. It is a fellowship not merely with nature seen in terms of its four kingdoms – mineral, vegetable, animal and human – but a fellowship that includes three invisible elemental kingdoms. Even more, it is a fellowship with living forces that are neither remote abstractions nor anthropomorphized entities. Through this fellowship we may experience the thrill of the discovery that within the human body there is a universe intimately bound up with a vast universe which includes many more worlds than what either visually or conceptually we call the cosmos. Deep, steady and regular meditation, supported by the integrity of self-study, becomes after a point as natural as breathing. It becomes continuous with the whole of one's life, and then a person can never be lonely in the ordinary sense, because one will be unafraid. If there is no limiting conception of oneself which makes one vulnerable, there is nothing to fear.

To explain this in detail would be futile because an explanation would say nothing to someone who does not have some experience of it. The best way to understand it is to focus one's consciousness, within the solitude of one's own life, upon those passages in the great devotional texts which give the capacity – within the alembic of one's purified imagination, the matrix of one's serene ideation, and the warmth of one's expanding heart – to tap through meditation the ideation, benevolence and compassion of beings who have gained enlightenment. An infallible test of whether one has truly entered the stream is that one recognizes one's predecessors, the *Tathagatas*. People who only attempt meditation for a while, and keep pretending that they have the last word or the final answer, are pitiable failures. The individual who has an authentic inner life feels a profound veneration for a vast brotherhood of beings who have walked that way before. Many people experience a comparable feeling on trips to the mountains, especially when they are alone for a long time. They experience an exhilaration at seeing another human being. There is a comradeship which we can experience but are not ready to verbalize.

We can find in such fruitful encounters preparatory anticipations of the solidarity experienced through the discipline of discipleship, meditating as steadily as a spinning top, while also engaged in creative action. Enjoying comradeship with the Brotherhood of *Bodhisattvas*, the disciple is strengthened by his constant awareness of Their boundless compassion. Simply to think of their infinite sacrificial wisdom fortifies him. This is a profound experience, and anyone can earn it by making the necessary effort. But in the sacred realm no false coins will serve, and there can be no cheating or manipulation. As in Rene Daumal's *Mount Analogue*, the only thing that entitles one to go further is being able to extract a particular kind of pearl-like substance that one can only get by risking great danger, coming close to precipitous waterfalls and crashing cascades. Progress is made solely by daring, the willingness to go through repeated trials, and by magnanimity.

Though depicted in different ways by many teachers throughout vast ages, the trials of a disciple are very real. No strength is gained by any who are unwilling to be tested and tried, or who are afraid of trying. This will always be the case, as long as the universe has the integrity necessary to accommodate the continuities between great beings and every person alive. In a universe of law, the only way in which it is possible to go through the journey is step by step. As suggested in the story of Job, one's burden will never be greater than one can bear. But at any given time, the trial one is undergoing will seem as if it is too much. Jesus exemplified this at his supreme trial when he faced the thought that he might have been forsaken. Even though such thoughts may occur, the disciple can persist. Faith will triumph over doubt, and *Kama Manas* will finally be sloughed off like the skin of a snake. The new self emerges at that very point where one is willing to let go of the whole assemblage of past limitations. But this cannot be done once and for all. It has to be done repeatedly.

There will be many trials, and, for those who are simply not able to understand what is involved, the warning is given at the outset that this is the Path of Woe. The Rosicrucian motto enjoins: "Know, dare, will," and, above all, "remain silent." If candidates are willing to fulfil such precise qualifications, they will be able to travel the whole Path. It is that kind of journey where, if one gains a self-sustaining measure of growth on the Path, a point is reached, earlier than one might think, where there is no more anxiety or concern about one's own good. When that point is passed, one is truly fortunate, because then it is possible to keep going while seeing beyond the calculus of consequences. A faith can be fostered which is founded in understanding and reinforced from within by a high resolve embodied in the realm of sacrificial action, depicted forcefully in the *Bhagavad Gita.* Inevitably, one may appear to lose ground at times, but a person who is ambivalent and dithering cannot augment his faith. All despondency has to be cast off. While this cannot be done at the beginning, it will be required as one grows. It can be done provided one always keeps looking ahead to that which is beyond oneself, and which encompasses all other human beings.

One must show a warm gratitude to those pilgrims on the path who, having gone further up, are beckoning to the persons below. This is little understood in the world of inversions or in the language of lower *Manas* which has tarnished all images of the truths of the spiritual life. We can become ready for more and more, however, by using every increment of authentic experience. It is the constant effort to bring many individuals to this hunger for genuine learning and to give them some meaningful hope, that constitutes the great sacrifice of the *Mahatmas*. Their ceaseless and magnanimous work is vaster at all times than any individual can comprehend, but at the same time it has precision in relation to the law of cycles. They work with vast cyclic forces and know what can be done in any year in any place at any level in relation to the greatest good of all. One will make marvellous discoveries as one climbs more, finding that the precision, detachment and selflessness needed are truly awe-inspiring. But a person will be proud to have become worthy even to know this much, and if he looks back at what he was a long time ago or sees those still struggling below, he will recognize a profound kinship and want to help in every way.

There is another telling insight in *Mount Analogue*. Pilgrims find they reach a stage where they cannot take the next step forward, where they have to sit and wait until those who are still struggling below have come up to their level. Those who would not do for others what has been done for them will never make further progress in the spiritual life. The door will be shut. Such persons may build up a pattern where, in their concern to keep going, they forget what they have already been through. They fail to empathize fully with those who are still struggling. A balance must be struck on the Path which can only be genuine and dynamic when produced by a rhythmic alternation between withdrawals and involvements, *nivritti* and *pravritti*, meditation and skill in the art of action, solitude and relationship. Disciples can integrate solitude into every week, into every day, and eventually integrate it into themselves so that they are within their spheres all the time and can see in all particular relationships mirrorings of vaster relationships with all living beings. They begin every week by deliberation in regard to what they can do for someone else and by self-study with regard to how they may apply what they have learned from others and how they may correct various sins of omission and commission. A person who regularly undertakes this can carry it out everywhere, even in the simplest relationships.

The most unspoken, intimate relationships reflect the very highest relations, which at the pinnacle of the spiritual life is that of disciple and teacher, but which at the cloud-obscured peak of enlightenment is like that between a child and a mother. The *chela* directly experiences these sacred relationships, which are inconceivable to human beings as they are. Yet, we can see them mirrored even in the awkward stumblings of ordinary men. Hence, as suggested in the great images given by Plato, those who recognize that the ladder of love extends into the elusive realms of the ineffable, can also see the reflections of that divine magic in its simplest manifestations among ordinary people. When a person can do this, there is no more dichotomy between authentic relationship and inner solitude.

An evolving human being and a developing disciple experience that which seems mysterious – what it is to be of the world and one with it and yet out of it and not in it at all. When we experience this in sufficient measure, we may more readily understand what it means to be a being who can remain awake during *pralaya* and yet also be uninvolved whilst fully engaged during manifestation in the work of the world. We come to see that for an ascending consciousness there are levels upon levels of negation and affirmation. This pair ultimately become like two poles that are symmetrically related to a higher pole which is beyond because it can never manifest and is unconditioned. This is most meaningful when seen, not as an image or a metaphor, but as a living reality within, pointing to the One beyond and above the Waters of Space, which "breathes breathless." It is possible to remain in that ground of Being which is Non-Being. It is feasible to understand the vast meshing of karmic causation and at the same time, while standing outside it, to feel no sense of separateness from the most ignorant beings, toiling and hurting themselves and somehow through their stumblings, growing towards a greater freedom than they can recognize while still hiding in the shadows. Those who approach these transcendental recognitions will truly feel it a sacred privilege to "profit by the gift, the priceless boon of learning truth, the right perception of existing things, the knowledge of the non-existent."

SIMILITUDE

As when with downcast eyes we muse and brood,
And ebb into a former life, or seem
To lapse far back in some confused dream
To states of mystical similitude,
If one but speaks or hems or stirs his chair,
Ever the wonder waxeth more and more,
So that we say, All this hath been before,
All this hath been, I know not when or where";
So, friend, when first I look"d upon your face,
Our thought gave answer each to each, so true –
Opposed mirrors each reflecting each –
That, tho" I knew not in what time or place,
Methought that I had often met with you,
And either lived in either's heart and speech.

Alfred Lord Tennyson

Hermes, June 1977
Raghavan Iyer

COGNITION AND FREEDOM

If anyone says that the Tathagata comes or goes, sits or reclines, he fails to understand my teaching. Why? The Tathagata has neither whence nor whither, and therefore he is called the Tathagata.

The Diamond Sutra

All growth in self-conscious beings is based upon self-determination checked by karma, the consequences of past causation. The immortal soul, as a self-subsisting being, is engaged in an awesome pilgrimage within a vast Circle of Necessity extending over an immense period of time. Within this manvantaric matrix, each must give meaning to the assumption of responsibility in the light of the central teaching of the *Diamond Sutra.* Over millennia myriads of human beings are involved in elaborating modes of perception and awareness which generate diverse emphases in thought-forms, in language, and in ways and means of interacting with those abstractions called institutions, roles and rules. Archetypally, these divergences may be seen in relation to the invisible centre of an invisible circle, which is also the topological centre of an equilateral triangle. There is no priority to any of the angles made by any two lines of the triad. At the same time, there must be a fourth point, in relation to which the triad may be seen as a whole. The geometry of the universe involves an appearance of stability which masks the living arithmetic of ceaseless development.

To begin to ponder upon the wisdom of the *Diamond Sutra,* the climactic message of the Buddha, we should reflect upon the fundamental identity of all monads. Every human being knows that in the context of the collective interdependence of beings under law, all discriminations between persons become illusory and irrelevant. Death does not discriminate between persons; an epidemic does not favour some and punish others. Men who sail on long voyages are silent witnesses to the majesty, impersonality and profound impartiality of the ocean, which is often compared to the whole of life. "Law" is merely a word given to the totality of interdependent relations that constitute a world or a system. One of the core statements of the *Diamond Sutra* is that the system is no-system. Consider any example – a school, a nation, an economy – and look at manuals, rules, and diagrams of edifices. Anyone can be induced to see a spatial field over a period of time in terms of determinate points and discrete relationships. Nevertheless, there is a freedom and an unstructured quality in human relationships. There is an indefinable improvisation in the relationship between a mother and her child, between a husband and his wife. These designations merely indicate persons in distinct roles, relative to particular contexts.

In the *Diamond Sutra* the problem of specification is raised by the wisest of the Buddha's disciples who have mastered the divine dialectic of Buddhist ontology, which negates the substantiality of visible forms and the rigidity of discriminations relative to objects of sense-perception. Most people entertain an unphilosophical notion of some kind of timetable or guide book for travel in terms of a predetermined starting-point and a fixed terminus. Yet anyone who wanders in the mountains or roams about like a nomad, neither threatened by nor dependent upon maps, knows that all of these are arbitrary localized representations in what appears as a boundless field from a high altitude. Anyone from a great city who merely happens to fly over its towering structures experiences a sort of release from overdrawn lines and discovers something of the lightness of a bird on the wing. Every human being is capable of a certain freedom and largeness, a magnanimity which is beyond the possibility of specification and analysis, and transcends all formal limitations. At the very moment someone says he is this or that, the object of the statement is becoming something else. We are always living some sort of parasitic and derivative existence because of restrictively conceptualizing consciousness, which itself is essentially as unbounded as the sky, as free space, as the vast and unfathomable ocean. Even the concepts of law and evolution merely refer to a process of ceaseless breathing in and out, a cyclical manifestation in time, which itself cannot be caught within the circle. We can never see a circle from outside if we are identified with any point in the circle.

Immense implications would emerge for the daily lives of human beings if they could seriously ask whether the *onus probandi* is in the wrong place all the time. They could look at babies and try to work back in consciousness to a time when they were less confined. Look at a person before he is obsessed with grades and degrees; watch a person over a weekend when he forsakes the distinctions that men make during the week. Every human being senses that he or she is more than all the conventionalized distinctions, which are devices for the solidification of matter and thereby a conceptual prison for consciousness. Human beings must give themselves the opportunity, deliberately and self-consciously, to focus their attention upon the forgotten truth that the mind cannot ever encompass reality. The very thought of space reaching out in every direction has a purifying and liberating effect upon the mind. This is because of fixed presuppositions and assumptions in relation to matter and spirit, which are merely two aspects of one and the same homogeneous substance-principle. Although called by many names, in the *Diamond Sutra* it is depicted as the fusion of the void with the white heat of thought bursting its own boundaries. The separation of inner from outer, man from the world, the infinite space within from the dimensionally defined though limitless space without, has a corrective and therapeutic function in relation to recovery of self-awareness within the context of shared awareness. If we think of many centres of light blended together, counting and differentiating become irrelevant. One experiences the joy and the thrill of a flood of light, but even this is only from the standpoint of the sense-organs. What looks like a flood of light may in fact be only a mirage, a film or veil upon that incredible voidness of absolute darkness which is necessarily true light.

In delivering the *Diamond Sutra* the Buddha was stretching the serene minds and spatial perspectives of those few disciples gathered around him who already sensed that plane of consciousness where the Buddha abides even while in manifestation. They were able to accommodate the magnitude of vision of the Bodhisattvic state. The *Bodhisattva* is a being who has mastered the wisdom of compassion. Wisdom manifests as an unmodified state of calm consciousness. Everything else in relation to it is like an evanescent bubble. Thinking about this untrammelled perspective can help us to understand our own time. What individuals have failed to do on their own is happening collectively: there is a shared experience of voiding old forms and the past criteria of frozen meanings, all of which can no longer be maintained because the very will to impose them has weakened, and the defensive will to react against them is on the decline. The moment individuals try to capture this awareness of voiding the old in terms of isms or nihilisms, they experience the painful gap between soul-awareness and the cool capacity of spiritual wakefulness to master and radiate through every mode of expression with the precision one would find in music or mathematics. The Buddha was, in effect, extolling the music of the Soundless Sound, the mathematics of the zero. He was an artist speaking and singing, but also gently chiding. He effortlessly embodied, in an inimitable manner, the inexhaustible plenty of the boundless ocean of wisdom *(Prajna)* and compassion *(Karuna).*

If a person really begins to see simultaneously from alternative standpoints and can make this a living reality in consciousness, while recognizing that this is still based upon a relative but always mistaken assumption of separate selfhood, then he is doing what is suggested in one puzzling place in the *Diamond Sutra.* The question is asked, why is the Absolute in persons? This is philosophically strange when so much has been said to void all attributes of

Absoluteness. Any person can, as much as any other, embody and maintain self-consciously the serene awareness of the whole. This suggests that though our language and thought are riddled with pairs of opposites, the activity in itself, *tathata,* the thing in itself which is truly a process, is so overwhelmingly profound that it creates a Buddha-field. How is this possible? When people get together they collectively create a shared but nonetheless dependent sense of reality, but the moment a sufficient number of persons lose interest in that form of sharing, the entire field becomes absurd. This is a fact about human consciousness which requires and presupposes differentiation. The differentiation is constantly cancelled by the interaction which cannot be sustained except in terms of the false supports provided by the seeming continuity and substantiality of what is unreal unless beings attach and assume a reality to it. This is only a way of saying that a human being can never stay still. No man can ever experience total immobility. If he did, he would cease to be alive. Equally, the mere fact of always changing does not by itself mean anything in relation to the motive of unfolding the five eyes of which the *Diamond Sutra* speaks. Motive itself is the vast motor-force of *Fohat,* an ocean of energy in ceaseless motion.

If the entire universe is a golden egg in which there is a fructifying principle of expansion, a breathing outwards, then all particular acts and motives are as unreal relative to the pulsation in the cosmic egg as an appendage which imagines it exists on its own, that it is not in fact wholly dependent. Every organ and cell of the human body depend upon that incredibly intricate network of nerve centres and invisible capillary streams of electromagnetic threads in subtle matter that binds together all light-atoms. The thought is overwhelming because human beings normally settle for less. Whether they talk a moral language, a seemingly philosophical idiom, or a scientific-mechanistic jargon, they are engaged in some sort of collective self-mutilation. One might think, as Tolstoi wrote in *War and Peace,* that there is no set of reasons sufficient to convey the rationale behind the bizarre course of history. Is there really free will? Tolstoi asked of the Napoleonic war whether it was all caused by one particular man with his obvious limitations, or whether perhaps there was a vaster force operating. When we seem to sense that greater force at work, it matters little who fills the role for the consummation of the collective Karma of the aggregates of human beings that masquerade as nations and races. We come to see what Schopenhauer stressed in the nineteenth century. The notion of personal will is possibly a tragic illusion. To this extent the behaviourists are right, but only from the standpoint of differentiated separateness which dilutes and destroys the mind. What behaviourists are doing in one direction is similar to what drug addicts are doing in another. There is a common, desperate need to wipe out some essential features of consciousness and experience.

Supposing a man, when he looked at his life, saw that he could not particularize, did not plan, or deliberately intend most of what he did. When he begins to make experiments with the vast storehouse of energy that is the universe, with every centre of which he is linked through one of the various elements and substances in his being, he attempts to do what Nature does and becomes an alchemist. Every such apprentice alchemist will soon discover the extraordinary powers of concentrated thought and of controlled creative imagination. Few persons today think that the problems of some years ago, which at the time seemed so impossibly cosmic, were more than turbulences in teacups. Given the logic of identification, this is part of the ineluctable process of the prismatic scattering of undifferentiated consciousness into seven rays, which soon become obscured in a kaleidoscopic shadow-play. There is, in Platonic language, a series of reduced reflections, rather like an array of poor reproductions from a negative. There is a deep sense in which all human beings are dreamily involved in a secondary kind of existence. When men begin to wake up to the vastness and potency of cosmic will –

rather than fear a grotesque God whimsically manipulating the world – they will see that there is nothing greater on earth than the sovereign dignity and majesty of self-consciousness. There is an amazing plasticity, power, flexibility and range to human consciousness, but also myriad possibilities of polarization through a perverse disinclination to focus steadily on a worthy goal. We drift into false assumptions about "I" as "Mr. So-and-So", deciding now to do this, and to do that tomorrow. There is a recurrent constriction of consciousness. There is ever the danger of losing our awareness of the internality which must be unbounded in relation to the unending variety of fields of cognition. It was recognized even by someone as inverted in spiritual perception yet insightful as Hobbes, who said that cognition is rather like conceiving or giving birth. Imagining, on the other hand, is not like conceiving. The imagination is so fertile, capable of such an immense progeny, that one cannot limit its richness in terms of certain strenuous acts of cognition.

Our very language comes in the way of becoming self-consciously aware of what we already know. If we did not already know it, no communication would ever convey to us the consubstantiality of consciousness, behind and beyond possible focussing points of perception, and the intelligent, boundless universe as a vast though arbitrary aggregation of innumerable possible fields. This is the most difficult and crucial of all subjects for reflection. One can initially understand it by application to specific matters and then by learning to be free-wheeling in thought. This makes real the connection between unconditioned and conditioned. If a person has thought this through – engaged in *dianoia* – he finds that the whole notion of motive is transformed. While the universe cannot protect one's private intentions, through thought one can insert anything one chooses into the total good. Even though one does not fully know what that is, one can recognize it. One can equally visualize going in the opposite direction, unless one has blinded oneself to the point of enjoying a psycho-physical death-wish. We find we cannot explain easily the gesture of Jesus to Dostoevski's Grand Inquisitor. We cannot fathom the smile of a Mona Lisa or the inscrutable expression on the face of the Egyptian Sphinx. If a person suddenly did something without quite knowing why, in an atmosphere of acceptance and hope, with a great deal of give and take and a freedom from the burden of judgement, he or she would be astonished at how much human beings can improvise. And yet, they do it all the time when they care for each other. But when the demon of judgementalism, mired in a self-destructive shadowy self, and therefore a desperate insecurity, slithers like a snake into the picture, then nothing looks quite right. Everything is open to suspicion, so human beings torture themselves and nourish illogical attitudes.

The tradition that goes back to Gautama the Buddha and before, and which came down through teachers like Pythagoras and Shankaracharya, venerates the universal mind, the jewelled storehouse of all thought. At one with it any human being is invincible, but separated from it a person is a playground of illusions, inversions and deceptions. When anyone really thinks through the message of the *Diamond Sutra,* he soon finds that the meaning of life is totally different because he was overlooking that which was obvious from the first. There is an omnidirectional reflection of light in even the rough-cut diamond. Each is reminiscent, in its own way, of the Kohinoor – the renowned 108 carat "Fullness of Light". Many have wondered about its enigmatic history traced through many kingdoms. Its story is shrouded in the secret annals of Initiates. There exist beings capable in consciousness of maintaining a boundless field of awareness in a manner that can be hooked to any point in space-time. The human mind when perfected in its powers is capable of impressing matter at a noumenal level merely by the magnetic touch of a finger or through a deft rearrangement of life-atoms. Nature is itself the carrier of myriad impresses across millennia, converting coal eventually into a diamond.

In *Gupta Vidya* there are no such firm distinctions as we tend to make between metaphysical, mythic and metaphorical. Reality is one. The sages speak in terms of a total knowledge of all correspondences, and at the same time they can make endless substitutes and conversions because they effortlessly handle all the polarities – north, south, east, west, above, below – and yet they know that all of these are relativities. The *Diamond Sutra* is addressed to the Diamond Soul in every man, the hidden centre of the limitless light of awareness. We may be misled by physical analogies, but this noumenal light of mental awareness can create, sustain and dissolve entire fields of cognition. We know from common experience that few things can survive when totally ignored by all, and also that when human beings seize upon something, they lend it verisimilitude. The truly wise man both negates and affirms as he walks through life. Having found meaning and reality in abiding as a motionless being clothed in refined matter, he is like a person who has gone back into the egg. This is a puzzling phenomenon because we do not have physical representations which adequately depict the magic and beauty of self-transformation. When we reflect upon the diamond and the sun, we can conceive of subtle interactions over immense distances in time and of space. Yet a meteorite suddenly penetrating the atmosphere of the earth can instantly convert into diamonds whatever comes in its way. The laser beam of Buddhic perception can reach to the core *(tattva)* of anything and everything because it bypasses the region of dependent and secondary causation. It penetrates to the very root.

The *Diamond Sutra* teaches that any person can, in principle, see to the core of conditioned reality. He can do this through a clear-sighted recognition of the dimensionless cause of unconditioned reality within himself and everyone else. The jewel is within one's reach; one has to use it. When a person is ready to replace angular views with a rounded vision, he can activate the magnetic sphere of influence around him. At all times human beings, on all planes, either speed up or slow down. They exhibit either restlessness or inertia and cannot move equally in all directions at the same time. As one moves away from homogeneity into the realm of the differentiated, what one man cannot use, another man will appropriate. This applies not only to human beings but to all whirling centres of energy. Nature abhors a vacuum. There is nothing that is wholly unused except on the visible plane, and even this is mayavic. One's whole conception of the world of which one is a part can be profoundly altered. To the unfolding Buddhic perception of a person who is truly awake, the logic of relations in diverse realms of matter and consciousness has nothing to do with those eyes and ears which Heraclitus designated as false witnesses to the soul. If human beings had always trusted to the unreliable reports of their physical sense-organs, there would have been no real knowledge of any kind. It is thanks to the light of intelligence and self-reflection that there is knowledge. Souls that are fully awake radiate the inimitable lustre of the diamond through the magical fusion of wisdom and compassion. Buddha exemplified the sovereign human capacity of voiding the seeming full whilst also showing an unspoken, ever-present sympathy for everything that lives and breathes.

Whenever a person realizes the self-subsisting nature of truth, he enjoys the ineffable freedom which commands the power to see through the eyes of others, with and for them. He finds exhilaration in the expansion of consciousness that encompasses myriad perspectives. A point comes when one can do this not intermittently and by degrees, but ceaselessly by going to the very core, like the sage on a mountain who forgets there is a mountain, who sees no distinctions amidst the plains and between souls, but is replete with cosmic affirmation from what looks like bare negation in a limitless, azure expanse. These are imperfect representations of noumenal realities in the realm of consciousness. Every person has within him or her the possibility of coming closer to the Diamond Soul, the true Self of all. It is transcendent and need not be transfixed one-dimensionally or in as many dimensions as one may count, because it has a solidity and depth inseparable from the void. It is that which constantly rediscovers the voidness of the seeming full – the striking keynote of Buddha – and thereby prepares a person to do that which Krishna taught – to see the fullness of the seeming void. To bring these two archetypal modes together is the noble prospect and the divine destiny of the forerunners of the Aquarian Age. This is a time which spares no illusions or shadows, but which is spacious and fertile in opportunities for such expansion of awareness as may attract credible and sharable representations from the realm of *Akasa* into the free spaces among human beings.

Hermes, May 1978
Raghavan Iyer

INSIGHT AND ENERGY

The universe really is motion and nothing else
Plato

Energy is generated by cosmic ideation within the ever-potential field of cosmic electricity. On the subtlest levels of abstraction there is an incredible rapidity of rhythmic motion in a diaphanous, undifferentiated, homogeneous material medium. At that level of cosmic unity there can be no sharp distinction between ideation or thought and motion or electricity involving atomic particles. *Alayavijnana*, cosmic consciousness, is the storehouse and the penultimate source of all the energy moving on all planes of awareness and matter through descending degrees of differentiation and varying rates of motion, elaborating different curves of cyclic origination, alteration, decay and destruction.

When contrasted with this cosmic perspective, the early modern distinction between kinetic and potential in the natural sciences, stemming from crucial moves made in the eighteenth and early nineteenth centuries – especially in the contributions of Young who connected energy with work – is inadequate. Even at a physical level, problems remain in regard to what is potential and what is actual. Potentially, there is energy in a suspended object to the extent to which it has not fallen. If it were to fall, it would release energy, but if it is fixed in place, it is not going to fall. If it has potential energy in terms of the notion of a falling object though it is an object that is secured, what kind of energy is in fact involved though it is not visible as active energy in motion? It might be said that gravity exerts a measurable pull upon it, but what is that? A person may thus try, in a Socratic way, to ask the sorts of questions which the pioneers of the modern natural sciences raised, but now in reference to the conceptual framework of contemporary mechanics, biology or chemistry. Galileo once puzzled in church about the uniformity in the time intervals of the oscillations of a pendulum despite the diminishing of the arc of oscillation.

Beginning to ask basic questions with the help of examples will show that the distinction between potential and actual is relative to those who are at a certain point in a realm of actualization. For someone at a point of stasis or standstill, all motion is relative to that position, and as objects move at the same rate along parallel lines, each appears motionless to the other.

In a Leibnizian sense, all possible worlds exist in the divine mind, but there seems to be only one particular world of which we are a part. This world must be a complex manifestation, through myriad monads, of one primordial monadic essence within the divine light. If, for example, one took a blank sheet of paper and set down three variables in relation to some problem, a number of models or different combinations of possible alternatives could emerge. If the problem is simple enough and one is sufficiently logical at that level of simplicity, it is possible to exhaust the alternatives. This soon becomes tedious for a thinking person who wishes to see what further permutations and combinations could be made. Meditation is a constant cancelling in thought of crystallization inherent in particularization. Non-attachment is a logical pre-condition for self-consciously handling matter at a rate of extremely rapid motion, like the speed of light, and shaping out of homogeneous substance a suitable vehicle for the concentrated noetic energy that streams forth from an ever-present awareness of the unconditioned and the unmanifest. Noetic insight is much richer than merely handling alternatives in a dry-as-dust, arid manner wherein an attenuated scheme of logic results in circumscribed logical possibilities.

Self-conscious thinkers are aware that through every thought they produce a progeny, that through every image they emanate a whole procession of elementals. This is not very difficult to imagine when one knows that merely by dropping fifty cents on the floor a million ergs are released. The erg is a minute unit of measurement and yet a wealth of energy and motion is involved. More generally, the earth's entire energy resources, the focus of many self-elected prophets of doomsday, are miniscule in comparison to the energy released by the sun. In about fifteen minutes the sun radiates upon our planet more energy than the whole world consumes in a year. Here one directly confronts the poverty of conventional categories of thought in relation to demonstrable evidence for the tremendous plenitude in regard to solar heat, light and electro-magnetic energy. Contemporary science is still crude, awkward and assertive due to its state of adolescence.

In a metaphysically impoverished climate, merely to say that people ought to think of logical possibilities will not help them to tap noetic energy. We might enlist a concept like vision from religion and myth. The advantage of the term "vision" is that everyone can understand the use of the eyes, and knows at some level what is involved in seeing even though most have not really thought much about it. Even without being an artist, a person knows that one critical element in seeing is perspective. A more crucial element is the capacity to be able to handle different perspectives over a period of time. Still better, though more difficult, is the ability to handle various perspectives simultaneously. Even on the physical plane there are rich imaginative possibilities which are forfeited through fixation or through having a wandering eye. Most people are simply not able to exercise the full potential of the godlike faculty of sight on the physical plane. When people think that by the aid of a drug, a technique, a text, they could suddenly have a vision, see sights, forms and sounds, and even have some sensation of light, the word "vision" becomes so plebeianized, even in its mystic sense, that many hazards are connected with its use. There is no cognitive content to that kind of concept. People who have had what they sincerely believe are valid and beautiful visionary experiences may very quickly trivialize them by depicting them in the language of emotion. Does this give one real knowledge? Does it permanently transform one's view of the world? At one level, it does give the recognition that the world of superficial appearances is a lie and that much so-called knowledge is empty and pretentious. This recognition has a certain value but it is not very constructive.

Although it is a useful exercise to insert a philosophical notion like logical possibility or vision into the common conception of potential and kinetic motion, this moves us no closer to a grasp of higher states of consciousness. Such states cannot be unlocked by any stolen key because they presuppose a distinct moral requirement – disinterested, altruistic, detached receptivity. It has to be disinterested to release a high level of energy. It has to be altruistic, for unless one can release pure energy one would be burnt up at the higher levels. This is a merciful protection because few could truly handle the power of a cosmic vision. With Nietzsche, many might say, "Let the veil remain." The larger the vision, the greater the corresponding compassion required. The more penetrating the insight, the greater the necessary detachment and the single-minded concentration needed. One must be sufficiently strong and unafraid, not wanting anything for oneself that is not legitimate and which cannot be effortlessly secured like the breathing of air or the drinking of water. The moral requirement for tapping high energies is not an arbitrary imposition upon self-conscious beings by some capricious authority. It is actually a psychological pre-condition for being able to maintain a poise which is needed to sustain subtler vestures in realms of consciousness wherein the crucial distinction is not between actual and potential, but rather the ontological distinction between potentiality and potency.

Metaphysical imagination, continuous reflection and deep meditation are required for real understanding. One could learn by looking at Nature, the inimitable teacher. Nature is a servant of Adepts, but a teacher to everyone else. Even on the physical plane, potential energy has something to do with height. Consider what happens to the immense electrical energy potentially available in the downward trickle of mountain streams. Where does it come from? It represents nature's work as an alchemist in taking the moisture in the ocean and evaporating it through heat. Through the evaporation and raising of moisture to a sufficient height, nature is able to convert alchemically that water so that it is not energically the same as it is when at sea level. There are only a few drops where a stream begins, but there is a vast potential energy present. Yet that potential energy is in fact an actual energy in relation to the potential energy which went into the whole process of alchemization begun by heat and which will also be present when the process is complete.

There is something in higher states of consciousness analogous to the experience of a condition which is neither hot nor cold, but where there is a vivifying participation in the cool blue flames of a soft light which can release a steady stream of energy and which could be used at will in any direction on any plane beginning with ideation and working downward. One soon reaches a point where one has to relinquish conventional distinctions and also recognize the poverty of all mundane concepts. There is some similarity between the image-making power of a newborn babe, innocently floating on the ocean of life, and the disciplined imagination, gently guided by a benevolent will, of the detached and all-seeing Adept. There is more similarity between these than between the disciplined imagination of the Adept and the impressionistic visions of excitable prophets. These latter are chaotic, and have only a limited validity in relation to the illusions of men in the realm of so-called reality made up of divisive and tortuous, impotent and aborted, actualizations. Confused visions are not merely crude and delusive, but actually generate a perverse and demonic energy.

Patanjali's *Yoga Sutras* refers to two kinds of energy. One kind of energy, which might be called a sort of higher *prana*, gives one level of understanding. The other kind of energy cannot remotely be tapped, except through a serene continuity of consciousness called *sama* or similitude. In such a state, a person can consciously make luminous the sphere surrounding his *rupa* and effortlessly sustain self-luminosity. This is only possible at a high level of ceaseless meditation upon the one secondless, universal source of divine light. It involves the theurgy wherein a person sees all beings as spheres of light within a vast universe which is a limitless, boundless sphere of light. From this perspective, one would be able self-consciously to transmute every atom of one's grosser vestures and radiate out, from above below and from within without, that supreme self-luminous noetic energy which can light up the atoms and arouse the potentials that slumber in human beings. No society, group or civilization can self-consciously harness this energy – even for the sake of the collective good – without fulfilling the moral and psychological prerequisites that are needed. There is no possibility of access to *Akashic* energy without fulfilling the ethical pre-conditions that prevent its misuse. People might, however, in a misguided search for the *vril* foster a multitude of delusions. Strictly speaking, all the psychic states are shadowy and insignificant in relation to the wisdom of noetic insight.

One could, with unwavering detachment, profound disinterestedness, and unconditional benevolence towards all, sustain a higher indifference in relation to every aspect of this world of manifestation, and yet see all relativities from the standpoint of unconditioned consciousness in which the self-luminosity of the divine is ceaselessly present. It is necessary to discriminate between the turbulent atmosphere of divisive, separative thought coalescing with psychic forces and the pellucid strength generated by the noetic energies of sustained altruistic thought. Proximity on the physical plane has nothing to do with co-adunition and consubstantiality on higher planes of consciousness. Human beings carry their own problems around them, creating and living in their own world. Maya or deception accompanies the notion that because people are close together on the physical planes they therefore share a common access to the same current of ideation. The situation is quite different if persons are consciously aware of the thoughts and energies they release. At the highest level, there is no real distinction between thoughts and feelings and noetic energies. They are intermeshed. They are emanations which involve noetic thought, Buddhic feeling and spiritual energy. These emanations will always bless, but especially those who are willing to expel from their own vestures chaotic and befouled energies.

All aspirants must do something on their own. It cannot be done for them. They must aid in the conscious and continual purgation of these muddled matrices, the fuel of their *Kama Manas*, so that the void can be filled by streams of noetic energy. But this would be very misleading if a person expected it to happen suddenly: hence Plato's metaphor of the leaky jar in *Gorgias*. If a person made it a habit of allowing himself to be filled up with foul matrices only to eliminate them, merely out of soul-disgust, and then was able out of unconscious receptivity to receive a great outpouring of higher energy – it could not be retained. One cannot retain noetic energies if one has cut astral grooves that can only channel lower emanations. One would be like a leaky jar that has been so befouled that every time it is emptied, and pure fresh water is put into it, the fresh water gets contaminated. In the process of dynamic interchange of life-atoms, the fresh water would be expelled by evaporation.

A person has to do those basic things which will help produce more fundamental, stable, reliable and long-term changes in his vestures. One must establish points of contact and connections between the highest thoughts, feelings and states which one can maintain in daily life. One can experience the vibrant ocean of life-energy when at sunrise or at sunset one is able to experience the majesty and joy of the burgeoning light hidden behind the vast vista of nature's wealth of manifestation. Old cultures practised self-conscious modes of purification. What is the equivalent on the mental plane to bathing, to becoming ready to receive the manna that one hopes will fall from heaven? What is the equivalent of wanting to share it on the plane of thought and feeling with those who need help, or with those whom through the natural course of events one could help? One's own integrity and honesty, as well as toughness, are involved. Fearlessness is the defining characteristic of spiritual strength, and is the only basis upon which one could release truly noetic energy. No man could suddenly jump from being a concatenation of fears to supreme fearlessness. The very fact that one wants to jump means one is somewhere afraid of failure, hoping for spiritual favours or that partiality will work on one's behalf. What is that self that one is so anxious to protect, and on behalf of which one has to be so afraid and to seek favours?

In the *Bhagavad Gita* one could see unlimited applications of the central teachings, not merely to life conceived in terms of events, external decisions and particular duties, but in terms of a noble and noetic consciousness that must be vigilantly maintained with increasing detachment and without fear or wish for favour. Then, in a state of inward receptivity, one could enter the world of divine light, the light of the Logos within every man and behind and beyond the universe, a world in which every thought and feeling is instantaneously translated into altruistic action for the sake of all.

Hermes, January 1978
Raghavan Iyer

POLARITY AND DISCRIMINATION

As a lamp in a windless spot does not flicker, so is the man of subdued thought who practises union in the Self.

Shri Krishna

It is intrinsic to the complex nature of man that though he necessarily participates in the ever-present polarity of the three qualities *(gunas),* he is always capable of mirroring spaceless wisdom in the theatre of time. According to the ancient teachings of the sages, man is essentially aloof from all the modifications of his mind. Man is more than the medley of bodily movements, more than the sum-total of his desires, and stronger than the torrent of thoughts that rush forth in a frenzied procession before his inward eye. Man is vaster than his variegated states of consciousness. Every person is beyond all possible modes of manifestation, for at the root there is an inmost core of consciousness wherein one is free from the familiar pairs of opposites. There is hardly a human being who does not savour golden moments of release and reconciliation, a deep feeling of joyous freedom, a firm sense of the falling away of fetters. There is not a person who does not experience, while tossed between the polarities of inertia and impetuosity, intervals of rhythmic, harmonious movement. Every person, in principle, is conscious of boundless space, ceaseless motion and eternal duration. These transcend the clumsy categories into which human life is conventionally divided. Man has the potential power of going beyond yesterday, today and tomorrow, here, there and everywhere. It is this central truth, as Krishna suggests in the *Bhagavad Gita,* that makes man capable of union with the Universal Self. Each can become a true man of meditation, with an inalienable freedom from captivity to the *gunas* as well as a creative participation in the three qualities – in illumination, in the desires and passions of the world, and in the enveloping fog of obscuration, darkness and ignorance. At all times, the immortal soul is uninvolved.

In Buddhist literature the elephant symbolized the magnanimous potentials of human nature. The impersonal majesty, gentle friendliness and steady reliability of elephants are familiar to all, and there is scarcely anyone who cannot appreciate the story of the six blind men and the elephant. One of them clasped the tail and concluded that the elephant was a rope; another held the trunk and decided that the elephant was a huge serpent; the blind man who grasped a leg thought the elephant was like a tree; stroking the ear, another surmised the elephant to be a fan; touching the elephant's side, the fifth man took the elephant to be a wall; and finally, seizing a tusk, the sixth man feared the elephant was a spear. So they all came to conflicting views. A seventh person, standing apart and clearly seeing that there are six paradigmatic standpoints corresponding to north, south, east, west, above and below, could cherish a synthesizing insight. All six perspectives are partially true, but none of them expresses the whole truth. The Buddha often spoke of the elephant as signifying the *Bodhisattva*, with his wisdom and compassion. The *Bodhisattva*, like the elephant, is incapable of forgetting anything which is relevant to what he needs to know. At the same time, he is suffused by supreme detachment. The *Bodhisattva*'s eyes, like those of the elephant, are gentle and full of tenderness, gladdening all around. The *Bodhisattva* teaches what it is to be truly human, to be abundantly affectionate, to love generously. Just as little children can approach elephants with no fear of being hurt, so too may all men and women approach the *Bodhisattvas*.

The elephant displays a marvellous blending of the three qualities. The elephant is tamasic; no one who sees a quiet pachyderm weighing four tons is likely to regard the animal as restless. There is a tremendous stability to the elephant. At the same time, though it is tamasic, it relishes harmless pleasures, as every child knows who has had the satisfaction of offering bananas to an elephant. Yet the elephant is proverbially patient and long-suffering, with a majestic indifference to the curiosity of passers-by. In this way the elephant indicates the enormous potential strength of soul, mind and character in every human being. Furthermore, the elephant shows the most harmonious movements, swishing its tail or swaying its trunk. When it raises its trunk, it salutes the boundless sky, its tusks ever pointing upwards. To take an elephant's-eye view of the world is to appreciate the immensity of what is above by saluting the vastness of the sky while at the same time standing very firmly on the ground. When in motion the elephant is an enchanting sight. Bartok, commenting on a delightful passage in one of Beethoven's symphonies, said that it was like the stately yet playful movement of elephants dancing. Such music employs the bass notes of heavy instruments and at the same time conveys to intuitive listeners a quality reminiscent of those haunting times in history when great events converged. Elephants are symbolic reminders of the momentous changes that are gestating today on the globe, seminal movements which are the unacknowledged reflections of the sacrificial ideation of *Bodhisattvas*. Remaining rooted in immovable contemplation upon the spaceless, the soundless, the boundless, they are also motionless in mind and in will, yet rhythmic and deliberate in thought and creation. They participate in the vicissitudes of historical cycles sufficiently to understand human beings who are still captive to the bonds of matter, but at the same time they remain in a seeming state of non-activity because they have no incentive or motivation to act for the sake of results. They simply do not live for the fruits of action, and are beyond praise and blame, while effortlessly exemplifying the Religion of Responsibility.

The *Bhagavad Gita* intimates that perfectibility is a meaningful ideal because it is rooted in the very ground of one's being. In effect, Krishna's teaching is echoed in the injunction of Christ: "Be ye therefore perfect, even as your Father which is in Heaven is perfect." If every human being can summon an active faith in the possibility of perfection, then each can vitally participate in the vicissitudes of space and time, the perplexing imperfections of this world. If one can avoid consolidating through guilt-ridden tamasic obsession or precipitating through the intensely rajasic and disordered buzzing of the brain, or seeking self-satisfaction through a static, sattvic equilibrium, then one may become an apprentice in the art of alchemical self-transmutation. One could repeatedly rise above the three qualities and thereby recognize in this great teaching an assured basis for the principle of indefinite growth in the context of cool detachment and joyous renunciation. So long as the three qualities are not merely properties of matter and mind but also grounded in the very nature of differentiated reality, human beings can self-consciously seek the One in the many and then discern the many in the One. Eventually a point is reached when it is possible simultaneously to see the One in the many and the many in the One. The *Bhagavad Gita* blends three types of knowledge with the three *gunas*. In the fourteenth and seventeenth chapters the three qualities are differentiated at many levels, including faith, charity, action, knowledge, the discriminative faculty of *Buddhi*, the power of steadfastness and the potency of meditation.

In regard to discrimination of duty Krishna offers a dialectical teaching that can accommodate a variety of situations owing to its central logic. Quintessentially, it is a philosophy in which there is no intrinsic separation of the knower from the known. Anyone with a strictly conventional view of his obligations is apt to be attached to results. He becomes so conditioned and conditional that he can attempt something solely in the hope of reward. This is magnified unmistakably in an effete commercial culture where one never initiates anything unless it can be weighed and measured, bought and sold. Today many people are waking up to the absurdity of the logic of the cash register when applied to human encounters. Those who perform duties in a rajasic sense have no real discrimination. They are ever agitated by the desire for results, and, therefore, can only discharge their duties by setting false values upon them. They have somehow to set apart certain acts and duties from all others. Not only are they inflexible, but they are also preoccupied with the language of comparison and contrast. They soon start comparing and contrasting, whether in self-awareness or meditation, in drug-taking or erotic activity, in stocks and shares or success measured in terms of dollars and cents. As they are constantly involved in making comparisons which are misleading, they cling to a derivative and parasitic conception of duty. They cannot generate the supreme, serene sense of obligation of the truly free man who voluntarily binds himself by a fundamental commitment and chooses to honour it through every trial.

Alternatively, consider the person who decides to remain true to a sacred teaching and to a fundamental negation of false values. Here one may sense the strength of clear-sightedness brought over from previous lives in order to carry out a line of inward resolve. Such souls show the power of calm discrimination between essentials and non-essentials. The more tough-minded a person remains in preserving a pattern of self-chosen obligations – or as Krishna says, in doing *only* what is necessary – the more he is always, in every situation, ready to negate the superfluous while concentrating on what is needed. This produces a level of discriminative wisdom which is rather like the use and enjoyment of light. Some mystical poets compare this to the light that radiates from a red-hot piece of glowing coal. *Tamas* would be the same coal when it is inert. When a fire is put out, there is a death of rajasic radiance and there results a stone-like state concealing an inner process of disintegration. Discriminative wisdom exists at many levels. Herein lies the great strength and generous hope of the teaching of the *Bhagavad Gita.* Every rivulet of discrimination enhances the active power of *Buddhi.* Even if one merely has a few drops of the waters of devotion and humbly consecrates them at the inmost altar of Krishna, it is possible to negate in advance any attachment to consequences. Engaging in action in a sacrificial spirit, with pure joy and the willing acceptance of pain, the true devotee will certainly be delivered from a network of errors and miseries. In the progress of time he will surely experience tranquillity of thought. "*Dharma*" in Sanskrit has a very different connotation from any strenuous conceptions of duty, Calvinistic or Teutonic. There is instead a firm yet relaxed sense of obligation which is self-sustaining and also spontaneous. In the *Bhagavad Gita Dharma* is ascribed to fire, the sky, all objects in space, all phenomena in time, and the categories of selfhood. *Dharma* is that which *holds:* anything which holds up a human being, anything which sustains him, anything which helps him to keep going – is rooted in his duty. If *Dharma* upholds every person, anyone can regulate and refine *Dharma* through Buddhic discrimination. This is the sovereign talisman of every human being.

All persons inherently possess godlike faculties of imagination, creativity, freedom and serenity. All are capable of exalted conceptions of calm, and can expand their perspectives and horizons while at the same time bringing a godlike faculty of intense concentration to every task. The great Teachers of mankind have always reminded all of the privilege of incarnation into a human form. Many people, however, are liable to be so rajasic at the moment of death that they will soon be propelled back into incarnation in circumstances they do not like. There are also those who are so receptive in life to the summerland of ghosts, demons and disintegrating entities, *pisachas* and *rakshasas*, that at the moment of death they are drawn into the underworld of psychic corpses. Human beings are innately divine, but there are myriad degrees of differentiation in the manifestation of divine light. The light shines in all, but in all it does not shine equally. By using whatever in consciousness is an authentic mirroring of supernal light in the concrete contexts of daily obligations, one's own light will grow. The rays of truth can fall upon those who ardently desire to rescue the mind from the darkness of ignorance. It is critical for human beings to keep relighting themselves, to wipe out the ignorance that consolidates out of inertia and delusion in that pseudo-entity absolutized as the personal self. In the eyes of the sages there are only rays of light accompanied by long shadows masquerading as personalities.

Krishna speaks in the sixteenth chapter of those who are born with demonic qualities, and provides a perfect portrait of the contemporary dying culture in *Kali Yuga*. He also offers a compelling picture of the graces and excellences of those who evoke memories of the Golden Age. The demonic qualities, resulting in spiritual inertia, are the product of misuse in previous lives. Everyone who abused any power must face the consequences in the future. For three or four lives he may find his will blunted, his faculties castrated, his potencies circumcised, until he can thoroughly learn the proper use of his powers. There is a compelling passage in *The Dream of Ravan* wherein we are given a graphic analogy between states of mind and diseases. Theosophically, all ailments are caused in the realm of the mind; all ailments are rooted in the subtler vestures. *Sattva* corresponds to the *karana sarira,* the causal body, comprising the most fundamental ideas of selfhood in relation to which one generates a sense of reality. There is a correspondence between *rajas,* the principle of chaotic desire, and the *sukshma sarira,* the astral form. When this is irradiated by the Light of the Logos, it can show a reflected radiance. In all human beings there are glimmerings of noble aspiration, the yearning to do good. This is the source of fellow-feeling, the kindness of a mother for her children, the solicitude of a doctor for a pregnant woman whose baby he is delivering. These are mere intimations of that sattvic quality which can make a human being magnanimous, noble and free.

The astral body is lunar and is affected by the phases of the moon. It is vulnerable to pollution, especially through self-hatred, perverse ambition and self-dramatization. This is accompanied by the ever-thickening anxiety which deep down in the soul represents the fear that one may not return in a human form. With the disconnection between what the soul knows in sleep and what the mind fears in waking life, there is an acute sense of being unworthy of the rich resources of life. This enormous sense of inadequacy is coupled with the terror of loneliness, aggravated by the inability to share the joys and sorrows of others. It is pathetic to be preoccupied with success and failure. There is nothing more tedious than continuously adding up the figures in one's own account. When such a person gives himself a rest, he mistakes chaotic images in the brain for thinking, or the mechanical borrowing of sounds and gestures for sacred mantrams. Mantrams must be intoned with tremendous deliberation. When persons find that they are like leaky jars and at the same time suffer a painful inner congestion, they must recognize that there is no release except through fundamental measures. There is no protection for the lazy and the weak, nor for those who indulge in self-pity but who are perversely strong-willed. These spiritual and moral cowards, drawing on frustration and hatred from previous lives, would either like to rearrange everything instantly, or steal their way, with drugs or incantations, into the magic casements of mystical states of consciousness. Many, through memories from previous lives, would like to think that simply by holding a book they will be saved. Any possibility of redemption, however, depends upon the degree and continuity of their genuine concern for other human beings.

There is an enigmatic story in the *Bhagavatam* about a man who became wicked. He had several children, named after gods and goddesses, and at the moment of death he happened to cry out the name of his son Narayana. Because he uttered this divine name in a mood of resignation when the god of Death came, he suddenly began to see the light. The god of Death took counsel with the attendants of Vishnu, who asked, "Can you take him away when he has uttered this sacred sound?" Then they told this man that he could have another lease on life, but they warned him that henceforth no accidental sounding of the divine name would protect him. From now onwards he must deliberately and daily intone it. The gods knew that in his sounding of the name there was a residual sincerity reaching out to Lord Narayana, and that if he got another chance, he would deeply repent and generate constancy of devotion. There are few experiences that are so chastening as a narrow escape from death. Unfortunately, many people have not used their time to think through their fundamental view of life, but it is always possible to reflect that there are other human beings on earth, that the world is a wonderful place, that one's life is not one's own to throw away. One is indebted to one's parents and teachers for myriad opportunities to learn, and just because one fails to reflect calmly upon the good in oneself does not mean that one cannot grasp such opportunities or that one must continually brood on limitations. To do so is demonic. There are large numbers of people with abundant energies and considerable powers, but unable to use them effectively because of past misuse, owing to excessive meditation upon themselves and of extreme callousness in regard to means and ends. They have played the ancient game of gaining confidence at the expense of others, but for such there is no cosmic protection. He who seeks to gain at the expense of another is lost in life after life. But he who seeks to grow in the service and the loving acceptance of all others, can always reflect upon the good in all human beings, and thereby release the good in himself.

Demonic inertia arises through a whole way of thinking that is false. If one thinks that this world exists for enjoyment only, that human beings are merely the ephemeral accidental product of the pleasure of a man and a woman, that everyone is in competition for wealth and fame and status, and if one ceaselessly caters to all such absurdities and stupidities, one develops an asuric nature. Anyone who really wants to rise above this condition could do no better than to ponder upon the seventeenth chapter of the *Bhagavad Gita,* the philosophical nature of the three qualities, and the sixteenth chapter, which gives the portraits of the demonic personality as well as the godlike being. A sensible person who wishes to travel on the road to true discipleship, will find that simply by studying these chapters calmly he could see clearly the convergence of attitudes and qualities that strengthens the demonic or godlike nature in man. Instead of indulging in self-pity and self-contempt, the sincere seeker of wisdom will allow his whole nature to become absorbed in contemplation on the godlike qualities. The whole of the *Bhagavad Gita* is replete with magnificent portraits of sages. The magic of meditation is such that by merely focussing upon them, they can release a light-energy which streams downward, freeing a person from the bondage of self-created illusions and self-destructive acts. Rid of the specious notion that he is somebody special, he can freely accept his cosmic potential as a point in space and joyously deliver himself with the dignity of man *qua* man. It is only when he is ready that Krishna confers upon Arjuna the exalted title of Nara (man), an individual ray of Divine Light. When a person can truly witness the divine in every human being, he can also see that every time anyone torments himself, he tortures Krishna. No one has such a right. One's parents did not give a body simply for the sake of crucifying the Christos-Krishna within. One has to free oneself from all obsessive identification with the shadow and salute the empyrean with the cool assurance of one who does not fear the light or is not threatened by the fact that other human beings exist, and whose stance is firmly rooted in the Divine Ground that transcends the *gunas* and the playful polarities of *Purusha* and *Prakriti*.

Hermes, July 1978
Raghavan Iyer

THE NACHIKETAS FIRE

A hundred and one are the heart's channels; of these one passes to the crown. Going up by this, he comes to the immortal.

Katha Upanishad

Viraga – indifference to pleasure and to pain, illusion conquered, truth alone perceived – marks the beginning of the razor-edged Path. For reasons connected with the cosmogony of divine wisdom, human beings find the first step on the Path the most difficult. They must come to an initial standpoint of detachment from the world, with its false values, its glamour and attractions, its nightmares and anguish. Indifference simply means perceiving no essential difference between pleasure and pain because both arise from cerebral reaction to sensory stimuli. They are alike devoid of intrinsic meaning for that Self which nurtures its own transcendent conception of growth. Two individuals, from seemingly identical experiences of pleasure or pain, may come to contrasting conclusions and derive radically different implications. Consider two persons who enjoyed identical dinners, containing ingredients guaranteed to produce a stomach-ache, such that both experienced gastric pains the next day. Similar facts yield no insight into the diverse meanings that persons might ascribe to their experiences. This points towards the philosophical basis of self-reference and action. Man is a value-assigning agent, who needs minimal freedom from titillation and disturbance induced by pleasurable or painful experiences. Once this initial standpoint of philosophical indifference is established even to a small extent, one will find out for oneself that it points to the Path of inward growth.

When one averts attention from the chaos of external events, through the dawning realization that assigning meaning and value is one's own task, one aspires to gain greater knowledge and control. Yet, turning inward, one soon confronts a host of unresolved elements – repressed fears and fantasies – within what is often called the unconscious. Once they are set in motion, one risks slipping into alternating euphoric and terrifying states, losing hold over the real world of spiritual light which one seeks as well as the public world of shared sensory impressions. To dare to face oneself fully is difficult, because the more illusions one strips away, the more illusions crop up. The protracted and painful, self-reinforcing nature of persisting illusions is familiar, but they must be cut through. Sufficient detachment enables one to glimpse the central but undiscovered truth of Self, omnipresent and indestructible, shining behind and beyond the world. This truth about oneself is equally the truth about the Path, which must be trodden in secret. Only by taking each step is the next revealed. Like a winding mountain path which cannot be discerned from a distance, it cannot be traced without treading it.

One must foster steadiness, determination and continuity, remaining fixed in the recognition of the spiritual insignificance of the passing panorama of the subconscious and the supreme value of the single truth that one now partly sees and wholly seeks. When a natural detachment is secured at this level, one is ready to experience greater fearlessness and more penetrating insight. *Viraga* is "the Gate of Balance". Repeatedly at different levels of growth, through daunting trials at successive stages of spiritual life, one needs to establish a stable fulcrum reflecting a mentally constant standpoint of inward steadiness and balance. Though seemingly complicated, this is not unlike walking, or balancing on a bicycle or a tightrope. One only knows for oneself that it is possible to balance, or that it is necessary to have absolute faith in one's spiritual strength. A tightrope walker cannot mechanically teach someone how to balance and perform delicate manoeuvres upon a very thin, taut thread. The experienced tightrope walker can take all the appropriate security measures in regard to the wire, but it is the learner who must not move one iota from an absolute, immovable conviction that he can both maintain and restore balance, and that even if he experiences a sudden loss of equilibrium, he can still bring himself back to the state of balance. Existential equilibrium cannot be taught to someone who is not actually involved in the dynamic struggle for balance amidst ceaselessly shifting variables.

Yet the more one gains proficiency in the practice of *viraga*, the more it becomes as natural as breathing.

One must be yoked, by regular meditation and recurrent reflection, to the universal Self. That Self is veiled rather than revealed by compulsive speech and chaotic thought-patterns. One has to sustain in daily life a secret spiritual discipline which no one else can gauge from observation of externals. This discipline has to do with constancy in that standpoint which steadily sees the universal Self behind the mental furniture of the world and the manifest self. What is at first an exercise in repeated balancing can become, after a while, a mental breathing as natural as physical breathing, leading to the state of inmost tranquillity. *The Voice of the Silence* enjoins the disciple to be ready to find "thy body agitated, thy mind tranquil, thy Soul as limpid as a mountain lake". It is possible to realize this within oneself and remain continuously in those depths of spiritual awareness where there are no ripples, but rather a serene experience of the limpidity intrinsic to Atmic consciousness. This may be brought down into the realm of the mind in a manner that makes for self-tranquillization and self-regeneration, and it is compatible with vigorous incarnation in the sphere of active duty. Like all subtle delineations of detachment, these lines from *The Voice of the Silence* have an archetypal significance. They are relevant at the beginning, but they presage the efflorescence at the end, and they have applications all along the Path.

The *Katha Upanishad* teaches that once one hears of this Path, one cannot pretend life will be the same again. Once the flashing insight has torn away "the loathsome mask", the words of truth cannot be set aside as if they were never heard. All who enter the orbit of great Teachers are self-condemned: they will never again be able to nestle in the soft folds of delusion, for "the Hound of Heaven" will pursue them to the end. Not to realize this is either naive ignorance about oneself and the universe, or perversity in the face of the embodiment of spiritual light within the vestures and limitations of this deceptive world. Since balance in motion requires both vision and aim, when one is in right earnest about treading the Path, it will be found that one cannot keep one's feet on that Path without practising spiritual archery. This is the continual realignment of mental vision, symbolized in archery by the relation of the eyes to the target. The target is the indestructible, the invisible, the formless, the great Self, which is mirrored in the divine Triad within and beyond one's manifest identity.

As the Buddha taught, one realizes upon entering the Path that it is impossible to fall back into thoughtlessness with impunity. On the razor-edged Path everything is finely balanced and highly energized. The greater the knowledge, the greater must be the responsibility and courage to accept the consequences of thoughts, images and ideation. More and more, one must feel a profound and cool heart-awareness of identity with every being whose limitations have become, through ignorance, like the entwining coils of a serpent. Compassionate awareness cannot be sustained without making the teaching come alive. Teachers vivify the ancient teachings by the light of their spiritual wisdom and through their own effortless embodiment of the oneness of all and the transcendence of the divine Triad beyond all cosmic phenomena. It is only through them that the disciple has the opportunity of lighting up "the Nachiketas Fire" of discernment and daring. Once lit, it must be tended and guarded by the disciple himself, and eventually fanned into a bright flame. Established on this Path, a stage will come when indifference to earthly reward will be natural and easy. In the *Katha Upanishad* Nachiketas simply could not see the point of the various gifts Yama first offered him: riches, kingship, kingdoms and pleasures. All these had no meaning for Nachiketas because he knew they were the trappings of a life he had long since outgrown. He sought the secret of immortality and was unconditionally willing to honour the privilege of receiving the secret and living by it. Every skill and faculty is needed while climbing the steep mountain precipices of the Path. It must never be forgotten that the necessary equipment is within oneself, and that it will all have to be used, because this Path is like a razor's edge. Those who would understand what these things mean cannot do so except by the effort to attain some initial foothold on the Path. Having heard about the Path and having grasped that one cannot evade this recognition, however partial or fleeting, one needs to see the profound sense in which the Path is difficult to travel.

The great metaphors – indeed, the entire parable of the *Katha Upanishad* – have manifold layers and levels of meaning, all pointing to the secret spiritual heart. In *The Voice of the Silence* the Path is connected with *antaskarana,* the bridge between the impersonal and personal selves. A time will come when a person must choose between the two, for either must prevail. One cannot both be on the Path and also maintain the absurd but common misconception that there is a personal entity inside oneself, to whom things are happening and who is planning the course of life. This is the prime illusion in the eyes of Seers: no such entity exists; there is only a bundle of propensities and reflexes. The concatenation of elemental entities comprising the shadowy self are engaged in their own activity. The personality may have the illusory thought lodged in it that it is acting freely, but it is only a congeries of life-atoms pursuing their own ends. The celebrated metaphor of the chariot, also deployed in Plato's *Phaedrus,* is given a vast extension in the *Katha Upanishad* as it is applicable to cosmic as well as to human activity. The *Katha Upanishad* may be seen not only as a philosophical dialogue, but also as an alchemical text, replete with deeply evocative, enigmatic and magical mantrams.

The image of the chariot and charioteer symbolizes a hierarchy of cosmic and human forces bridging the unmanifest and the manifest. Rather than an abrupt and stark dualism, they involve continuous degrees of manifestation. Consider a great architect, potter or creative cook. In the translation of a mental conception to the physical plane, one may discover that some critical ingredient is unavailable. When improvisation is required, the greater the artist, the more he or she can turn a supposed set-back into a timely opportunity for innovation which enriches the art. The artist knows that a creative and resourceful mind simply cannot be confined by a *priori* specifications attached to any great conception. Layers, levels and hierarchies, constituting thought which is cosmic and undifferentiated, intelligence which is bound up with differentiated matter and specific forms, and mediating will-energy, recur at every level of spiritual gestation and material manifestation.

At some point one must mentally let go of the route by which one has come, what the Buddha called the Raft and *The Voice of the Silence* terms the *antaskarana* bridge. This letting go is depicted in the image of the complete sacrifice of personal existence to the impersonal Self upon the altar of the heart. For a *manasa* to be engaged in personal existence means that an impersonal universe has made an immense sacrifice. This is symbolized physically by the sacrifice of the father in giving of his life-essence, and mentally by the magnanimous sacrifice of a great being giving freely of his spiritual essence so that evolution may go on. It is also evident in the noble sacrifice of the mother who, over a period of painful growth, gives everything to the astral body of the soul coming into the world, just as the maternal matrix of *Akasa* nourishes the embryo of the world. The impersonal has sacrificed for the sake of manifestation on the personal plane. This must be deliberately reversed through an intent awareness of what one owes to one's father, one's mother, and to all of one's teachers, especially to one's spiritual parents and teachers. The deliberate reversal involves taking everything that one has, with all one's strength and limitations, and sacrificing it for the sake of the self-conscious reemergence on the plane of manifestation of the inward god, the inner sovereign, who otherwise would remain the silent Self. One must allow that Self within, who is no different from the Self of all, to assume kingship.

No one can tap the highest resources without becoming secure enough to want nothing for the puny, shadowy self. Moved only by desires that elevate the whole of mankind and the entirety of life, and established in that proper posture, one can abandon the *antaskarana* bridge, because one can re-create it at will. Seeing one's personal self as no different from other personal selves, one can do the bidding of the divine through the instrumentality of anything in nature, including, therefore, the use of one's *persona*, in which one has renounced absolutely all proprietary interest. Becoming aware of the life-atoms in that vesture, one realizes that there is no such thing as the "personal self" save in a metaphorical sense. Life-atoms are constantly streaming in and out as part of the ceaseless spiritual transmutation of matter on seven planes and the uninterrupted law of sacrifice within the seven kingdoms of nature. The true *hotri* is an alchemist able to send out beneficent emanations through a mighty current of thought, meditation, vision and universal compassion, quickening the upward growth of all the life-atoms that are available. To such a sage the *antaskarana* Path does not have its former significance, except as a drawbridge to be extended at will in the service of universal welfare.

The important thing for all seekers is to seize upon that teaching which refers to taking the first step. One may begin with the profound feeling of gratitude for all one's gifts. Even every limitation could be seen as an opportunity. This attitude of mind is certainly helpful for any person trying to gain an initial self-understanding before treading the Path. At another level, it is even more important to recognize, in the words of *The Voice of the Silence*, how great is "the priceless boon of learning truth". Nachiketas is an archetypal man, a Golden Age figure who lived at a time when many people were aware that nothing was more precious than the teaching of immortality and the standpoint of the Supreme Self. Men searched all their lives and went through many tribulations and trials simply for the sake of coming closer to anyone who belonged to the Brotherhood of *Mahatmas*. Now, in the Iron Age, only those who have devoted many lives to this Path can know the magnitude of what has already been given. The fire is being rekindled for the sake of nothing less than the community of mankind of the future, most of whom are still unborn. It would be a sad mistake not to take full advantage and to make the best possible use, within one's own limitations and situation, of the opportunity to make a grateful, reverential response to the teachers of Divine Wisdom. This can only be authentically achieved through the attempt to live by and embody the teachings. Though initial efforts may falter, the moment a person begins to nurture a holy resolve whereby one will neither remit nor run away from the task to one's last breath, even a modest effort at the beginning will be charged with meaning and significance by the unconditional nature of the affirmation.

The value of the first step is enhanced when a person, instead of starting off with a limiting conception of personal and individual success and failure, thinks instead of human need, human pain and human ignorance. The stakes are high for multitudes of souls in our time, and immense could be the harvest from seeds sown in the right places with a wise detachment toward results. Individuals, galvanized by spontaneous love of their fellow-men in great need, can be sustained till the last breath by a steadfast determination to persevere. When one truly wakes up and stands firm, then one may also seek spiritual instruction from those who bear witness to the Master-soul within. One can thereby increase one's own possibilities of conscious access to *Sat* or truth, *Chit* or ideation, and *Ananda* or bliss, which abide in a single triad of supreme and active peace within the quiet depths of every human heart. Even though one may feel, in personal consciousness, that one can never become wholly one with It, nonetheless, one must continually seek and yearn, keeping alive this Nachiketas fire of devotion.

To comprehend this teaching in terms of the spiritual heart, one must start from the cosmic and descend to the human. The pulsating rhythm of life can never be perceived until a person begins to inhabit those higher planes which permit conscious use of subtle matter, in relation to which the physical body is like a coat or a garment. The *Upanishads* teach that for a wise man death is not an event. No one would think that the shadow is alive in the same sense in which the body is. For the wise, the body is like a shadow of that which is subtler and which it reflects. This subtle body in turn is a shadow in relation to something still more subtle which it partially mirrors. The dialectical method of the Hermetic fragments and the neo-Platonic mystics requires that we keep rethinking our view of light and shadow at many levels as we travel inward and

THE NACHIKETAS FIRE   109

upwards. One may approach the vast mystery of life by sensing the sun as a great heart which is constantly beating. There is a systole and diastole to the cosmic heart of the sun, without which no single heart could beat. The thrill of life in every atom and mineral, in every plant and animal, and in every human heart, is merely a derivative expression of perpetual motion in the ceaseless, rhythmic breathing of the great heart of the cosmos.

Everything is sevenfold and acts upon seven planes. Descending by analogy and correspondence to that miniature solar system which is the individual human being, one discovers an outwardly disordered and disharmonious system. But this is only true apparently, not fundamentally. Every person consists of a hierarchy of dynamic and complex systems, among which the most invisible are the most harmonious. What is most visible is the most disordered, being the most heterogeneous. On the external plane there are many obscurations and many violent, discordant movements. Therefore, it is difficult to grasp the majesty and grandeur of the proposition that every man is a microcosm, a little universe. But the core of the teaching of *Buddhi Yoga* is that each individual is capable, from the realm of the disordered and disharmonious, of coming closer through a series of progressive awakenings to that realm where one spontaneously affirms the mantram of Jesus, "I and my Father are one." Manifested consciousness may be yoked to the unmanifest consciousness of the real, unembodied Self – the Spiritual Sun at the heart of all, which is eternally in a proper relationship to every planet and to the subtlest constitution of man.

Anyone may begin by cultivating the highest feelings of which he or she is capable. This unravels the paradox, for the Heart Doctrine is the only key by which individuals may unlock the chamber of the deeper teaching, which by definition must be secret, as suggested in the *Upanishads* and their commentaries. The word *upanishad* itself implies secret, direct teaching from Master to pupil. The Heart Doctrine must be felt before one will be ready to use freely the spiritual teachings about the inner analogues – in the realms of idea, emotion and vital energy – of the circulatory, respiratory and all other systems of the physical frame. A beautiful Sanskrit word for the heart occurs in the *Upanishads*: *guhya,* "that which is hidden, that which is in secret". It is like the *sanctum sanctorum* of an old Hindu cave temple, with its analogies to the human body. Even if one goes into the temple, and even if one is admitted into the *sanctum sanctorum*, there is nevertheless a mystery beyond that which is seen. There is a sense, analogous to the mathematical concept of limit, in which one will never quite arrive at the end. The wise know that this is the symbolism of the temple: even if one presses into the darkest place in the *sanctum sanctorum* of the temple, it is only a point of entry to other states. The word *guhya* refers to what anyone who grows self-consciously in regard to various sheaths of human nature is going to discover – that which may be called the astral brain and heart. None of the five physical senses is any more than a mechanical outpost for activities that are located in the astral body. There are astral senses, and those who develop them will experience their tremendous range and extension, along with appropriate problems which would not be intelligible in terms of the physical plane. So too with the brain and the heart. There would be a progressive series of discoveries of correspondences to the heart at different levels in the different vestures or sheaths of the Supreme Self. Anyone who feels that there is a divine spark in every human being, about which one could silently think and with which one could inwardly commune, taps the potential wisdom of the hidden fire within the heart. Those who at some level begin to live this truth in every thought and feeling-impulse that they generate, deepen their inmost feeling for the sacred cause of the spiritual elevation of the race, the deliberate pursuit of self-knowledge for the sake of all. The more they can light up and rekindle, deepen and sustain this heart-feeling as a continuous flame of devotion, the more they can take what might look like thin, frail candles and light up their hearts. In time, the Nachiketas flame blazes up and is established on the square platform of the altar in the sanctuary of the heart. There it can shine in its full, hidden glory as a continuous regenerator of the kingdom in which man lives and which is his share in the great kingdoms of nature. Thus the true beginning is in the sphere of soul-feelings. Unless one's heart can feel something of the generosity and compassion, something of the immense heart-pulsation behind the movement of all nature and the great Lodge of Perfected Sages – those *Rishis* who gave the *Upanishads* – one will not be able to light up one's own pathway. This heart-light will take the persistent beginner from the broad plains to the entrance of the true Path, for which many are called, but few are chosen.

Hermes, April 1978
Raghavan Iyer

ELEMENTALS

The universe is worked and guided from within outwards. As above so it is below, as in heaven so on earth; and man – the microcosm and miniature copy of the macrocosm – is the living witness to this Universal Law and to the mode of its action. We see that every external motion, act, gesture, whether voluntary or mechanical, organic or mental, is produced and preceded by internal feeling or emotion, will or volition, and thought or mind. . . . The whole Kosmos is guided, controlled, and animated by almost endless series of Hierarchies of sentient Beings, each having a mission to perform, and who – whether we give to them one name or another, and call them Dhyan-Chohans *or* Angels *– are "messengers" in the sense only that they are the agents of Karmic and Cosmic Laws. They vary infinitely in their respective degrees of consciousness and intelligence. . . .*

Man . . . being a compound of the essences of all those celestial Hierarchies may succeed in making himself, as such, superior, in one sense, to any hierarchy or class, or even combination of them.

The Secret Doctrine, i 274-276

The metaphysical basis of the doctrine of elementals is essential to understanding the relationship of man to the world. Both Man and Nature are composed of a complex congeries of elemental entities endowed with character and perceptible form by continuous streams of ideation originating in Universal Mind. Virtually everything perceived by man, virtually every faculty of action, is such an aggregate of elementals. All the various modes and modulations of active and passive intelligence in man exist and subsist within these fields of elementals, and no aspect of human life is comprehensible without some grasp of elemental existence. Sensation, for example, which is ordinarily thought of in a purely external way, has another side to it when seen from the standpoint of the immortal soul, and this involves the intimate presence of hosts of elementals composing the very organs of sensation and mind.

The entire quest for enlightenment and self-conscious immortality cannot be understood without careful examination of the relationship of human beings to elementals. It is necessary to know where elementals reside and how their inherent modes of activity relate to the different principles in man. Sometimes people who speculate about the hidden side of Nature and human life, either inspired by folklore or a dabbling in the occult, develop a fascination with elementals and inadequately theorize about them. Usually they do not see any significance to elementals beyond their connection with the *prana* principle; this, however, is grossly inadequate and unhelpful, if not downright dangerous, particularly when coupled with lower yogic practices or mediumistic tendencies.

An authentic approach to the doctrine of elementals must be motivated by a desire to regenerate oneself on behalf of all. Both wisdom and compassion are needed if one would master the ways in which a human being may work upon elementals and also be acted upon by them. In practice, this is an extremely intimate and detailed enquiry involving all the most basic activities of daily life. The real nature of home and possessions, of eating and sleeping, and of every other aspect of life is bound up with elementals. Naturally, this includes questions of physical and psychological disease and health, with all the fads and fancies, popular and private, that accompany them. Problems of drugs and depression, along with the other ailments of the age for which there are no available remedies, are bound up with the interactions of the human and elemental worlds. No amount of mechanistic manipulation by doctors, therapists, specialists or religious counsellors will be of any avail in curing these ills of individuals and society; all ignore the fundamental nature of human malaise.

Real human welfare and well-being proceed from within without, beginning in the mind and heart and enacted through responsibility in thought and speech before they are reflected in outward action. The collective regeneration of society, therefore, depends upon the efforts of individuals to regenerate themselves fundamentally – first at the level of their basic self-consciousness, and later in relation to their vestures. Working outward from what one thinks of oneself, this regeneration must involve existing elementals in one's own being and will have definite effects upon everything with which one has contact and relationship. One must do this without falling into increasing self-obsession. One must sustain a universal motive. Merely building a fortress around one's own virtue is incompatible with teaching elementals and giving them the sort of beneficial impress that makes them a healing force in society. To avoid this moralistic delusion and still carry out the work of self-regeneration, one must insert the effort to overcome one's own sins and failings into the most universal context of human suffering. One must feel one's own pain as inseparable from the pain of every atom, every elemental and every human being involved in the collective human pilgrimage. Instead of hiding in fear or withdrawing from it, one must remain sensitive to that universal pain and so become as wide awake as Buddha.

Metaphysically, the doctrine of elementals encompasses the wide range of *devas* and *devatas,* gods and demigods, on seven different planes of differentiated cosmic substance. Extending far beyond medieval lore about gnomes, sylphs, salamanders and undines, the true teaching of elementals begins with the root processes by which thought impresses matter with form through *fohat.* Much of this teaching is secret, but any aspirant seeking aid in the acquisition of self-mastery will find considerable help in the sacred texts of all the authentic spiritual traditions of the world. These, however, must be approached from the standpoint of the philosophy of perfectibility and the science of spirituality, with no quarter given to blind superstition and stale dogmatism. At the most fundamental philosophical level, the doctrine of elementals is indeed magical and mystical, but this magic is noetic and akashic. It has nothing to do with the morass of grey psychic practices that pass for magic among pseudo-occultists. Instead, one must begin with meditation upon the abstract Point and the Zero Principle. (See *Hermes,* February 1986.) Without a firmer grasp of principles and without a true mental confrontation with fundamental ideas, it is impossible to understand and use the teaching of elementals for the benefit of the world. Without these rigorous basics, one can only fall prey to secondary and tertiary emanations and so become coiled in nefarious practices and sorcery.

A secure beginning can be found in the recognition that a fully self-conscious sevenfold being is unique. Such a being is the crown of creation, the full embodiment of the macrocosm in the microcosm. In a very specific sense man is, at the essential core of his being, a pure and immaculate crystallized ray of light-energy. This light ultimately represents the radiation of universal self-consciousness, the light that brings together all the gods and all the hierarchies. It goes beyond all colours and numbers to the one clear white light, the secondless light hidden in the divine darkness and silence. Thus man is one with the rootless root of the cosmos, a differentiated being compounded of every conceivable element in every one of the kingdoms of Nature. All the seven kingdoms are in a human being. This, of course, involves not only the physical body, but a series of vestures or *upadhis* on several different planes. In all the vestures of the human being, there is not a single element of any of the kingdoms of Nature, or any of the elemental forces, that is not already present.

This complexity in human nature, spanning the unmanifest and the manifest, is the basis of the paradox that man is both the potential crown of creation and its curse. In the whole of creation, sevenfold man is the unique possessor of the pristine light which precedes, differentiates and integrates, but also transcends, the entire spectrum of colours, sounds, forces, energies and vibrations. At the very core, man is deific and divine. Yet this does not make man sublime or spiritual in a way that stones and animals are not, for the deific breath and the divine afflatus of the One Life is everywhere and in everything. What is crucial about Man is that he is the possessor of self-consciousness through the gift of the *Manasas* and *Agnishvatta Pitris*, a particular class of the highest gods involving the second and third of the four classes below the first. Man is thus able to synthesize and transcend all the elementals.

Since man at the core possesses a thread of self-consciousness antedating embodied life, man is the integrator of all life. This is, in a sense, what contemporary astronomy and cosmology have come to recognize in studying the hosts of stars and galaxies. They have begun to speak of an anthropic principle in Nature. This is not to be confused with the outdated and parochial notion of an anthropocentric universe. Rather, it is the recognition that one cannot understand life, even at the level of physical chemistry, or in reference to primordial matter on distant planets, without seeing it as part of a vast chain that must ultimately culminate in what we call the human being. Naturally, what is called "human" on this earth is not necessarily the only possible mode of human being. There could be examples of other, vastly more developed, types of human being on other planets. Indeed, when one takes into account the possible variations in consciousness connected with the possible modes of human existence, there could be human beings existing not only on other planets, but on other planes of matter, perhaps even now invisibly present on this earth.

To say that man is the microcosm of the macrocosm, whilst having the power of integration that accommodates the maximum diversity of elements throughout Nature, means that man is in fact a cosmos. Whilst that cosmos is deific at the core, it is also so vast that it would be hardly surprising if, at some stage, that cosmos were mostly chaotic. Man is a victim of his inability to master this cosmic complexity within himself. This task demands so high a degree of dignity, integrity, fidelity and control rooted in self-conscious awareness that most people flee at the mere thought of it. They would rather go to sleep or forget about it, exchanging their human prerogative for daydreams, contributing tamasic elementals to hapless rocks and stones. Hence the paradox of the human condition. When man resigns from the difficult work of self-mastery, he abandons his essential place in Nature. The illustrious Pico della Mirandola called man the pivot of Nature. This idea, sadly neglected or falsely interpreted since then, was central to the seven-century cycle of the Theosophical Movement initiated by Tsong-Kha-Pa in Tibet. That cycle has now returned to its original point, and the future unfoldment of spiritual humanity rests upon the restoration of the true dignity of man.

If man, who is the pivot of Nature, abdicates his role, he becomes a curse upon creation, more hellish and demonic than anything that exists in the external realms of Nature, or anything depicted by Hieronymus Bosch and the *tankas* of Tibet. Even the most ghastly tales of goblins, monsters, giants and fiends cannot compare with the actual evil that can exist within a human being. Certainly, one will never find anything in visible and invisible Nature that outdoes the terrifying evil of which human beings are capable. This does not, however, make man into a weak, miserable worm; it makes him into a depraved being, damned of human evolution, and a veritable devil. Deific at the core, man inhabits a cosmos which all too easily becomes a chaos. The most appalling aspects of the demonic side of man have to do with the larger story of lost continents and vanished races, eras when spiritual powers were deliberately misused. Every time a failed human being becomes an elementary, he becomes, as a disembodied entity, an agent responsible for more harm on earth than anything else that exists. This is an invisible but real and terrifying fact of modern civilization, involving all the victims of wars and all the bitter, frustrated victims of accidents, murders, executions and suicides.

If this is metaphysically true, however frightening, it is important to understand what will stimulate and give incentive and motive to a human being to rediscover divinity and dignity. What will strengthen a person, so that he will not abdicate responsibility? First of all, he must relinquish one of the greatest fictions besetting contemporary human beings: the Cartesian belief in an abyss between mind and matter. *Brahma Vidya* teaches that spirit is sublimated matter and matter is condensed spirit. There is no point in space where there is not a spark of universal spirit, and there is not a set of particles derived from primordial substance which is not alive with divine intelligence. The seeming gap between mind and matter is an illusion created by the sensorium. In one sense, this illusion is the cost of physical incarnation: human beings are imprisoned, and indeed self-entombed, in a body, according to the old Orphic and Platonic accounts. To some degree, this is an inevitable result of taking birth in a limited body, even though the best available in natural evolution. Nonetheless, it is not required by the programme of Nature that human beings become so inextricably caught up in the sensorium that they succumb to a fragmentation of themselves and the world. It is not necessary that their minds become so cluttered with nouns that they forget verbs, and lose through language all sense of their spiritual vitality. This corruption of thought through language has led most human beings to create a false sense of identity which is actually a dominant elemental. This offspring of pseudo-self-consciousness is made up of the lower four elements – earth, air, fire and water, both gross and astral – and it goes by the name of Mr. X or Ms. Y. The tragedy is that the souls who have conjured these elementals out of their identification with the sensorium mistake them for their own real natures, and confuse the elemental apparitions created by other souls for real human beings.

It is difficult for souls to wake up from this collectively reinforced delusion and recognize these elemental projections for what they are. It is especially hard at this time, when people have nothing but a fugitive sense of clinging to a personality and when the once-compelling names and forms of the past mean so little. The elementals people mistake for themselves know only one law and one language – that of survival at any cost and of self before all else. When one adds to this the competitiveness and callousness of modern society, one gets an elemental of truly monstrous proportions. No amount of external makeup will hide the hideousness of that elemental. It is part of the humbug of our time that behind the so-called "beautiful people" lie some of the ugliest specimens of inhumanity and pseudo-humanity that have ever walked this earth. Most cities and centres of modern "civilization" really amount to central places for manufacturing and cloning these monstrous elementals.

Such an elemental form, as Buddha taught, is ultimately a composite entity that must be broken up. It has no enduring existence but belongs to the false, parasitic and derivative "I". Only by denying a sense of "I" to this elemental can one release the true sense of "I-am-I" consciousness in the universal light, at the same time releasing these elementals from the torture of bondage to the delusions and modes of selfishness. Even though human beings may torture elementals for a while, they cannot do so indefinitely. In the long run, they are stronger and more powerful than their captor, who is actually the weak pseudo-man or pseudo-"I", full of sound and fury and signifying nothing. Such a nature lacks the strength of genuine human thought. It is inherently cowardly; unable to do anything against the elementals, the elementals will get their revenge over a period of time. All elementals are themselves specialized completely within one or other of the elements. This fact, which could work to the advantage of the higher sovereign spirit in man as the integrator of all the elements, becomes the exact opposite in the case of the delusive ego struggling for self-perpetuation. Such a being falls prey to a pathetic and impotent enslavement to elementals that are more intelligent, precise and concentrated than itself. Because these elementals are pure in their fiery, watery, airy or earthy nature, they have an integrity of action that cannot be diverted for long by the twisted deceptions of the false ego. They will eventually wreak their revenge for having been misappropriated on behalf of separative delusions through one form or another of ill health, mental sickness or depression.

Whilst the insecure will fixate on this predicament merely as it applies to them, the rectification of wrongs involving the elemental kingdoms is actually an enormous process encompassing the globe. At this time, owing to the Avataric impulse, all the hosts of elementals have been immensely stirred up and hastened in precipitating their revenge on their torturers. The object is to get these people off the face of the earth, so that there will no longer be such a preponderance of selfish beings. This may be the only alternative to nuclear annihilation if the earth is to be repopulated by real human beings, beings who know how to breathe gratefully just for the privilege of the air. This is an extraordinary time, calling for the reversal of long ages of degradation of the idea of Man and the freeing of Nature from an intolerable regime of domination by selfishness. Put in Christian terms, this means the reversal of the corrupt doctrines of original sin and vicarious atonement, which have obscured the true teaching of Jesus about the perfectibility of man. To understand this reversing process, one has to bring in the invisible world of devils and demons, the idea of a personal god and much else. This is a much older story than the brief history of Christianity and it has happened to every religion.

To come into line with the forward movement of spiritual humanity, individuals must bring about in themselves a fundamental transformation of mind. Through an irreversible *metanoia*, they must calmly and surely overcome the dichotomy between mind and matter, rooting their consciousness in that which is beyond all differentiation. That is why meditation is no longer a luxury, but has become a necessity for survival. Simply recognizing this, however, does not mean that it will be easy or that it will work. If the only meditation one knows is on one's lower self – the elemental – how can one expect that elemental to forget itself? That is impossible. For such beings it is not merely difficult to meditate; it is actually to ask for too much too soon in cases that are too far gone. But even though they seem to be many, they are still a microscopic minority of the whole of the human family. They are powerful because their poisonous pollution can spread fast and wide, weakening lukewarm, irresolute people in the middle who are not really doing any thinking. They can fool themselves for a while, fudging the issue of choice and responsibility, but they are eventually going to be sucked into the vortex of the times and go one way or the other.

All of this should be understood as following from the metaphysical basis of the doctrine of elementals. It is a crucial, if painful, part of its practical application to the psychological and meta-psychological life of incarnated human souls. Yet there is much more to the teaching of elementals than its application to the lower principles of human nature. Elementals, at the highest level, are the most etheric, divine elements that exist. They are sparks of divine flame. This is a part of the secret teachings that is only comprehensible through initiation. Yet one can understand theoretically that the Sons of Agni, the divine flame, are the highest beings in evolution, and that they released myriads of sparks of fiery intelligence which then, *pari passu* with the differentiation of primordial substance, became the elemental world of Nature. This process included the creation of a kind of elemental prototype of the human being, but one that will not consolidate or become self-conscious by itself. This must await the descent of the *Manasas*. Still other elementals remain permanently in the rarefied realm of *akasha*, higher than the ether, let alone the lower astral light. It is these hosts that Shelley intimated in his poetry. They are invulnerable, all-powerful and omnipresent.

Elementals reach out to the highest aspects of existence, which is why it is extremely misleading to link elementals merely to one principle, such as *prana,* in sevenfold man. All life-energy works through all life-atoms; there is, therefore, a life-current existing in human nature which may be called *prana.* It is a sort of sum-total or quantum of life-energy within the metabolic system of the human body or, more correctly, within the astral body. It flows in that body like a fluidic current, and one might say that the elementals participate actively in it, as if swimming in an ocean of pranic life-energy. This is where they get their life. They are repeatedly refreshed by it, especially during sleep, and this is how they regenerate themselves. Nonetheless, the elementals belong to each and every one of the human principles except the *atman.*

Only if one understands this can one appreciate the enormous breadth of the doctrine of elementals. At the highest end, it includes what are called the gods in exoteric theologies, hosts of the finest beings in existence, though they are not self-conscious human beings. If they were self-conscious human beings in a previous *manvantara,* they have gone beyond that and only have a collective function, like that ascribed to the *dhyani buddhas* and archangels. At the same time, elementals include the three kingdoms below the mineral kingdom. Paracelsus gave, perhaps, the best summation of the metaphysics of elementals and their connection with man when he said, "Man lives in the exterior elements, and the Elementals live in the interior elements." Through the mind turning outward, man becomes fragmented and abdicates his throne. Becoming totally caught up in the external details of life, man is living, so to speak, outside his own true home. In this sense he is an exile. His body is no longer his temple, for he has cast himself out of it. In truth all the elementals live within that temple, in the interior elements.

Looked at in this way, elementals may be seen to be close to the essential aspects of a human being, in every one of the senses, on every plane and in every vesture. The human mind has its own elementals, which one may call mental elementals if one likes, though in fact they are airy elementals. On the physical plane, man has mostly earthy elementals. Within each principle, there are further subdivisions, so that there are earthy-fire elementals, airy-fire elementals and so on. Even this traditional language of the elements is awkward and misleading at best, since the true meanings of these divisions and subdivisions cannot be correlated with merely visual data, much less with the ever-changing atomic language of modern science. Whatever the linguistic problem, however, there should be no difficulty in seeing that one is really speaking of a vast, shoreless, boundless etheric field populated by billions of elementals. This is the true population of the cosmos, far more numerous than human beings or any other organic beings in any of the kingdoms of Nature. This being so, there is no way that one can even begin to understand human life apart from elementals. All daily activities of human life thus take on a fresh colouration and vitality, a magical potency involved with invisible, interior kingdoms. Every thought, every breath, every feeling and especially every word is filled with magic. Every instant, one either blesses or curses, elevates or degrades, hosts of elementals; every moment, one either sinks downward towards the demonic or soars upward towards the company and presence of the Blessed.

If thou would'st not be slain by them, then must thou harmless make thy own creations, the children of thy thoughts, unseen, impalpable, that swarm round humankind, the progeny and heirs to man and his terrestrial spoils. Thou hast to study the voidness of the seeming full, the fullness of the seeming void. O fearless Aspirant, look deep within the well of thine own heart, and answer. Knowest thou of Self the powers, O thou perceiver of external shadows?

The Voice of the Silence

Hermes, April 1987
Raghavan Iyer

NOETIC DISCRIMINATION

Spirit and Matter, *Purusha* and *Prakriti,* are the primeval aspects of the Logos. The separation between spirit and matter, subject and object, is an integral part of the illusion or *maya* of manifestation. To every state of ideation there corresponds exactly a plane of substance. Every grade of consciousness is a stratum of matter. Spirit and matter are two modes of apprehension of one reality. The seeming contrast between spirit and matter increases as one moves downwards from the homogeneous to the heterogeneous. Those who see each other as bodies experience difficulty in meditation in seeing each other as rays of light, let alone as rays streaming from a single source in metaphysical space. What is difficult for human beings in general is an essential yardstick of human growth, perfectibility and spiritual progress. Upon each plane of manifestation there is a whole host of intelligences emanated from primal sets of hierarchies. Every human being, as an incomplete incarnation of the *Manasaputras,* is a self-conscious agent capable of summoning the hierarchies and commanding their emanations through the recognition of affinity with the highest aspects of each. At the exalted level of enlightened beings who have transcended the dualities and polarities inherent to manifestation, there is no sense of separation from each other because they have dissolved all separateness from the One.

At all times a thinking individual is either active or passive to a greater or lesser extent. Either one is impelled from outside by secondary emanations and elementals, by external forces and mental winds, by emotional currents and all sorts of reverberation in the universe, *or* one acts from within without on the basis of a continuously maintained self-awareness of the dignity of descent from the *Manasaputras,* the self-conscious gods hidden behind the screen of time. When one acts from the depths of silence tapped by meditation, with mature deliberation and cool precision, one becomes a serene master of all the vestures and the sovereign ruler of one's divine sphere. With the strength of noetic discrimination in the service of one's sacred responsibility as a Manasic being, one can engage in authentic thinking, willing and feeling. Or one may be obscured, forgetful of one's glorious human stature, acting as a semi-automaton, a creature of habit, viewing every jolt of emotion as a sign of vitality or as an uncontrollable stimulus. One could mistake the volition induced by the movement of life-atoms for a deliberate act of visualization which is creative in the context of cosmic unity and harmony. Every person has the prerogative of a thinking being, potentially capable of an intense interiorization that empties itself, while mirroring divine thought. Or one could merely function as a mind conditioned by memory and sensation, a passive instrument of fleeting impressions, past and present, which are devoid of real meaning. The more one does the one, the less one does the other. The longer one is involved in confused cerebration, the harder it is to rise to the plane of pure ideation. Thus there is a critical choice at each moment for every human being. Through daily meditation and calm reflection, the individual must generate the energy needed to reverse the polarities of the vestures and refuse to function as a creature of circumstance, thereby becoming an initiator who assumes the full burden of responsibility for every thought, feeling and act of will.

The Secret Doctrine is a rare guide to regenerative meditation. The Proem provides ancient glyphs and symbols which can aid meditation by showing an archetypal logic to the cosmic process of manifestation. At all levels the Mundane Egg signifies a sphere that is a collection of radii from a single centre. One's centre of consciousness at the beginning of the day can have a bearing upon one's state of consciousness throughout the day and at dusk, thus affecting the ensuing day. The radii emanating from the centre of consciousness within every human being are related to the hidden Germ in the Root. This pertains not only to every single mind-being, but to the entire totality of mind-beings on a planet, in a solar system and ultimately in the cosmos, which comprises myriads of galaxies. The arcane teaching is difficult as it presupposes the coadunition of many levels of subtle matter. Human beings mature in inverse proportion to the degree to which they materialize the concept of motion. Spiritual adolescence consists in imagining that one is active when one is merely running around. Ganesha, the elephant-headed god of auspicious beginnings, is seemingly immobile but is intensely active in the power of ideation, unlike Karthikeya, who circles the globe, riding on a white horse. The highest kind of energy can be generated through the most intense concentration. Any person could take physical breathing as an analogue to the systole and diastole of the universe, the ceaseless rhythm of cosmic ideation. Such meditation is so far removed from mundane concepts of cerebration and cogitation that one can only move towards it by negating every framework and model employed by the analytical mind.

When the *chela* is ready for initiation by the *guru*, he receives the instruction needed for radical transformation of his subtlest vestures. The ancient Catechism teaches that Space, the Germ in the Root and the Great Breath are all one. The conceptual separation between the three is only an accommodation to the limitations of one's understanding, which seems to need a sequential succession of states. Mundane consciousness is caught up in ordinary time, experienced as a succession of moments. But once one transcends the hypnotic illusion of momentary succession and gains some experience of eternal duration, one begins to see that space, potentiality and motion are interconnected. Eternal Space, the Germ in the Root and the Great Breath are metaphysically abstract but causally fundamental in comparison with all differentiated modes. It is necessary when one begins a day to recognize that there was a night before and there is a night ahead. When one initiates a stream of activity one should salute those souls that are leaving the earth and those that are waiting to come into incarnation. Most people can barely bring a modicum of significance to daily living, still less can they continually include within their horizon all beings, embodied and disembodied. When one is a little child one may readily recognize that there are old people, and when one is old, one should be actively aware of little children. As one grows, one

NOETIC DISCRIMINATION 127

may deliberately gain mental and moral strength from those who are younger and older. This idea is so far removed from what is normally called egotism that it does take a tremendous leap in one's entire conception of reality to be able to visualize these things. If one meditates upon the most abstract conception of space that one can generate, going beyond the galaxies, beyond all that is visible, and reaches as far as one can, including in that awareness space wherein there are no universes, one is spiritually awake. At the highest level one is most alive when in a state of total concentration, able by the power of abstraction and visualization to see beyond *manvantaras* to *pralayas* where universes are naught.

The unbroken ring or circle has its centre everywhere and its circumference nowhere. Nicholas of Cusa declared that one ought not even to speak on the subject of God until one has studied the mathematics of infinity. We need to give adequate attention to the relationships of meaning, assimilation and growth. The ratios are important, particularly the ratio of the amount of time one gives, while manifesting, to the unmanifest. This is the basis of depth. One may plumb the depths in thinking, feeling and willing only by remaining more securely in the realm of the unmanifest even while manifesting. One must attribute less and less importance to birth in the realm of the manifest while gaining a greater and greater sense of active awareness of the vast boundless Unmanifest. Then one can know mighty Men of Meditation, those Exemplars of endless compassion. They are Masters of the metaphysical algebra of the highest states of consciousness, which to them are as natural as breathing, but which to the ordinary human being are *terra incognita*, the realm of the unknown.

The noetic calculus encompasses a dynamic universe extending from the atomic to the infinite, bound together on every plane by currents that radiate from the depths of silence and non-being.

Almost five centuries B.C. Leucippus, the instructor of Democritus, maintained that Space was filled eternally with atoms actuated by a ceaseless motion, the latter generating in due course of time, when those atoms aggregated, rotatory motion, through mutual collisions producing lateral movements. Epicurus and Lucretius taught the same, only adding to the lateral motion of the atoms the idea of affinity – an occult teaching.

The Secret Doctrine, i 2

To place an atom, or an aggregation of atoms, in rotatory motion, and from rotatory motion to generate further lateral movements, would be like spinning a top, which then begins to travel horizontally while spinning. This happens to myriads and myriads of atoms. Today we encounter theoretical constructs like 'proton' and 'neutron', but their antecedents are to be found in ancient systems of philosophical atomism. The presupposition of these systems was that if one seeks to go beyond rotatory and lateral movements, one must grasp a basic principle at work, which is more fundamental than the second law of thermodynamics.

The principle of affinity is essential to those who are ready to understand the alphabet of magic, magnetism, purification and real control. All the hierarchies involve the most incredibly subtle and complex affinities in the universe. There must be one universe as everything is connected with everything else, but at the same time it is a complex whole, with immense variety and functional specialization. There are different pathways that establish channels of direct affinity. Nonetheless, there is but one electric pulsation, one *Fohat*ic attraction, throughout the cosmos, primarily on the plane of thought. There is also a veil upon that *Fohat*ic motion on the physical plane. To be able to get to the core of this principle of universal affinity means to heighten spiritual awareness. This principle is prior to the pair of opposites called attraction and repulsion because they are the obverse and reverse of one kind of affinity. Through dislike one is bound up with that which one dislikes. This is pervasive in the arena of emotions, which differ from true feelings.

People have positive and negative tendencies, and the more they become thinking beings, the more they can experience conscious control over polarity. A time may come when they can polarize at will the medium of reflection so that they can beneficently magnetize everything they contact. Above all, they must polarize their own subtle vestures. Anyone who seeks to grasp the root of the connection between affinity and energy should reflect upon the Platonic etymology of the Greek term for Deity.

> Plato proves himself an Initiate, when saying in Cratylus that θεός is derived from the verb θέειν , 'to move,' 'to run,' as the first astronomers who observed the motions of the heavenly bodies called the planets θεοί , the gods.... Later, the word produced another term, ἀλήθεια – 'the breath of God.'

The Secret Doctrine, i 2

In Greek the verb is more important than the noun. When one can see the integral connection between divinity and motion, one can self-consciously divinize and make sacred everything one perceives, while manifesting a deep and unspoken awareness of the unmanifest immortal Self. Real affinities are so noumenal that they have nothing to do with the realm of externals. They involve the most delicate tuning of the subtlest vibration in one's being to the rhythm of the noumenal cosmos reflected in myriad ways in visible nature. This attunement can only be brought about through one-pointed meditation upon the Triad, the higher Self and the *Mahatmas.* One cannot meditate upon *Atma-Buddhi-Manas* of the *Guru* without entering into the One. If one were to meditate intently upon the Triad, one will also come closer to the *Guru.* As Gautama taught, the Buddha, the *Dhamma* and the *Sangha* are one. A person who comes to see the three as one has become a pilgrim and entered the stream. Those who have not entered the stream engage in wasteful disputation. Just as the babe has no sense of the harshness of the boundary of the personal ego, one who has entered the stream dissolves egotism in its purifying waters.

The *Mahatmas,* the *Vajrasattvas,* the Diamond-Souled, who have overcome all *Ahankara* and fused the sixth and the seventh principles, use the fifth principle of cosmic ideation called *Manas* to become one with *Mahat.* Merging the *Atman* and *Manas* into *Buddhi,* they are *Bodhisattvas* who are both Atmic and Manasic, and then they become full *Mahatmas* merged with the Absolute. At that level they are *Anupadaka,* parentless. Because the One is self-existent, they are self-existent, one with the universal Spirit, *Svayambhu,* that which generates itself ceaselessly. The mystery of the *Anupadaka* is also the mystery of how the *Dhyani Buddha* on the seventh plane emanates a *Bodhisattva* on the sixth plane. Such a *Bodhisattva,* seen only by the developed intuition of awakened *chela*s, projects the *Manushi Buddha* into the world of time. A *Manushi Buddha* in a form is the visible representative of the hidden *Bodhisattva* overbrooded by the *Dhyani Buddha,* each accessible on the appropriate plane of consciousness when the seeker is consubstantial with and receptive to the great heart, the great mind, the diamond-souled *Vajrasattva* of the *Vajradhara* – 'he who holds the *vajra*'. This concerns the sublime experiences of progressive initiation.

In the long history of Eastern philosophy these mystical states have been partially intimated in different schools of thought, resulting in various dialectical interpretations. In the protracted debates between the Yogacharya and the Madhyamika schools, some of the Madhyamikas stressed the immense chasm between the One and the many. Like Parmenides in Plato's dialogue, they insisted that the One without a second cannot have any relationship whatsoever to the many. Between the One and the many there is an unfathomable abyss. For many people with authentic but conditional aspirations, this teaching is cold and remote. It is hardly surprising that most people settle for a simple dualism of subject and object, spirit and matter, and then hope to be saved by some god or saviour. There are also those who try to be subtle in a middle course, but end up by using monism on behalf of dualism. In the Yogacharya school of Aryasanga, which was originally esoteric though in time it did become exoteric, it was recognized that *Alaya,* the state of voidness, is the basis of everything visible or invisible. Though eternal and immutable in its essential nature, it is reflected in every object of the universe. It is also reflected in what may be called the mind of Nature, yielding *Alayavijnana,* the storehouse of eternal ideation, sometimes called *Akasa.* This is the divine energy-field that begins where *Mulaprakriti* ends and which in its highest aspect is *Daiviprakriti.* In its lowest fourfold aspects it becomes what is called the pure as well as the polluted astral light.

The importance of the Yogacharya teaching for the individual is suggested in the following statement:

> In the Yogacharya system of the contemplative Mahayana school, Alaya is both the Universal Soul (Anima Mundi) and the Self of a progressed adept.

The Secret Doctrine, i 49

The Adept has a golden vesture which is consubstantial with the golden egg of the universe. While this must be mysterious to the finite mind which thinks in terms of physical space, at the level of the noumenal one is dealing with light-energy and subtle consubstantiality and different conceptions of space-time. There is so high a level of mirroring that it is not reflecting as normally understood. There is so great a coadunition of the luminous egg of the universe and the luminous sphere of the *Mahatma* that the two are essentially the same.

> He who is strong in the Yoga can introduce at will his Maya by means of meditation into the true Nature of Existence.

The Secret Doctrine, i 49

The Yogacharya school pointed to those *yogins* who by the act of *dhyana,* deep spiritual meditation, are able to generate at will the energy-field of the cosmic egg. Their potent ideation reverberates throughout all three worlds. It not only awakens and enlightens every plant, stone, mineral and atom, but also the whole earth, "the great globe itself", as well as the minds and hearts of all the monads who constitute one single family. Immense are the powers of such a *yogin.* Any person who wishes to enter into the states of consciousness symbolized by the fifth, the sixth and the seventh must in the fourth principle create the germ of *bhakti.* Not only devotion, gratitude, loyalty and love, but also hunger and thirst for

Divine Wisdom and Divine Life are the graces of the self-regenerated. When these become the constant, unuttered, inaudible hum of the heart, then a *chela* may become capable of receiving the light-energy that flows in and through every atom touched by the thought, the will and the feeling of the *Mahatma*. This is a profoundly sacred teaching, which draws attention to the Knowers of the Secret Doctrine *(Gupta Vidya), Brahmajnanis, Tattvajnanis, Brahmarishis, Mahatmas, Dhyani Buddhas, Bodhisattvas, Manushi Buddhas*, the great Teachers of all humanity. From the Teaching to the Teacher is an ancient axiom, which may be used as an infallible mantram.

Hermes, March 1980
Raghavan Iyer

REGENERATION

Expansion from within without, from the subjective to the objective, may be seen at many levels, from the smallest bud, moistened by the dew, gently opening in the dawn, to the gestation and emergence of a human vesture for the incarnating ray of an immortal soul. It is expressed archetypally in the mysterious birth that takes place within cosmic matter, giving rise to new centres of energy, planets and systems of worlds, initiating varied cycles spanning vast periods of time. Creative expansion is central to the sacred process of self-regeneration through spiritual wisdom. To understand this metaphysically, at the highest level of homogeneity one may begin by drawing a circle in the mind and then dissolve its boundary through visualizing a series of ever-expanding concentric circles that extend as far as possible in every direction. To do this intently in thought is effectively to change one's state of consciousness as well as the corresponding grade of matter. Having withdrawn from the outer sheaths to the subtler vestures, one becomes completely absorbed and concentrated in a steady, serene state upon that which is without any differentiation, without any beginning, alteration or end. Once established in this equipoise, one might calmly reflect upon the bare sky, without boundaries, seeing all the stars as one belt of light but absorbed back into the primordial darkness.

Primordial matter is coeval with infinite space and eternal duration – indestructible, impartite and without conceivable division. In deep contemplation, the mind becomes absorbed into it and empties everything into the divine darkness, and one experiences a complete voidness of the sense of self. Those who persist in this will find that they become aware of noumenal light and of myriads of scintillating sparks streaming forth between different forms in nature. There is a palpable fullness to this void, an inexhaustible potentiality. Most of it will never be tapped because beings in incarnation have become limited through identification with fluttering shadows and fleeting events, leaving them wholly absorbed with bubbles of foam that drift amidst the flotsam and jetsam on the surface of the shallower parts of the ocean of being. To plunge one's mind as far as possible into the very depths, and to do this again and again, is to generate a sense of reality which is so potent that one readily discerns that this subjectivity is without limit and can be objectified only on the noumenal plane at the subtlest level. To touch this plane is to awaken an awareness of non-being. This occurs on an objective plane of noumenal matter where there is a reflection and a radiation. Yet that objectivity would seem like darkness to the spiritually blind, since it has neither relevance nor reference to those who are habituated to limited sense-perceptions and who abide in the light and shadow of the physical sun. The range of perception of human beings in general is enormously narrowed, and this is the price they pay for taking an inordinate interest in the detail and furniture of the physical world.

Limitless subjectivity can never become limitless objectivity on this plane. But if one has experienced the rapid transformation of limitless subjectivity into limitless objectivity on the noumenal plane, one can then come out into the everyday world and perceive many possibilities which are commonly overlooked. One can enlarge the perspectives of other human beings simply by the noetic power of concentrated thought. Pinched views of existence, fear of physical pain or the moment of death, and narrow notions of success or failure are all the offspring of personal consciousness which obscures the true life of the immortal soul. For the soul there is no 'mine' and 'thine', no success and failure as understood in ordinary terms, and no significance in the effusions of other beings which are called opinions and sometimes aspire to be judgements. All of these are irrelevant because the immortal soul has come through an immense pilgrimage in which it feels at home with the spiritual solidarity of all beings. The ineffable experience in meditation of this boundless subjectivity would be akin to the feeling of a mountaineer upon an exalted promontory, who sees the manifold activities of human beings as part of one great and single enterprise. He can understand and identify with all of them because he is in a state of silence which is closer to what is abstract and undifferentiated.

The more unconfined one's sense of subjectivity, the profounder one's sense of objectivity. Though people wish to come closer to the *Mahatmas*, this is impossible if one's mind does not to some extent share in the ideation of the *Mahatmas*, who do not see past, present and future, and do not function in terms of physical changes and clock-time. Similarly, one cannot come closer to the *Mahatmas* if one's heart is unable to show love to the person next door, for the *Mahatmas*' heart pulses with a constant and controlled compassion for everything that lives. They continually emanate powerful and beneficent ideas into the *Akasa* at that level of the astral light where there can be mirrorings accessible to human beings who are struggling in confusion and desperation. Many human beings have experienced the feeling that they cannot go on any further, yet surprisingly, they do. It is because of the compassion and the ideation of the *Mahatmas* that the will to survive becomes feasible for vast numbers of human beings who find Fate inscrutable and life unbearable. If they go on, it is because of the compassionate outpouring from the *Mahatmas* who, from the limitless subjectivity of the plane of consciousness which they inhabit, are able to give hope, energy and the will to persevere to all human beings imprisoned within the Orphic tomb of the personality. The *Mahatmas* live continuously upon the subjective plane of the immortal Triad, which most people contact only in deep sleep. Without this daily contact, existence would be impossible. The hum in the heart would cease if a person went through a sufficient period without sleep because the person would be denied *sushupti*. There would be no way of continuing in the astral form that is bound up with the physical body. This is why sleep, which "knits up the ravelled sleeve of care", is the ordinary person's approach to meditation. It is possible to enrich the quality of sleep through conscious contemplation every day. One can make significant connections, heighten self-consciousness, and in waking life change the ratios of the objective and the subjective. One can take that which is abstract and make it a focal point for a matrix which may be deposited into the astral light and thus serve as a friend, philosopher and guide to other beings in need. It is possible, by making a difference to one's capacity to connect daily meditations with nightly *sushupti*, to become more self-conscious, and that self-consciousness will in time become more universal. This means that subject and object as ordinarily understood are radically altered.

Initially a person is a disordered subject in a chaotic world of changing objects. There seems to be a harsh and hostile gap between the individual mind which is fatigued and bewildered, and the external world which is like a great track on which there are many fast-moving beings caught up in grossly objective sensations. Where one experiences the closeness between limitless subjectivity and limitless objectivity, one has no sense of separate existence as normally understood. One merely confers an appropriate sense of transferred reality to living in a body, growing up, moving from birth to death. One maintains this sense of relative reality out of compassion and for the sake of communication with other beings. The ability to do this is perfected in the *Mahatmas*, who over myriads of lives have woven out of the subtlest matter living matrices that can channel the electric energy of compassion. Those grateful individuals who are quickened by the life-giving ideation of the *Mahatmas* and who wish to gain conscious control over their lives on the path of selfless service to humanity, can begin by learning about the subjective and objective correlations of *Fohat*.

Prior to the appearance of the objective cosmos, *Fohat* in its purely subjective aspect is said to 'harden and scatter' the atoms. Primordial electricity galvanizes into life and separates primordial stuff or pregenetic matter into atoms, the source of all life. There is at the highest level of abstraction an intensely charged field of cosmic electricity, wherein the spiritual life-atoms are quickened. This dynamic field is so different from what we call electrical currents that it is extremely difficult for one to imagine. Nonetheless, the effort to do so is directly analogous to what is involved in visualizing the physical vesture of an enlightened being, which is so highly charged that it will make an ordinary person's astral body disintegrate unless protective shields are provided. The Adept does this, yet minimizes physical contact so as to specialize his magnetism. The whole way of life of the Adept is based upon exact knowledge of the nature of electrical activity on the highest cosmic plane where there is the possibility of scattering a homogeneous field, separating it out into seemingly separate points of life-energy. Linked with this subjective activity of *Fohat* is its objective capacity to gather clusters of cosmic matter and give them an impulse to set them in motion, developing the required heat and then leaving them to their own growth. This is followed by the expanding and contracting of the web – the world-stuff – from within without and from without within, the pulsatory motion of the infinite, shoreless ocean of the noumenon of matter which causes the universal vibration of atoms. The objective activity that is centred upon the physical sun is a pale reflection of the deeper subjective activity involving the Spiritual Sun and cosmic consciousness. That activity represents the possibility of maintaining the universal vibration of atoms ceaselessly in motion during an immense period of evolution. This is why it is possible for there to be growth, transformation and the beneficent dispersion of atoms that human beings call death. All these are only changes of state that enable beings to assume new vestures to continue the spiritual pilgrimage of the immortal soul.

All objective change corresponds to this ceaseless subjective vibration or pulsation taking place upon a noumenal plane. Since all beings have degrees of intelligence, and since all participate at the most causal level in that noumenal plane, there are sparks of divine light in the eyes not only of human beings but also of all other beings. Because this light is capable of charging and benefiting everything that is seen, one must be careful to shield it and to keep it unpolluted by negative forces. On the plane of manifestation everything is dual. One cannot have the positive without the negative because the universal vibration of atoms produces its corresponding and very complicated repercussions in molecular motion which are responsible for change, growth and decay. On an even more fundamental and pregenetic level there is the possibility of sundering the homogeneous into the heterogeneous, which involves the subtlest concept of cosmic electricity. A perfected being who has gained the knowledge pertaining to this would be able at will to send forth as many *mayavi rupas* as he wishes out of his astral form. This has been symbolized in accounts of how, when the Buddha sat in profound meditation under the Kumbum tree, every leaf of the tree received the imprint of the Buddha's form, so potent is that cosmic ideation.

A person who cherishes this teaching will seek to intensify and purify his or her own field of ideation. One of the purposes of the Theosophical Movement, especially at this point in the early dawn of the Aquarian Age, is to teach people the exacting sense of moral responsibility that they will need if they are not to be pulverized at higher levels of noumenal action. To come into the stronger field one has to become far more sensitive, far more deliberate, far more responsible than before. Otherwise, if one enters this higher field and brings into it any selfish concern, the polarity of its intense energy will be reversed, becoming the messenger of death. The dual aspects, active and passive, positive and negative, of the universal agent are always mixed with each other in manifestation. "Od is the pure life-giving Light, or magnetic fluid; Ob the messenger of death used by the sorcerers, the nefarious evil fluid." A person can become charged with life-giving magnetic energy through intense meditation and continuous contact with the Divine Wisdom which is consubstantial with the formless *Akasa.* If a person came in contact with the azure empyrean of pure thought, it is essential to maintain a profound calm and serene freedom from self-concern. Where there is a deep oceanic calm, one can hold that energy level, but if one becomes excited or mixes the atmosphere with hostile or anxious thoughts, there will be an explosion, leaving an aperture open to the nefarious evil fluid that may be sent by sorcerers or spiritual vampires. Human beings live in a dangerous universe which is both life-giving and death-dealing. When individuals become capable through deep meditation of tapping the electromagnetic field of their subtler vestures and the planes to which they correspond, they could disperse the lunar form at will, extracting the essence out of all experiences and summoning creative combinations, thereby giving a forward impulse to human evolution.

The progressive unfoldment of the powers of *Manas* involves not only the shifting boundaries of selfhood but also the primordial feeling of self-consciousness. This is rooted in unbroken awareness of the "Incorporeal man who contains in himself the divine Idea – the generator of Light and Life . . . . He is called the 'Blazing Dragon of Wisdom' . . . the *Logos*, the *Verbum* of the Thought Divine." Every immortal soul is a spark of the Central Fire. Close to the Central Fire there is the possibility of self-conscious synthesis of the septenates that emanate out of the third *Logos*, for every human being derives his divine spark of immortal awareness from that hebdomadal heart. The principle of continuity in a human being is the *sutratman,* which enables one to know that one is essentially the same person through a lifetime. This sense of continuity must be strengthened through meditation and tested during the subjective phases of sleep, until it becomes profound and powerful. When one can experience what it means to pass through myriads of lives, one can effortlessly put oneself in the position of vast varieties of beings whose states of consciousness correspond to whatever one has already experienced. To attain such a high level of continuity requires great detachment and mastery over the art of non-involvement, *pancha shila.* One must learn the art of non-interference because one knows that global Karma is vast and one is determined to add to the sum of human good by the power of meditation. To walk unobtrusively through life, minimizing the creation of karma, is a mark of wisdom. If the *sutratman* becomes activated, then one comes closer to Oeaohoo, who "contains in himself the Seven Creative Hosts... and is thus the essence of manifested Wisdom". One comes closer to what sometimes is called the Ancient of Days, to the primordial givers of wisdom. And therefore it is said, "He who bathes in the light of *Oeaohoo* will never be deceived by the veil of *Maya*."

The objective world constantly entices one to exaggerate the sense of reality that belongs to what is only partially alive. People make a great deal of fuss over minor detail relevant only to the instrumentality of the physical body and are much deceived by the glamour of *maya*. If one thinks that the main factors in life are likes and dislikes, one is going to be agitated by antipathies and sympathies. One will live not as a noetic, discriminating, immortal individuality, but as a vociferating, volatile persona. If one knows this danger at the moment of birth because one has already glimpsed the light and entered the stream of spiritual wisdom, one has gained self-consciousness in reference to the *sutratman* at the moment of death in a previous life. If one could bring this knowledge through the subjective phases of existence between lives to the moment of birth, then one can readily recognize that one cannot really participate in the *maya* that people mistake for the real world. One would develop devices to leave people's illusions undisturbed wherever possible, and keep oneself undistracted by those illusions. One would create a magnetic orbit in which it is possible to move with ears attuned, as Thoreau said, to another drummer, to the music of the spheres, to *Brahma Vach*, the *Verbum*. Then one could become conscious of the sacred company of the Men of the Word. The Vedic *Hymn to Vach* makes reference to the extraordinary companionship of those who have knowledge of what is and give measure to worship:

> When, O Lord of the Word, the Wise established
> Name-giving, the first principle of language,
> Their inmost excellence, pristine and pure,
> Hidden deep within, was brought to light through love.

When the Wise created language with the mind,
As winnowing ground barley with a sieve,
Friends acknowledged the essence of friendship;
Upon their speech was impressed the mark of grace.

With devotion they walked the path of the Word
Which they saw abiding within the Seers.
They drew it out, ordering it all ways,
The Word which the Seven Sages exalt.

The mysteries of initiation intimated here are hidden through many veils and are genuinely accessible only to those who have sought through deep meditation to open the eye of Wisdom. Divine discrimination requires us to look upon seeming events, not from the locus of the perishable personality, but from the impartial standpoint of the immortal soul. Each experience must be assimilated not only in terms of its present meaning, but also in its relation to the moment of death. Those privileged to hear the Word must understand all things in relation to the ability to summon it to consciousness at the moment of death. To live in this way is to cherish the constant aim of selfless regeneration. Those who do so in any appreciable measure will in time develop an unspoken awareness of the sacred meaning of the mysterious Serpents and Dragons of Wisdom:

The primitive symbol of the serpent symbolised divine Wisdom and Perfection, and had always stood for psychical Regeneration and Immortality. Hence – Hermes, calling the serpent the most spiritual of all beings; Moses, initiated in the wisdom of Hermes, following suit in *Genesis*; the Gnostic's Serpent with the seven vowels over its head, being the emblem of the seven hierarchies of the Septenary or Planetary Creators. Hence, also, the Hindu serpent Sesha or Ananta, 'the Infinite,' a name of Vishnu, whose first *Vahan* or vehicle on the primordial waters is this serpent.

Within the subjective vestures of awakened spiritual consciousness the neophyte will begin to understand and experience the different aspects of the process of regeneration.

"The mystery of apparent self-generation and evolution through its own creative power repeating in miniature the process of Cosmic evolution in the egg, both being due to heat and moisture under the efflux of the unseen creative spirit . . ." Heat on a purely subjective level would refer to the spiritual fire activated by meditation, and moisture would pertain to the compassion of the *Bodhisattvas*, the archetypal equivalent of rain falling upon the earth. The serpent in philosophical and religious symbolism is "an emblem of eternity, infinitude, regeneration, and rejuvenation, as well as of wisdom". If a person deeply meditates upon this idea, it will provide the basis for raising the simple process of sifting through experience to a refined art whereby, in the alembic of ideation and imagination, one may burn out the dross in life and alchemize what may be transmuted into potent energies that are capable of reproducing benefit for all living beings.

Hermes, May 1980
Raghavan Iyer

SELF-EMANCIPATION

BUDDHI YOGA

Every form on earth, and every speck (atom) in Space strives in its efforts towards self-formulation to follow the model placed for it in the 'HEAVENLY MAN.'

The Secret Doctrine, i 183

Monadic evolution aims initially at establishing individuated centres of human self-consciousness. Once millions upon millions of these have emerged under natural law, the distinctive purpose of human evolution thereafter is to arouse and activate universal self-consciousness through a series of progressive awakenings. The Monad "in its absolute totality and awakened condition" as "the culmination of the divine incarnations on earth" represents a critical state which will be fully perfected at the end of the Seventh Round by the whole of humanity, under the common cosmic laws of growth and retardation. In this long process there are many casualties and tragedies, but there are also shining examples of truly heroic, Promethean self-emancipation by moral geniuses. Having sunk into the depths of matter, such exemplars have pulled themselves up by self-effort and emerged through creative suffering into exalted states of enlightened consciousness, through which they could keep pace with the Avataric Saviours and Teachers of the entire human race. At all times the spiritual vanguard at the forefront of human evolution points towards the noetic possibilities of human life and architectonic perfection in spiritual consciousness. Every creative advance in monadic evolution depends upon the critical range and potent fullness of self-consciousness. Through its depth of perception in reference to the world, it impels a natural movement towards the Heavenly Man, the Divine Prototype, the Daimon of the immortal Self in every human being. By withdrawal from the selfish clutches of the grosser vestures and the demoniac tendencies, the human Monad reascends through *Buddhi Yoga* to the state of transcendental union with its parent Self, the universal *Ishwara*, the Logos in the cosmos and the God in man.

The degrees of differentiation in the Monadic Host below the human kingdom, as well as the distinctive marks of the human Monad, are conveyed by H.P. Blavatsky in a critical series of propositions which commences with a reference to the earliest period in the ethereal formation of the earth chain:

> The Monadic Host may be roughly divided into three great classes:
>
> 1. The most developed Monads (the Lunar Gods or 'Spirits,' called, in India, the *Pitris*), whose function it is to pass in the first Round through the whole triple cycle of the mineral, vegetable, and animal kingdoms in their most ethereal, filmy, and rudimentary forms, in order to clothe themselves in, and assimilate, the nature of the newly formed chain.
>
> *The Secret Doctrine*, i 174

These Monads come over progressively from the previous lunar chain in a series of stages in order to animate all the nascent forms in the coalescing matrix of the earth chain. These lunar forms, extremely subtle and refined in the First Round, incipiently belong from the first to the seven different kingdoms. Then come "those Monads that are the first to reach the human stage during the three and a half Rounds". This great descent of the Monadic Host does not take place all at once, but over immense cycles of manvantaric time, and according to the innate characteristics of these Monads, reflecting an inherent sevenfold division. Owing to the degrees of development that have already taken place, all human Monads roughly fall into seven classes connected with the seven cosmic hierarchies, the seven planets and other sets of seven in nature. They come therefore in a certain order, and those Monads that are the first to reach the human stage during the three and a half

Rounds become Men, or attain to self-consciousness, by the middle of the Fourth Round. These constitute most of Humanity.

The key to the internal continuity of this entire process, linking together these various stages and phases on diverse planes and globes, is given in the ideational power of the Monad, manifesting as self-conscious intelligence:

> The MONAD emerges from its state of spiritual and intellectual unconsciousness; and, skipping the first two planes – too near the ABSOLUTE to permit of any correlation with anything on a lower plane – it gets direct into the plane of Mentality. But there is no plane in the whole universe with a wider margin, or a wider field of action m its almost endless gradations of perceptive and apperceptive qualities, than this plane.

The Secret Doctrine, i 175

The term 'mentality' is used here to indicate *Manas* or self-consciousness, and has little or nothing to do with what is normally called mind or brain-power. Manasic beings function on a plane of consciousness saturated with inexhaustible possibilities for mental creation acting through ideal projections, pictures and images. Through this power, or rather through its truncated specialization on the plane of incarnation, all human beings, most of the time unconsciously and ignorantly, are constantly creating affinities with different classes of living centres of energy. Since there is no intrinsic difference between Spirit and Matter, but only an extrinsic difference of degree, the two are inseparable, and one can neither find ideation without substance nor energy without form. This continual coalescence or interaction of energy and form, of ideation and substance, is a pervasive principle in this dynamic universe of ceaseless change and has an intimate bearing upon the whole course of human evolution. Not only do human beings experience alterations of state in the brain-mind and modifications of the vestures at every moment, but correlative changes are also experienced at the level of cohesion in the mineral kingdom, and at the level of instinct in the animal kingdom. In the human kingdom these interrelated changes encompass emotion and feeling in the realm of 'affect', the sense of comparison and contrast, identification and differentiation, in the realm of intellectual awareness, as well as the power of noetic discrimination in recognizing subtle nuances of meaning and in the continual interplay of light and darkness.

These evolutionary processes on the plane of mentality produce the human sense-organs, which are perfected through imaginative precision. Indeed, they must be contemplated calmly and carefully, as without proper mental attention they will remain under-utilized. Most persons are barely able to tap all that is possible even within the entire range of the seven sense-powers. Most people barely hear, barely see, barely touch, barely taste and barely smell, much less activate higher sense-powers. As an obvious example, anyone who develops a refined ability to differentiate the most subtle fragrances will regard the ordinary sense of smell as extremely crude. This would be true not only in regard to herbs or perfumes, but especially in regard to the familiar experience of cooking. It is quite possible to develop and refine the capacity to recognize the invisible essences underlying what seems to be physical food, and to be directly aware of the myriad effects of different combinations of spiritual essences upon the sevenfold human constitution, with its latent forty-nine fires. Such sensory refinement has to do with wise magnetic attunement, and vitally affects the vestures in both their constitution and composition. The alchemical process of distilling the combinations and correlations of essences in each of the invisible vestures proceeds through *etherealization* which must necessarily work through the Spiritual Will.

The Spiritual Will alone is constantly able to alchemize, renovate and refine the life-atoms of the vestures, increasing their lightness and porosity to Divine Light. When the vestures are suffused by that Light, it becomes possible to think, feel, act, breathe, smell, taste, touch, see and hear benevolently. One is enabled to employ Divine Wisdom as a science governing every relationship to the atoms that one touches and blesses. The process of refinement involves the full and vast range of Monads that have passed collectively through the various kingdoms at different levels, coming down from the most ethereal in the early Rounds to the existing fourth stage with its kaleidoscopic variety of alternative opportunities for apperceptive and perceptive consciousness. Passing this mid-point, the cycle of monadic evolution moves upwards again to that plane which was in the beginning a state of spiritual, and intellectual unconsciousness for the Monads, but which must become the plane of universal self-consciousness for perfected Monads by the end of the Seventh Round.

Behind and beyond all these changes of state and form there remains, unchanging and intact, one and the same Monad. It is an inward centre of light which does not participate in all the many alterations that affect the vestures. To put it differently, there must be beyond all the material vestures the perpetual motion of the *Atman*, which is the indwelling noumenal and invisible core of every Monad. Those who regularly meditate derive much benefit from the instruction of the Catechism of the *Gupta Vidya*, which teaches one to draw inwards in consciousness to an inmost noumenal centre or point, which then immediately becomes a point in a line, a point in a cross, and finally the central point in relation to all possible forms. By entering into the Divine Darkness of pure abstraction, by becoming a Point without extension and receding behind all the planes of differentiation, one removes all awareness of forms and all evidence that there are many Monads. In the absence of manifest light, one experiences a deeper sense of the unity of all Monads and fundamentally destroys the all-pervasive illusion that there are many different beings separate from each other, sitting or moving in their separate bodies. Krishna teaches that the Eye of Wisdom has the intrinsic capacity to distinguish Spirit itself from a world of diverse objects and ultimately destroys the persisting illusion of manifold objects. When noetic consciousness has majestically risen above separations of objects and forms, it now experiences the world differently, omnidimensionally and in depth, entering the noumenal realm of what is unmanifest on the illusory plane of contrasts, beyond which there is the homogeneous plane of radiant matter, which lends luminosity to the subtlest vestures of the immortal Soul. This elevation of consciousness to a *laya* point is an experiment through which one can visualize at a preliminary level the plenitude of the field of noetic ideation, but it may be taken even further and simultaneously applied to all classes of human beings throughout the earth. This requires the progressive deepening of one's perception through intense meditation, so that over a period of time one may gain a greater sense of the noumenal depths of life-energy, and the magical properties of the Alkahest, the universal solvent.

The Monad, which is essentially ever the same, participates through the various vestures in succeeding cycles of partial or total obscuration of Spirit or of Matter. Everything occurring in daily life could be seen entirely in terms of the continuous ascent or descent from the One, or in terms of obscuration and illumination, but these could pertain either to Matter or to Spirit. Once one has grasped this philosophical and metaphysical basis for comprehending the complex scheme of monadic life and transformation, one can reckon with the fact that there are seven kingdoms of Monads:

> The first group comprises three degrees of elementals, or nascent centres of forces – from the first stage of differentiation of (from) Mulaprakriti (or rather Pradhana, primordial homogeneous matter) to its third degree – i.e., from full unconsciousness to semi-perception; the second or higher group embraces the kingdoms from vegetable to man; the mineral kingdom thus forming the central or turning point in the degrees of the 'Monadic Essence,' considered as an evoluting energy. Three stages (sub-physical) on the elemental side; the mineral kingdom; three stages on the objective physical side – these are the (first or preliminary) seven links of the evolutionary chain.

The Secret Doctrine, i 176

Between the three elemental kingdoms on the subjective side and the vegetable, animal and human kingdoms on the objective side, lies the mineral kingdom. Poised in the fourth, or balance position, the Mineral Monad becomes crucially important. Indeed, one cannot understand either Evolution or Magic without apprehending the process of immetalization through which the abstract *Monas* reaches a maximum of condensation in the mineral kingdom. After this stage there comes a rapid dispersion, a continuous loosening up, which then produces the three kingdoms on the ascending arc. Viewed in one way, there is "a descent of spirit into matter equivalent to an ascent in physical evolution".

The more Spirit descends into Matter, the more there is conscious evolution on the physical plane. This is part of the cosmic sacrifice, because the bringing down of Spirit into Matter enables the latter at a greater level of density to evolve further and thus be quickened by noetic intelligence. If, for example, one handles with natural reverence and spiritual wakefulness any so-called object, which may seem to be a book, a piece of jade or a wristwatch, but which is actually an aggregate of elementals and life-atoms, then one can wisely instruct and initiate. Those who are truly awake spiritually can take anything, and with selfless love they can quicken latent intelligence, vivifying active awareness and higher self-consciousness. It is not as if there is not much to do in this visible universe. At any given moment one can touch and elevate every sentient point of energy. Looked at in this way, all life becomes extraordinarily meaningful, holding innumerable opportunities to aid monadic life in a re-ascent from the deepest depths of materiality (the mineral) towards its *status quo ante*".

Since reascent implies a corresponding dissipation of the concrete organism, it is frightening to most people as it means the renunciation of identification with the sense of being in a body. Hence it is a disadvantage for them to have clocks and calendars. By thinking in terms of the distance or closeness in years to birth or death, and the waste of time since the birth of the body, little indeed is done for the care or tendance of the immortal soul. Seeing this makes many people nervous, but this is to lose the proper perspective. One must see all life in the context of the invisible whole. One cannot reascend consciously without a progressive series of dissipations and a continual breaking up of *skandhas* accumulated throughout a lifetime. For instance, an emotional person needs to reduce the liabilities of the lower vestures to certain basic patterns of consolidation and break up these unhelpful clusters at their very core. Whence the need to belong? What is this concern to appropriate? Whence the desire for material or psychological security? One must burst the consolidating sources of emotion in order to keep pace with forward Manasic evolution. Humanity is in the Fifth Race of the Fourth Round, the long epoch of *Manas,* and to be emotional is only to go racially backwards. To catch up with the forward impulse of humanity in the Fifth Race means becoming a self-sufficient being of creative thought and deep meditation, freed from the evanescent impulses of mere emotional reaction.

In order progressively to dissipate and dissolve the elements by which, through the desire for consolidation, people limit and bind themselves, the persisting root of illusion must be sought in the mind. The mental image of oneself as separate from other human beings, feverishly moving places but periodically depressed if not ascending all the time, is entirely false. Each human being is merely one of myriads of centres of sensation and observation, but while such centres in the lower kingdoms have a certain precision, humans are all too often lazily and inefficiently trying to observe and record on the basis of mayavic conceptions amidst a kind of day-dreamy existence. It is an important and difficult task to cut through this veil of illusion, and this can only be done by coming down from the cosmic to the mundane. First, one must rise upwards to a cosmic perspective and perceive the whole universe from a unitary standpoint. Then one can come down to oneself and one's daily orbit of duties and obligations. Human beings are assuming an impossible task when they attempt the opposite, starting with the lower self and then trying to dispel their root illusions. Only by ascending to the universal and then descending to the particular can one find greater meaning in every atom and every aspect of oneself, as well as every event upon life's journey and the soul's pilgrimage.

Hermetic wisdom holds that everything in the universe follows analogy, that as it is above, so it is below, and that man is a microcosm of the universe. H.P. Blavatsky expresses this axiom in exact terms which clearly show the critical relevance of the evolution of human mentality to corresponding transformations in the subhuman kingdoms: "That which takes place on the spiritual plane repeats itself on the Cosmic plane. Concretion follows the lines of abstraction; corresponding to the highest must be the lowest; the material to the spiritual." Pointing to the dangers of the anti-intuitive, or below-above approach to the task of liberating consciousness from the bonds of form, she warns: "It would be very misleading to imagine a Monad as a separate Entity trailing its slow way in a distinct path through the lower Kingdoms, and after an incalculable series of transformations flowering into a human being." To think in such a limiting and linear way is to repeat the error of nineteenth century Darwinian speculation, effectually cutting oneself off both from the prospects of emancipation and the possibilities of service to the entire life-stream of evolution – monadic, mental and astral. To think of oneself and a tiny pebble, and to suppose that the pebble or stone is a separate entity which will eventually become an equally separate human being, is essentially false.

The Monadic Host is a collective host below the human level, working conjointly, by descent of Spirit into Matter, to raise all that which has become differentiated to a higher power of porosity or luminous reflection of intelligence. Until the human stage the indestructible monadic spark of the One Central Fire is only collectively involved in evolution as part of the great Monadic Host. At the human stage it becomes creatively capable by the potent power of self-reflection, *Svasamvedana,* of being able to consider itself as an object of its own thought and imagination. This is an extraordinary power, denied to the animal, which the human being has, the sacred gift of visualization. Thought is an essentially divine power belonging to human beings, and when exercised properly it can become an irresistibly potent agent of transformation in human nature and Nature in general. The collective Monadic Host in its descent is only a vast collection of creative centres because the atom "is not a particle of something, animated by a psychic something, destined after aeons to blossom as a man. But it is a concrete manifestation of the Universal Energy which itself has not yet become individualized." The human Monad is that same universal energy, not separate in any way, but individuated.

Many of the problems that arise in trying to understand this process are due to thinking in terms of terrene rather than aquatic analogies. When one thinks of the ocean, it is clear that there is no less differentiation there than on the earth. But the untutored and ungoverned senses are practised liars. Hence there is a profound need for true science. Occultism begins in the recognition that raw sense-perceptions not only tell nothing, but are actually poor reporters of inaccurate information. They falsely convey an impression that there are myriad separate things 'out there'. This is why people who close their eyes and begin to meditate work hard from early on to destroy this delusion. It is sometimes held that this misconception is strong in human life because of the deception of language and the actual activities of naming and particularization, but these themselves arise merely from a prior consolidation in consciousness of one's image as a separate being. These psychological differentiations exist only as incomplete reflections.

In essence, there is no differentiation. All drops in the ocean are within one great collective being, and the moment one speaks of 'drops', this is only in relation to some water taken out of the ocean and put in a jar. These are ephemeral 'drops'. What applies to the ocean also applies to the earth and everything else, contrary to what the casual eye reports. To understand this truly at its root requires the return, through the power of abstract meditation, to the noumenal source of consciousness, and then smoothly descending in concentrated thought. One thus takes hold of a single torch in the darkness, lighting it up, and through it one may light up other receptive beings. In a sense this is mayavic because all Monads are exactly the same, whether manifest or not, whether illuminated or in darkness. Yet, to recover a sense of true being independently of what has happened in the external fields of sensory contrast, material disaggregation, seeming cohesion and dispersion, and mayavic manifestation, is to recover a noetic sense of the entire ocean and its invisible, unfathomable depths. Then, as a *Manasa*, one may readily appreciate the depth of responsibility implied by the statement that "The ocean (of matter) does not divide into its potential and constituent drops until the sweep of the life-impulse reaches the evolutionary stage of man-birth."

The seemingly unbridgeable gap between the human and the other Monads is no more than the deceptive difference between the drop within the ocean and the drop outside the ocean. The teleological significance of the drop having been taken out of the ocean is that the cosmic power of that Monad, consciously to mirror the whole, is greater when it is locked into a certain vesture, the boundaries of which it must burst by the power of meditation. There is a deep meaning to the Orphic saying, quoted by Plato and Socrates, that the human body is like a tomb. The body is a temple, potentially, but in practice it is a tomb in which there is a confinement of the human Monad. Like a bird that is only freed from its cage at night, the Monad is ordinarily free only during deep sleep. Waking life is a kind of pralayic death to the immortal soul, and deep sleep, which is a temporary state of death or amnesia for the brain-mind, is truly regeneration and the elixir of life for the immortal soul. The soul is locked up and cannot come into its own except in deep sleep because its jailer, the brain-mind or personal ray, has assumed a parasitic false identity. Like a monkey or an automaton, it obscures the light which can only be gestated in silence. The personal ray is addicted to manifestation: the greater its desire to manifest, the longer and intenser the imprisonment of the immortal soul. From this, all the ascetic rules logically follow. The deeper the desire for meditation and calmness, for drawing within, and for self-forgetfulness in a state of active wakefulness to the noumenal realm of universal unity and life, the richer the possibilities for release of the spark of *Buddhi-Manas* from the *Atman* (the divine flame), and of establishing the still centre of one's inmost being, thus regaining the sovereign throne which has been usurped by *Kama Manas.*

If *Kama Manas* were an entity on its own, it could not ever displace itself. But *Kama Manas* is like an unruly child, an uproarious upstart in relation to *Manas,* a pathetic cheat that has stolen the light of self-consciousness and appropriated it on behalf of name and form. It did not mean to do all of this, but it caught the habit in the company of other people doing the same thing. During what is called 'growing up', it became inextricably involved in the extraordinary exaggeration that there are different and competing actors out there. Then, through compulsive consolidation of the personal consciousness, this became a dangerous habit. The child is bewildered when it first goes to school because it is expected increasingly to identify itself with something external. It may have already been given much aid in separativeness at home, especially where there were other children from which to differentiate itself. This banal phenomenon is somewhat unavoidable, but it is a spiritual hindrance to the incarnation of the immortal soul. Hence the importance of being able repeatedly to recollect, in a Platonic sense, one's true awareness of who one is as an 'I am I', an invisible centre of divine light-energy, essentially independent of all external impressions, conceptions, perceptions and forms. The mystical ability to release the potency and will of the indwelling Monad in waking life is the defining mark of spiritual wakefulness. When one sees rays of light, not forms, and when one sees oneself only as a ray of light and never as a form, then the human Monad begins to become progressively self-conscious in waking life. A truly self-conscious being in the midst of people who are not self-conscious can, while maintaining total silence, have an alchemical effect upon other people. At a minimum, they will be more apologetic rather than boastful about being bound up with the sensorium. If one maintains inward continuity of spiritual wakefulness, one can be a potent force for lighting up latent self-consciousness and giving spiritual life to all other beings.

This sacred privilege, exemplified by all the Avatars, is the fruition of the life-giving power of the perfected Monad. "As the Monads are uncompounded things . . . it is the spiritual essence which vivifies them in their degree of differentiation." There is that golden germ in the immortal Monad which vivifies even while it differentiates. The power to give life is always derived from the higher principles, which is why science will never be able to fabricate a living being through genetic manipulation. The divine power to give life derives entirely from the spiritual essence of the highest principles in the cosmos and in Man,

> which properly constitutes the Monad – not the atomic aggregation, which is only the vehicle and the substance through which thrill the lower and the higher degrees of intelligence.

> Leibnitz conceived of the Monads as elementary and indestructible units endowed with the power of giving and receiving with respect to other units, and thus of determining all spiritual and physical phenomena.

> It may be wrong on strictly metaphysical lines to call *Atma-Buddhi* a MONAD, since in the materialistic view it is dual and therefore compound.

The Secret Doctrine, i 179

One should not imagine rigid Aristotelian rifts between *Buddhi* and *Manas*, between *Atman* and *Buddhi*, or between *Atman* and *Buddhi-Manas*. These are really the three hypostases or aspects of one abstract reality. All the human principles should be seen as specializations of a supreme principle, different kinds of lenses through which one central light can be focussed at varying degrees of differentiation. This fundamental fact is itself the enduring basis of analogy and correspondence in nature, and hence of the myriad opportunities people have, with the help of simple analogies, to recognize how the same light is focussed in different ways in all beings. But all seekers must apply these sacred analogies to themselves through the practice of *Buddhi Yoga*. "As Matter is Spirit, and *vice versa;* and since the Universe and the Deity which informs it are unthinkable apart from each other; so in the case of Atma-Buddhi." One cannot think of light in the human constitution apart from the Light of the Logos in the cosmos and the Divine Darkness beyond. And if one thinks of the Light of the Logos, the noumenal light within *Mulaprakriti,* the *Ishwara* and the *Paramatman,* then one will readily salute the inward light in *Buddhi-Manas,* in every human being. Everything at any given degree of differentiation is simply a specialization of a higher principle manifesting through the matrix of a different lens or focussing medium. To realize this fully is irreversibly to alter one's way of looking at the world and oneself.

Darkness from the standpoint of the sense-organs is metaphysically closer to Light, and primordial Light is permanently hidden within the Divine Darkness. Upon entering a condition of visual darkness, by analogy and correspondence one may experience resonances of a deeper state of spiritual darkness wherein meditation upon Non-Being results in an ineffable experience of primordial Light. Since all nature can be understood in terms of analogy and correspondence, everything on the physical plane is not only isomorphic, but also isodynamic with something on a higher plane. On the physical plane artificial light generates an illusory kaleidoscopic world, in contrast with which the darkness of abstraction is closer to the noumenal; so with the noetic mind that meditates. But mere exposure to the evocative power of physical darkness will not alter the ephemeral mental conceptions of human beings. This is why most people, though they go daily into deep sleep and come closer to the ideographic language of the immortal Soul, find that it avails them naught the next day. They have little basis for believing during the day that only the previous night they entered into their ancestral kingdom of Divine Light. There are blockages in bringing back the noumenal light of true knowledge gained in deep sleep through the chaos of *swapna,* the chaos of fascination with form, mostly arising through ignorant fear and wishful thinking.

So long as there is in human beings a compressed, congested view of the separative self, conceived in terms of innate deficiency, such blockages will persist. They derive from millennia of mutilation of the nimbus of human beings and have to do with causal factors connected with the misuse of magic, with creedal religion and exploitative social structures, but also with the persistent if pathetic refusal of many persons to accept fully their own responsibility and consequent karma. There is a stark alienation between human beings and their myriad opportunities for good in each life because as they learnt language, like Caliban in *The Tempest,* they learnt faster to curse than to bless. The recent story of humanity is a complicated and sometimes sordid tale of base ingratitude arising from fear and guilt, owing to many golden opportunities being misused through the failure to share them with others. Humanity thereby engendered certain ingrained patterns, so that the fresh opportunities given frequently in deep sleep or at certain waking moments will not make a lasting difference unless there is a calm and careful recognition of the diverse modes of karmic bondage.

Put simply, two distinct requirements must be fulfilled: *first,* one has to get beyond oneself, going in consciousness to the core of what is common, cosmic and transcendent until one can come down and be wide awake in the world of particularities and contrasts, the arena of illusion, ignorance and delusion; *secondly,* one must also acknowledge in detail, at least unto oneself, one's persisting delusions, because if one looks for commonality at the expense of fruitful diversity, one evades one's ethical responsibility. If one is unduly caught up in the world, one is running away from the One Light, but if one vainly tries to grab instantly the light of spiritual will, one is running away from past karma. Therefore one has to recognize frankly that every moment is a precious opportunity to learn, that everything which comes in life is really one's *guru* in disguise. At every moment of each day, the stream of life is rushing in to teach the soul if it is willing to learn. If one takes proper advantage of these golden opportunities, one can clean and polish the lenses of the vestures. By working upon one's different vestures in deep meditation several times a day, and also by going beyond them during deep sleep, a point will come at which one is refining them deftly from both ends rather like a person who is both visualizing a plan for a new arrangement in a room and also cleaning out objects as they are. The one activity need not preclude the other. One can have some time each day to think out a new way of arranging everything, and new ways of thinking. Meanwhile, one can also dust each object as it is, keeping things as neatly as possible within the existing arrangement.

Applying the analogy to the vestures, one can simultaneously increase slowly the porosity of the grosser vestures to the light while also working through the subtlest vestures to invite the beatific descent of the Divine Light. As the grosser vestures are continually renovated and cleaned, and as the subtlest vestures experience through meditation the infusion of noumenal light, a point comes at which the two processes can be brought together, realigning all the vestures from a fresh standpoint. This process must be renewed and repeated again and again. The search for the spiritual is really hard work, and while it is good that so many people have rebelled against a social structure which was using labour as a means of confinement to a narrow bourgeois conception of the world, the deeper purpose of this widespread and anomie rebellion was not to encourage indolence and indiscipline. Work and discipline can be done in an Aquarian mode, as a form of silent worship and spontaneous sacrifice, flowing forth a selfless motive to be of true service to humanity and to elevate human and global consciousness, thus furthering the noble impulse of monadic evolution.

Light on the Path teaches "Kill out ambition . . . Work as those work who are ambitious." Taken up in isolation, this is indeed difficult, but where it is done on behalf of the whole, without concern for any rewards to one's precarious self-image, it is much easier. This does not mean that there is no longer any ambition whatsoever. The diseases of the soul are still there to be healed, but where individuals work collectively, there is a quantum jump to a point at which they are less concerned with living a banal life of petty personal ambition. Yet, to work as those work who are ambitious is truly difficult for many weak-willed individuals. To work mainly for a loftier purpose, to generate a tremendous energy but out of a cheerful sense of obligation and as a modest contribution to the whole, even though there is no payoff to the personal ray, is hard for the persona. One must replace lunar emanations by solar energies. The sun does not wax and wane, but ceaselessly emanates light, life and energy so that in and around every human being there is a magnetic field of self-sustaining motions of the Spiritual Will, the Spiritual Heart and the Spiritual Mind. All that waxes and wanes, participating feebly in the vicissitudes of change, is secondary and instrumental. It is ephemeral and relatively unreal when seen from the noetic standpoint of the Spiritual Sun, mirrored in *Atma-Buddhi-Manas.*

Atma-Buddhi is the invisible sun in man, the *Atman* being like the invisible disc itself, and *Buddhi* is its centrifugal light. *Manas* is the centripetal organ for focussing that light, the seat of pure thought and spiritual will. What is below is like the moon which receives reflected light from the sun. *Manas* would be rather like Venus, the fixed star in highest heaven, Lucifer-Hesperus. This has nothing to do with the personal mind, which is extremely fickle and volatile, ever-changing and in a constant state of self-obscuration. The ordinary mind has developed into a perverse instrument because it is fiercely gripped within the cruel claws and greedy tentacles of the demon of selfish desire. *Kama manas* is like a motor-power driving the personal man to a pseudo-life sustained by futile fears of death and the obscure past. Inwardly, these fears stem from the loss of the birth vision. People become vulnerable to plausible but absurd eschatologies because in every human soul there is the sad loss of an earlier vision which can only be recaptured by conscious effort. Until it is sufficiently recovered, one is necessarily subject to a creeping fear of the divine judgement which comes at the moment of death. Yet, there is much truth to what Shakespeare says, that life is but a poor shadow that struts upon the stage for a brief hour, full of sound and fury, signifying nothing. For the immortal soul there is little benefit, typically, in most of what is called earthly life. Therefore, the immortal soul must indeed make the most of a few moments of time in daily meditation and deep sleep, so that it may become capable of sustaining its own pure visions of the Good. This does not mean that at other times there is no creative activity, on the subtler planes of non-manifestation, but all this has little to do with the reflected ray. Until its periodic pain becomes the basis of a life of search for meaning, and until it is blended through *Buddhi Yoga* with the vaster suffering of all humanity, one cannot hope to awaken to the real life of the immortal Monad. When one enters what *The Voice of the Silence* calls the Path of Woe, then one will eventually come to discover the ineffable *ananda* of the Divine Light streaming forth from the Divine Darkness, the changeless *alpha* and *omega* of monadic life beyond all form, stretching until the farthest shore of formless existence.

The Dewdrop slips into the shining sea.

OM MANI PADME HUM

Hermes, November 1980
Raghavan Iyer

DELIVERANCE FROM BONDAGE

Perhaps the most widespread and universal among the symbols in the old astronomical systems, which have passed down the stream of time to our century...are the Cross and the Fire – the latter, the emblem of the Sun, The ancient Aryans had them both as the symbols of Agni. Whenever the ancient Hindu devotee desired to worship Agni...he arranged two pieces of wood in the form of a cross, and, by a peculiar whirling and friction obtained fire for his sacrifice. As a symbol, it is called Swastica, and, as an instrument manufactured out of a sacred tree and in possession of every Brahmin, it is known as Arani.

The Theosophist
H. P. Blavatsky

Throughout the immense pilgrimage of humanity, Avatars, Initiates and Adepts have recorded and also incarnated the spiritual meanings and initiatory potentials of sacred symbols and glyphs. Each evolutionary advance of the human race depends upon a timely recovery and fresh realization of the insights hidden within archaic records of arcane wisdom. Not only do symbols enshrine matrices of forces in visible and invisible nature, pointing to the complex interpenetration of planes of substance and consciousness, but they also reach to the indestructible core of spiritual wisdom within every human being. Therein lies the pristine seed of immortality, waiting to be quickened to life by the blazing fires of purification and illumination. Every new turning of the Wheel of Law offers appropriate avenues for growth for all soul-atoms nestled in the cosmic vestures of the *Logos*. Under the watchful eye of Krishna-Buddha-Christos, each human soul has the golden opportunity to insert itself into the forward movement of human evolution. Through the power of spiritual reminiscence, through minor and major awakenings, each may find its place in the awesome *Guruparampara* chain that binds together all human souls. So vast has been the variegated diffusion of sacred symbols through space and time that every human being has myriad sources from which to sift and select, with reverence and devotion, in seeking an authentic reminiscence of the sacred purpose of human existence. There are few human beings on earth, for example, who are not familiar with the figure of the Buddha. There are millions of copies of statues of the Buddha, ranging from the massive Kamakura Buddha to small reproductions readily available to the humblest devotee. Whether one is privileged to see a majestic and monumental representation of the Buddha in the ancient centres of Buddhist culture in Asia, or one cherishes a modest image of the Buddha in one's own home, anyone can make it a focus of concentration and compassion. The vital question is, even if one makes this a daily practice, how may one evoke through it a summons to self-enlightenment?

In order to awaken true reminiscence through the aid of a symbol, it would be helpful to associate a powerful idea with a pleasing image. For instance, if one were to associate the Kwan Yin Pledge with one's contemplation of the statue of the Buddha, and at the same time deepen and concentrate all one's feelings of gratitude for everything that one has received in life, this would begin to give life to the symbol. By linking the idea of renunciation with a potent and sublime image – whether it be of the Buddha, of Christ or of Krishna – one may gradually gain the ability to see one's life not merely in terms of past, present and future, but *sub specie aeternitatis*. When one comes to live consciously within the rays of compassionate light and ideation streaming forth from the enlightened Teachers of Humanity, one can augment the power to alter the patterns of association of one's ideas and images. Just as the seven colours of the rainbow give way to many subtle hues in nature and on the painter's palette, so too the compassion of the *Bodhisattvas* unveils varied modes of attunement accessible to human souls. Like the visible sun, which provides light and nourishment to innumerable leaves extending over an enormous range of greenish tints, the Spiritual Sun radiates a continuous stream of spiritual sustenance capable of sustaining human beings in every circumstance. The chief barriers to receiving benediction from this constant illumination are lack of meditation upon the light, ingratitude for its warmth, and fear-ridden selfishness originating from a life lived in the darkness. By associating the ideas of *Buddhi Yoga*, thanksgiving and renunciation, with the sacred image of the Buddha, even though one may know little about the life of Gautama, one could begin to see through the shadows of limited and imperfect associations which bind the soul. By taking a symbolic image as the constant focus and repository of one's calm reflections, one can build fresh constellations of ideas capable of serving as a salutary guide to action in daily life. One may even restore the multi-dimensional quality of the mind, ready to contemplate universal themes and to translate them into apt applications. Gradually, one will overcome the propensity of the mind to be distracted, to move towards dichotomous thinking, towards proliferating *foci* of personal concern, and steadily reorient it towards wisdom.

Since all spiritual discernment is necessarily connected with ethical practice, the true test of learning is the ability to strengthen and mature one's concern for the welfare of others. There are in the world today innumerable individuals with intuitive powers, and one must become a silent member of their hallowed ranks, quietly labouring to alleviate the misery of mankind. As one's meditation upon the sacred symbols of the *Gupta Vidya* deepens, one will begin to discern, amidst the cacophony of worldly events, fruitful opportunities for effective service to others. What is wisdom in Shamballa is seldom seen as wisdom on earth, and though the potent seeds of the New Cycle are burgeoning in the soil everywhere, this will not be evident to those who are entrapped in anxious self-concern. With the good earth groaning under the burden of personal greed, what may seem like oppressive karma to the personality is, in fact, from the standpoint of the soul, beneficent karma. The acute sense of alienation from life caused by this gap in consciousness can be overcome only by turning the mind around and redirecting it away from the constricting circle of the separative personality towards the luminous sphere of the immortal soul. It is essential to reach in consciousness to the core of the idea of renunciation, and this is impossible without eliminating every trace of greed from one's nature. Even the minutest residue of greed is incompatible with the pristine spirit of gratitude exemplified by the galaxy of *Bodhisattvas*. One must learn to test oneself daily, to scrutinize the quality of one's desires and dreams. Unfortunately, the capacity for constructive self-examination has been attenuated through neglect. The primal power of desire itself has been diffused and dispersed, leaving individuals incapable of true philosophic contemplation, a deep love of ideas. They find themselves subject to random and mindless associations of ideas, a desperate reaching out to delusive alternatives that are false solutions to the basic needs of their lives. Through this fragmentation the fires of mind and motivation have gradually waned, and the electric current of ideation has ebbed. Rather than vainly seeking what seem to be pleasing solutions to problems, one must make a strong effort to rekindle the fire of self-consciousness within oneself. Although no one can do this for another, each must do it for the sake of all, and every person has the enormous resources of nature and the sacred Teachings to aid the attempt.

The restoration of the vital connection between the embodied self and the higher mind, and true communion between mind and spirit, requires soul-reminiscence. The right use of memory is aided by the pervasive compassion of Nature, which refrains from burdening any soul with those memories of errors and mistakes in past lives which might prevent it from doing what it needs to do in this incarnation. Nature mercifully veils the unneeded details of the past. It is, therefore, an utter waste of time to daydream or speculate about past lives. Proper understanding of the deeds and misdeeds of previous incarnations can come with the exactitude of the mathematics of the soul, but this precision can never be gleaned from external sources. It must be sought from within, and the first step is to take full responsibility for one's moral nature. One must learn to draw from memory and from one's abilities only that which one can truly use for the good of all. One must discover and enrich those activities which one can do right. A proper beginning must be made upon the path of the six virtues, the steep path of the *paramitas*, which culminates in that sublime condition wherein one is constitutionally incapable of deviating from the right way. One can discern within oneself the enduring basis of that harmony which ultimately makes one stand without variableness or shadow of turning. To learn to stand like a steady flame burning on holy ground, one must emulate the regulated motion of the sun and the planets. One must become one-pointed through the power of vows repeatedly taken and constantly observed over lifetimes. The concentrated moral effort to enact the ethics taught by Krishna, Buddha and Christ is the meaningful attempt to mirror the metaphysical harmony at the root of invisible Nature.

> The Central Point, or the great central sun of the Kosmos, as the Kabalists call it, is the Deity. It is the point of intersection between the two great conflicting powers – the centripetal and centrifugal forces, which drive the planets into their elliptical orbits, that make them trace a cross in their paths through the Zodiac. These two terrible, though as yet hypothetical and imaginary powers, preserve harmony and keep the Universe in steady, unceasing motion; and the four bent points of the Swastica typify the revolution of the Earth upon its axis.
>
> *The Theosophist*
> H. P. Blavatsky

As participants in a world marked by social decay and disorder, individuals must learn to accept universal responsibility for the general state of malaise, which is the result of past actions in previous lives. They must meditate upon what it is to be worthy of living in a human temple. The ethical integrity of the cosmos requires individuals to accept the consequences of their former deeds as made manifest in existing conditions. They must be willing to engage in the painful process of sifting the good from the bad, the wheat from the chaff, in all that they have brought from the past, and be prepared to embrace the fiery heat of *tapas* emanating from the central point in the swastika. It is through the expiatory power of Agni, the focus of life and light and heat in that central point, that individuals may remove the obscuring mass of illusions and delusions which beset humanity, crucified upon the cross of matter. Once the cleansing and purifying fire has accomplished the work of purgation, the crystalline ray of Spirit may vivify and fructify the matrix of matter, bringing with it the restoration of a true sense of purpose for human existence. Then the fiery light, acting as Lucifer, the Son of the Morning Star, will be felt as the illuminating power within the heart of every responsive individual. That which cannot be brought through the fires but must be cast off will, through the compassion of Nature, be used and refined by the lower kingdoms.

For the individual, the process of awakening soul-memories is similar to the sifting processes of Nature. The wise being is concerned only to remember that which can be used in the present and the future, because it has its roots beyond all time. Unwisdom consists in fancying something and mistaking it for knowledge or in confusing the lower psychic fantasy, containing mere shadows of forgotten truths, with authentic deliverances of Buddhic imagination. There is a sad tendency amongst those who have not properly meditated during life to drift into daydream as they approach the moment of death. If they have heard, at some level, of the doctrines of karma and reincarnation and of the existence of spiritual Teachers, they may be taken over by highly personalized fantasies regarding supposed relationships with those Teachers in past lives. Such delusions have nothing to do with soul-memory, but are ineffectual compensations for failures in the present life to approach the true Teachers through the inward path of meditation. Mistaking intellectual involvement with words and psychic involvement with images for the establishment of lasting connections in their inner natures, they cut off the possibility of spiritual contact with the Buddhas in future lives. Actual contact with spiritual realities can never be the result of passive association of ideas, however originated psychologically, but is the natural consequence of selfless motivation maintained consciously. Yet, on the other hand, there is hardly a human being alive today who has not in past lives received the potent seed of the Teachings. In moments of despair and despondency over the inevitable collapse of worldly delusions, and in times of distress at one's inability to aid the suffering of another, each has received gentle words of encouragement from the Servants of the *Bodhisattvas*. "Do not feel guilty. Do not seek to blame others. Life is full of pain but there is no need to be afraid. Each may seek right livelihood in the world and search for the Path." When in similar moments in the present life such memories stir in the soul, then one may begin to associate the idea of renunciation and purification with the vibration of the Teachers. This alchemical fusion is the beginning of spiritual maturation in the present life. It does not matter whether this takes place at the age of ten, thirty or sixty, for once one begins to put the Teachings to good use, then it becomes possible to discover better uses. Such is the Law. "The books say well, my brothers. Each man his prison makes", taught Gautama Buddha, and each may also unmake his prison. The primary need is for deep reflection upon the root ideas of renunciation and bondage. Since the world will not teach one how this is to be done, the spiritual Teachings are brought again and again to orphan humanity through the compassion of *Bodhisattvas*.

Whether one understands it in terms of the image of the Ashwattha tree depicted in the *Bhagavad Gita* or in terms of the image of the deadly *upas* tree, the world binds the soul with coils upon coils of ignorance. Krishna taught that this tree must be cut asunder at the root with the sword of spiritual knowledge sharpened by devotion. Whilst one cannot hope to do this fully at one stroke in this life, for that would imply that one had done so many times in previous lives, it is still possible to make a sufficient dent in the world tree that one may find space and time in the rush of life for deep thought and meditation. Anyone with a modicum of courage, as the sword of wisdom cannot be wielded by those with fear, may set aside every rationalization, at least for a few moments, and engage in earnest thought upon universal ideas. From such efforts one will find the strength to be able to help others, whether it be to render aid to an old person who is dying or to give gentle words of encouragement to a small child that is crying, and from these sacrificial acts one can gain further strength to engage in meditation.

When one finds within oneself the power to help others, one simultaneously discovers the power to help oneself to grow spiritually. Thus the wheel of the Great Law is turned and the endless stream of learning moves towards the universal ocean of wisdom. Through silent obedience and humble obeisance to the voice of conscience, one gradually builds a bridge in consciousness linking the experience of the outward nature with the wisdom of the soul within. In a small way one can come to mirror the *Mahatmas*, the paradigmatic exemplars of learning who are eternally and effortlessly obedient to the *Maha Guru* and ceaselessly engaged in exploration for the sake of implementing the modes of the future races. As the Light of the *Logos* is ubiquitous throughout the universe and present in each soul, the fundamental requirements of learning and the essential opportunities for growth are universally the same for all beings. Krishna-Buddha-Christos is present everywhere and eternally available to all who turn inward towards the light. No soul enters or leaves this world without the aid of the *Logos*. The modes of instruction of the Brotherhood of *Bodhisattvas* have nothing to do with the superficial and obsolete methods of mass modern education; they reach into the hearts of human beings and give them that which will come back to them in times of need. Every soul is whispered into at the moment of birth and whenever one is in real difficulty one is helped. Once one begins to realize this, and is ready to see the universality of the impulse towards spiritual enlightenment, then one is naturally much less entranced by the delusions of the world tree. Through thought and meditation, through contemplation of sacred glyphs and symbols, one becomes oneself a glyph – the glyph of man thinking. This inward transformation and restoration of one's true estate as a son of the *Manasas* is the real meaning and holy purpose of the presence of *Gupta Vidya* in the world of woe.

For the sake of recollection, the glyph of man thinking may be represented diagrammatically by the figure of a cross surrounded by an aureole of lambent flames, with a bridge forming a connection to a base below, the whole like a glowing lamp upon a secure stand. The object of thought may be represented by the glyph of three triangles surrounding the points of a central triangle, which together form the figure of a hexagon in the centre. The two glyphs – of the thinker and of thought – must be associated and made concentric, even though their geometric representation in space requires that they be distinct. Contemplation will reveal that the stand of the lamp is not essential to the process of thinking, any more than the clothes of the body are essential to its biological functioning. Just so, the physical human body is not the thinking self. In order to appreciate man thinking, one must dwell upon the nature of the cross, the fire and its rays, the triad, and their mutual relations to each other. Concern with the lampstand, whether through positive or negative forms of attachment, only serves as a distraction from deep reflection upon the essential meaning of the glyph. Unfortunately, many people rarely rise above or even reach the level of the bridge linking the lampstand to the golden light. Through mental and moral laziness, fear and inertia, they fall prey to delusions and fantasies preyed upon by those purveyors of pseudo-occult theories who masquerade under the name of hypnotists, depth psychologists and the like. These pedlars and their victims constitute a matrix of pollution stemming from misuse of the sacred. From the one side, practising a nefarious craft through the corruption of words, and from the other side, seeking to gain spiritual value through payment with worldly goods, the two may seem karmically to deserve each other. Here as in every case of pollution, one must not succumb to judgementalism. Certainly in the compassion of Agni, the fiery divine dragon of wisdom, there is a precise knowledge of the virtually infinite mathematical complexity involved in the karmic curves of purgation of individual souls, but this may not be judged from outside. In a time of universal purification and renewal, nothing is wasted, and even as the sweeping fires burn away the excrescences of the past, there are always soul-lessons to mitigate the agony of those who have made themselves the victims of self-hatred. Even the burning of the dross releases resources for the lower kingdoms.

The mystery of man thinking has been obscured in the modern world by its crude conceptions of progress. The cosmos has always been a macro-electronic universe, and for the past eighteen million years mankind has been living in a macro-electronic age. Recent expansions of human capabilities and innovations of thought are only seemingly new. They are, in fact, rather superficial applications of fundamental principles long known and taught by the Adepts. The sense of collective scientific advance and discovery in the modern age is a permissible illusion, particularly amongst people who without such encouragement would be drawn back into the violent and self-destructive tendencies of medievalism. Yet although this idea of progress offers some hope for human advancement, its danger is that it could eclipse the underlying reality of universal humanity and the logic of human evolution, which has nothing to do with external tokens. Anyone who has stopped to think about the nature of material progress soon realizes that the true amelioration of the human condition does not depend upon external inventions but rather upon an internal transformation in man. The Great Work, as it was called by the Renaissance alchemists, is far more demanding than any of its materialized representations in so-called exact science. The inward symbolic synthesis, the alchemical process of becoming a true glyph, moves through precise phases and stages, represented as dissolution, sublimation, condensation and coagulation. This is true not only for the individual but also for the entire human race.

An important aspect of this universal work of transformation is the drawing together and synthesizing of all the lines of good karma from the ancient sacred orders and the manifold symbol systems of antiquity. The self-conscious synthesis into the threefold path of the Philosophy of Perfection, the Religion of Responsibility, and the Science of Spirituality is a central task in the present cycle. Particular systems of glyphs and symbols, each of which has its own period of effectiveness, are being drawn together to provide the basis for soul-recollection for the maximum possible number of human beings. Heralding the progress of this restoration of the inheritance of humanity unto itself, H.P. Blavatsky spoke in the last century of the work of diligent students of the Mysteries:

. . . these students, though none of them has yet mastered all the "seven keys" that open the great problem, have discovered enough to be able to say: There was a universal mystery-language, in which all the World Scriptures were written, from Vedas to "Revelation", from the "Book of the Dead" to the Acts. One of the keys, at any rate – the numerical and geometrical key to the Mystery Speech – is now rescued; an ancient language, truly, which up to this time remained hidden, but the evidences of which abundantly exist, as may be proven by undeniable mathematical demonstrations.

Lucifer
H. P. Blavatsky

In the present period the further recovery of the mystery language depends upon the willingness of individuals to engage in selfless and lifelong learning. Anyone who is willing to ponder calmly, with an immense feeling of gratitude to the Teachers, upon the heavens and the omnipresent *Logos*, can contribute to the restoration of the sacred glyph of man thinking. Those who are wise will pursue this solitary work with no thought of selfish reward or recognition. Nor will they allow themselves to be captivated by the spectacle of the collapsing old order based upon blood covenants and vengeance. They will not be caught in the doomsday extrapolation of the record of disasters precipitated by those caught in self-contempt engendered by their desecration of the sacred. Rather, like children, they will seek to discern hieroglyphs in the sky and in the human heart, and treasuring their vision in silence they will look for means to connect the good in themselves and others with the innumerable rays of good flooding in on all sides.

The time has come for a self-conscious restoration of awareness of the original programme of human evolution. That programme and its meaning for the future are intimated in the symbol of the bird of everlasting life mentioned in *The Voice of the Silence.* The future of human evolution is bound up with the guardian race of Hamsa, the qualification for which is *ahimsa* – total non-violence in thought, word, feeling and will – the absence of any trace of self-assertion or egotism. This is the sacred tribe of *Bodhisattvas* surrounding the pavilion of the *Logos*, ceaselessly engaged in learning the teaching of Hamsa through the power of reverence and devotion. They are the exemplars *par excellence* of the truth taught by the Buddha that uttermost self-surrender and reverence are the only means to deliverance from bondage. Ceaselessly engaged in learning, they are the true recorders of the enactment of divine truth by the *Logos* in the cosmos. As the custodians of the archives of spiritual humanity, they recorded the original esoteric texts from which the entire plethora of exoteric religions are derived. Having realized within their own inner natures the rich meaning of the signature of the *Logos* in nature, they have given out from time to time, in veiled allegory and parable, glyphs and symbols which may serve as a bridge and ladder in consciousness for those vigilant souls ready to tread the path leading towards initiation. The deepest secrets of initiation have not been and indeed cannot be transmitted, but must be discovered by the disciple within the sanctuary of the soul. The timeless truths of divine nature are eternally enacted in the heart of the Ever-Living Human Banyan that is the core of humanity, and this enactment is intimated in the hoary tradition of the *Puranas*. Therein one finds the allegorical story of Vishvakarman, the Omnificent, the Vedic god who is the architect of the world and who sacrifices himself to himself, having offered up all the worlds in a *sarvamedha* or universal sacrifice.

> . . . his daughter Yoga-siddha "Spiritual consciousness", the wife of Surya, the Sun, complains to him of the too great effulgence of her husband; and Viswakarma, in his character of Takshaka, "wood cutter and carpenter", placing the Sun upon his lathe cuts away a part of his brightness. Surya looks, after this, crowned with dark thorns instead of rays, and becomes Vikarttana ("shorn of his rays"). All these names are terms which were used by the candidates when going through the trials of Initiation. The Hierophant-Initiator personated Viswakarman; the father, and the general artificer of the gods (the adepts on earth), and the candidate – Surya, the Sun, who had to kill all his fiery passions

and wear the crown of thorns while crucifying his body before he could rise and be re-born into a new life as the glorified "Light of the World" – Christos.

Lucifer
H. P. Blavatsky

None but *Mahatmas*, perfect embodiments of the truth, are really capable of understanding the full meaning of the divine enactment of the Mysteries or the mysterious avataric descent of the *Logos* into the world. They alone are permitted to record the archives of the Teachings of Hamsa, and will permit no pseudo-esoteric packagings of the truth to persist. Every sincere and devoted individual who is willing to become an apprentice in the arduous art of transcendent concentration and selfless meditation upon universal good is invited to enter the orbit of the *Mahatmas*. If one reads the *Bhagavad Gita* carefully, one will discover that Krishna always is surrounded by *Mahatmas*. It is only the consciousness corrupted by materialization and externalization which would mistake the allegorical scenes of the Mahabharata War for events constrained by the limits of physical space. The true locus of events is a matrix of divine Logoic ideation surrounded by the fathomless waters of invisible space, wherein *Mahatmas*, in their *vamanas* or aerial cars of inconceivably refined subtle substance, surround the *Logos*. They alone can see the invisible form of Krishna, and therefore they alone can tell the tale. The geographical space and colourful scene surrounding Krishna on earth is a form of *maya* hiding the "invisible garment of God". Within the invisible form of the Avatar there resides a galaxy of *Mahatmas*. Seated in ceaseless meditation and constant adoration within the matrix of the body of the *Logos*, they constitute the constellations, indeed the entire universe of enlightenment. Nothing of this can be known by going from without within, but something of it may be gathered by the intuition through contemplating Buddhist *tankas* showing myriads of *Bodhisattvas* surrounding a central figure of the Buddha like an aura of wisdom-light.

Once this central fact of human evolution is widely grasped, it marks the end of recorded history with all its pretentious pseudo-esoteric and secular accounts of the meaning of human existence. When the glyph of man thinking is realized within to be identical with the matrix of the *Logos* surrounded by the galaxies of *Bodhisattvas*, it is no more possible to be taken in by the trumped up stories and packaged accounts of spiritual life promoted by the failures in human evolution. Stripped of illusions, nothing remains but to insert oneself by the power of one's own mystic meditation into the universal vision of Shamballa. This is the vision of the One Flame and its innumerable rays streaming forth, each of which is like a jewel in the Logoic form of Shiva-Krishna or Nataraja-Narayana. Every diamond-souled *Mahatma* is an eternal witness to this sacred truth, and no concession can be made to any lesser vision. It has long been known in Shamballa that the time would come when there could be no further accommodation either to the ill-intentioned or to the passive which would obstruct the inward spiritual growth of humanity. It has always been inevitable that at some point the fiery divine dragon of wisdom – the living Word of Truth – should burn away the obscuring dross of past error. This is a necessary preparation for the entry of the good gardeners of nature, who will prepare the soil for the future Garden of Eden. Those who are so fortunate to earn under karma, through decades of striving, the golden privilege of thinking the right thoughts at the moment of death, may also be so fortunate as to reincarnate again in a human form at some point in time when they may hear of the actual presence on earth of a new humanity. To be worthy of the rare good karma of returning to the earth at this distant time, one must begin now to nurture the seed of the Buddha-nature through *Buddhi Yoga*, through gratitude and renunciation. Then one may hope to experience the immense thrill of being alive in those far-flung aeons when Men of Meditation, masters of the mathematics of service to humanity, will walk the earth openly and all human beings alike understand that the only purpose for being in a human form is to be a true servant to humanity.

Through understanding the real purpose of meditation upon sacred glyphs and symbols, which has to do with the inward invocation of the fires of self-purification and illumination through self-transcendence, one may come to appreciate the truth of what Hegel once said about history, that the dialectic must have its joke. In a sense, at this point in history the joke of the divine dialectic is the only significant fact in history. The dialectic is smiling the smile of the Buddha. It is playing the flute of Krishna. It is also seated in divine meditation like Shankara. The dialectic, at the same time, is accelerating the disintegration of the thought-forms and entities of the past for whom the hour has struck. There is an increasingly widespread recognition that the old order is nearing its end, and that the Aquarian task of self-regeneration has begun.

> Lodging the purified inner powers in the Self, the witness, who is pure illumination, gaining steadfastness step by step, let him fix his vision on the fullness of the Eternal.

Shri Shankaracharya

Hermes, October 1981
Raghavan Iyer

RENUNCIATION AND RESPONSIBILITY

Renounce and then enjoy this world.

Isopanishad

Starting upon the long journey immaculate; descending more and more into sinful matter, and having connected himself with every atom in manifested Space – the Pilgrim, having struggled through and suffered in every form of life and being, is only at the bottom of the valley of matter, and half through his cycle, when he has identified himself with collective Humanity. This, he has made in his own image. In order to progress upwards and homewards, the "God" has now to ascend the weary uphill path of the Golgotha of Life. It is the martyrdom of self-conscious existence. Like Visvakarman he has to sacrifice himself to himself in order to redeem all creatures, to resurrect from the many into the One Life. Then he ascends into heaven indeed; where, plunged into the incomprehensible absolute Being and Bliss of Paranirvana, he reigns unconditionally, and whence he will re-descend again...

The Secret Doctrine, i 268
H. P. Blavatsky

The immortal individuality of every human being is overbrooded by a luminous Dhyani, and it persists as a distinct Monad during its entire Manvantaric pilgrimage of myriad incarnations in mortal vestures. As *Atman*, the Monad is one in fiery essence with *Paramatman*; as the Buddhic *vahan* it is the Dhyan Chohanic light-energy; and as self-conscious *Manas*, the individual Monad is an integral portion of the Great Sacrifice – the mysterious *Adhiyajna*, the ensouling Mind and Heart of all Humanity. Immovably fixed at the highest pole of the spectrum of consciousness, the Divine Prototype is both the noumenal cause and Silent Watcher of its successive projections into the shadowy region of phenomenal change. The partial incarnation of the immortal Monad in every personality is a sacrificial participation in the shadowy side of existence. It carries into every descent a luminous spark of the supernal light of compassionate awareness, thus endowing each of its lunar vestures with the personal prerogative of reflective consciousness, choice and discrimination, moral conscience and responsibility. All self-consciousness is inherently ethical in essence, and is made possible through the voluntary sacrifice of the Immortal Triad. And yet, much of what is sensed and mirrored by the human Ego in its incarnation into a mortal vesture cannot serve the moral purposes of its immemorial pilgrimage, owing to the recurrent subversion of Manasic ideation through the sway of unregulated *kama* and attendant rationalizations of weakness and servility. For the human being the grossest plane and enslaving principle are not the physical, with its molecular matter constructed out of countless elemental "lives", but the chaotic astral plane of frustrated cravings, fears and foolish imaginings. These form clouds of vapour which obscure mental perception and obstruct the noetic capacity to focus the Buddhic light of the *Atman* with alertness and awareness, deliberation and detachment, calmness and creativity.

To render the priceless privilege of noetic insight relevant in daily life requires strength of concentration, serenity of feeling and skill in action. This creative state of being necessitates the withdrawal of the wandering mind from the hypnotic spell of nebulous sensations, compulsive reactions and repressed emotions. The analytical mind must be yoked to a still centre through the persistent negation of the false identity gleaned from the succession of humdrum events and the melodramatic moods of the shadowy self. The self-sacrifice of noetic consciousness enables the reflected rays within the lunar realm of heterogeneous matter and cloudy confusion to draw back to the parent sun and profit from its cosmic splendour. Everything turns upon true self-consciousness, which is the Manvantaric gift of the God in man as well as the grace of the Guru given to the selfless devotee in any auspicious cycle of growth.

The profound challenge to human beings moving in the realm of the mortal and the conditioned is to awaken a therapeutic awareness of the potential and the unmanifest. Each and every human being is invariably helped in deep dreamless sleep when the

Immortal Self is in its original state of timeless consciousness, analogous at its own level to Paranirvanic unconditionality. Thus it is possible for everyday life to go on even amidst the psychic confusion, the complicated enmeshing of events, and the karmic burden of all the misused and contaminated life-atoms that make matter seem sinful. The daily replenishment from the inner reserves of noetic consciousness is made possible through the magic of *sushupti.* To sustain this vibration in waking life and utilize the resources of deep meditation in the sphere of mundane *Dharma,* one needs continually to let go of all mental habits of narrow self-reference. One must break up the inert assemblage of ingrained tendencies which consolidate into a shallow conception of isolated identity. Even when through moralistic discipline this conditioned self becomes increasingly righteous, bound up with ostentatious virtues, with self-protective habits, with worthy resolves and pious aspirations, it still acts as a fragile crystallization of fickle identity and an arbitrary limitation upon the attributeless Self. The Path of true spiritual self-consciousness commences at that crucial point where one is ready to live in and through diverse human beings. This is neither the natural stance of humanity in general nor the mental posture of many human beings who have a fleeting attraction to the Path of self-redemption. Nevertheless, every person has some implicit sense of human growth, some elementary empathy which enables language itself to be meaningful. The unspoken reciprocities that make everyday interaction and humane understanding possible even at the simplest level presuppose a primary receptivity and intuitive intersubjectivity in self-consciousness. This is the unmanifest Mahabuddhic potential behind collective evolution at every level, but to be able to get beyond its instinctual and outward modes, individuals must consciously and confidently identify with the Mind and Heart of all Humanity.

The silent martyrdom of self-conscious existence becomes real enough with the cool recognition that everyone's limitation is also one's own. The harrowing pain at the inability of higher consciousness to avail itself fully of vestures provided under karma must be experienced by the awakened individual as a mere instance of universal pain. The intense realization of human suffering is not a once-and-for-all attainment, but a continuous Buddhimanasic expansion of awareness and a quickening of sensitivity together with an intense longing, on behalf of the entire human race, for Divine Wisdom. One must learn to keep awake and to sleep, to eat and bathe and work cheerfully on behalf of all living beings. One must enjoy traversing the daily round of familiar duties and sacrificial obligations, consecrating all these to *Lokasangraha*, the welfare of the world. Above all, one must discover the disarming simplicity of joyous devotion through selfless acts, sacred studies and deep meditations offered, like a leaf, a flower or a fruit, to Krishna, the Great Giver. This unconditional love and ceaseless sacrifice must be attempted by all those who would wish to come out and be separate, in the words of Paul, who would like to relinquish their illusory existence and begin to live anew, immersed in the potent current of spiritual evolution. The true martyrdom of self-conscious existence necessarily entails the total renunciation of any possible concept of personal identity and also of individual progress. Monadic individuation has validity and meaning solely in the sacred act of, and entirely for the sake of, intelligently focussing the universal light of the *Atman.* It has no other function. To be able to renounce this individuality completely, relinquishing at the core even the seed-idea of any conception of personal virtue, individual excellence or spiritual progress separate from the whole of humanity, is to blend the mind with the soul, and even more the light of the soul with the luminous Paramatmic essence of the *Adhiyajna,* the Great Sacrifice. *Agniyoga* burns out the root illusion of individuality in the fires of self-purgation.

When many first encounter the vast perspective and true proportions of the Secret Path of Renunciation, they become bewildered because they hastily assume they are inherently incapable of following it. The origin of this instinctual response is actually the delusive notion, deeply embedded in the unrefined psyche, that man is a fortuitous concurrence of atoms fatigued by external stimuli, involuntary emotions, incoherent thoughts and the appalling waste of energy through pseudo-knowledge. The personality is reinforced by a defensive posture of false omniscience at the mundane level which is nothing but mulish obstinacy and a pathological refusal to see the light. This arises from the fear-ridden reluctance to learn from others, to risk the pain of growth in awareness, to give moral shocks to the lunar vesture so that it can be shaken out of its automatic and habitual responses, all of which are based upon intertwined illusions in relation to time, space, motion, causality, karma, and above all, selfhood. To let go of such mental trappings and emotional reactions, learning to recognize the subtler and specious forms in which they reappear and relinquishing them yet again, must produce a triple revolution in awareness – in the subject of one's creative contemplation *(jnana),* in the object of one's constant devotion *(bhakti),* and in one's intrinsic capacity to consecrate the simplest acts of life *(karma).* This fundamental revolution in thought and feeling, word and deed, will alchemically transmute the ways in which one looks at the world and employs the sense-organs of hearing, taste, smell and touch. The more one can calmly sit down and, in the light of the potent ideal of universal compassion, concede the absurdity of much that many people call living in the world, the more one can give a radical shake-up to the entire system. One can quietly begin, in the silence after the storm, to induce a necessary state of separation of all the elements which have coagulated into ossified structures, breaking up the clusters and refining life-atoms through meditation upon voidness, *sunyata,* and fullness, *karuna* or compassion. By blanking out and refusing to give energy or indulgence to these many false identities or masks of the soul, one can reawaken noetic insight within a stream of consciousness of the sacredness of life and the One Source of Light-Energy.

Simpler peoples living in uncluttered cultures have often employed effective and graphic images to represent the corruption of consciousness through a false sense of personal identity. An angry person is sometimes portrayed as possessed by a malevolent red devil dancing upon his head. Children taught to think in terms of such powerful if intuitive images soon become aware that to fall into a state of temper is to give oneself over to some perverse manikin, to some demonic imp which may itself be a simulacrum or shadow of one's own unacknowledged fears. To think imaginatively of elementals in this way is to begin to see that a great portion of what one calls oneself and one's own is a costly delusion, for which the karmic negation is breakdown, despair and death. One's personal identity has no continuity whatsoever except through repetition of signs and sounds, and no intrinsic validity except through passive acquiescence or emotional reinforcement from the outside. Inevitably, Nature responds in the language of suffering, giving repeated shocks to the psyche, and in this way some progress is made in inward freedom from the inertia of delusion. If there were no suffering, which is the merciful teacher and stern awakener of consciousness, there would be no way for the cowardly individual to let go of obsessions. Thanks to therapeutic suffering there is at least some stimulus and hope for renunciation of outworn preoccupations. But as people relinquish illusions, they become so infatuated with a new sense of liberated selfhood that they resent any reminder of their past errors and persisting misconceptions of themselves and others. Thus they erect fresh barriers between their self-image and the rest of humanity, falling prey repeatedly to possession or obsession by elemental forces coloured by entrenched kamamanasic rationalizations.

How many people in the presence of children with temper tantrums think back to their own temper tantrums? How many people recognize in the illusions of those ten or fifteen years younger the reminders of similar snares in their youth? How many, when they see people ten or twenty years older who are trapped in a pathetic refusal to learn afresh from life, can see analogies with their own resistance to learn and their own crippling fear of coming to terms with their costly errors? Anyone so blessed by karma as to have heard the inspiring teaching concerning the Path of Renunciation should show the courage to overcome smug self-centeredness and enslavement to pride and prejudice. In a strictly unmetaphorical sense, the disciple's sojourn on earth should be a compassionate mode of wise participation in the lives of other human beings through the empathetic recognition of every possible illusion and its alchemical transmutation. Many people prefer not to recollect what they were five or ten years ago in negative terms, but would rather live in the undisturbed oblivion of their current self-image and thoughtless drift. This is a sad waste of their present incarnation, unpardonable in a would-be disciple, without any real benefit to the Immortal Soul. The higher principles cannot effectively incarnate and the Divine Triad cannot be invoked as a guardian and guide unless the individual purges his consciousness of whatsoever obscures the thread of moral purpose. The true seeker finds a firm basis for spiritual resolve by focussing concentrated attention upon a universal perspective, while gaining skill in action in the arena of daily duties.

The sacred task of purifying and perfecting Manasic self-consciousness, through effortless renunciation and sacrificial self-transcendence, takes many lives. Humanity, in general, will become fully Manasic only in the distant future, in the Fifth Race of the Fifth Round. The further development of *Manas* that should take place in the present Fifth and in the coming Sixth Sub-race of the Fifth Root Race in the Fourth Round is proportionately small for myriads of human beings who are half asleep most of the time. This is readily confirmed by considering how much of the potency of thought is untapped, because so little thinking is truly universal, and how much the volatile energy of volitional desire is wasted, because extremely little is expended on behalf of the immortal individuality. Most of what people call feeling is mere emotion, which causes wear and tear in the astral vesture. This wastage has as its ideational basis an arbitrary one-life assumption, which is only rendered hypocritical by those who pay lip-service to a salvationist belief in reincarnation but are actually captive to bodily cycles and a physical conception of age and vitality. Yet, while many human beings are not able to be highly Manasic, if any have drawn under the karma of former lives into the proximity of *Brahma Vach* or Divine Wisdom, the spiritual ideation of the deathless race of Seers and Sages, then great indeed is their privilege and its attendant responsibility. *Manas*, which descends from and corresponds to

Akasha, the fifth universal cosmic principle, can be existentially recognized in terms of the strong sense of individual responsibility: the more fully *Manas* is developed, the deeper is one's responsibility and the stronger one's capacity for choice. The full potential of *Manas* can only be intimated through an exacting conception of individual responsibility wherein one is accountable for every thought and feeling, and for every life-atom that at any given time is an integral part of one's vestures or merely passes in and through one's radius of influence. So immense is the Akashic potential of the fully awakened *Manas* that the perfected *Manasa* are literally responsible for the welfare of worlds.

Such a Promethean conception is far removed from the feeble notions of most thinking men and women of the present Round. It is downright alien to that noisy minority which is terrified of taking responsibility for the simplest things, for elementary errors, for past mistakes and present failures, for endemic and *tamasic* tendencies which act as mental blocks or emotional obstructions in the lunar and physical vestures. The refusal to accept responsibility, which is a cowardly refusal to become Manasic, is a vain attempt to be mindless, to become a retarded soul unable to keep pace with the high purposes of evolution. All of this has got to be paid for, not only through the tragic condition of the ray that gradually weakens its connection with the Divine Triad, but also through the immeasurable agony of those lofty souls who suffer for the sake of the whole, who do not have any sense of "mine" and "thine" in relation to the collective illusions of egotistic pride and ignorant selfishness of the human race. Those who truly aspire to the Path of Renunciation, also called the Path of Woe – mental woe for all souls trapped in the abject wretchedness of living death or indefinitely mired in ignorance and irresponsibility – should ponder deeply the sacred image of the cosmic sacrifice of Visvakarman in the steep Golgotha of life. Then, at the revelatory moment of death, they may come to have a flash of understanding strong enough to evoke a mighty resolve to return as early as possible in the next life into the spiritual service of suffering humanity. Hence the need for spiritual knowledge, self-study and daily meditation.

In a universe of justice the voluntary discipline of sacrifice presupposes the power of choice of every single human being. *Manas* spells moral responsibility, and it connotes freedom of choice as well as the fearless acceptance of the full consequences of past choices. A Manasic being welcomes everything that comes under merciful karma as a necessary consequence of choices in other lives, self-determination at the moment of birth, and the continuous stream of self-definition originating at the causal level of ideation. The truly Manasic being would never condescend to assign any portion of his character or circumstance entirely to an outside agency or source – whether heredity, environment, the collective Karma of society or humanity. All such alibis, excuses and evasions would be morally unworthy of a Manasic being. One might coolly consider these mitigating factors when one wishes to understand the unknown karma of other beings, especially as one cannot arrogate to oneself the vicarious burden of responsibility which other persons must assume voluntarily. It is with selfless humility and spontaneous reverence before the mystery of every Ego that the *Bodhisattva* seeks broader explanations for the sake of a compassionate understanding, a non-moralistic or constructive appraisal of the spiritual predicament of human souls. If one thinks seriously about the metaphysical basis of sacrifice, the ethics of responsibility would logically follow, including the moral codes of discipleship. Also, one would see with the clarity of compassion that what is customarily called living is largely a series of pathetic contortions based upon a sad legacy of fears inherited from past lives of irresponsibility and evasion. Persisting in such a course of self-destruction can only lead at some point to a total rupture of the connection with the Divine, unless there is a courageous if traumatic confrontation with these downward tendencies. For humanity as a whole, there eventually must come such a crucial moment of choice in the Fifth Round, but for individuals who have entered the Path, it can come much earlier than for the majority of mankind. When the twin gifts of *Manas* – moral responsibility and noetic choice – are strengthened through use by a burgeoning Buddhic awareness of cosmic sacrifice, then, as the *Stanzas* teach:

> The thread between the silent watcher and his shadow (man) becomes stronger – with every re-incarnation.

This is what should happen in every human life, and if it does not, there is something seriously wrong. In every incarnation the *sutratman* should become stronger between the Silent Watcher – the overbrooding *Dhyani* or Divine Prototype at the upper rung of the ladder of being – and the lunar shadow at the lower rung. *Gupta Vidya* teaches that the two highest classes of *Dhyanis* – the Watchers connected with the seventh principle and the Architects connected with the sixth principle – furnished the various races of humanity with divine Kings and Instructors:

> It is the latter who taught humanity their arts and sciences, and the former who revealed to the incarnated Monads that had just shaken off their vehicles of the lower Kingdoms – and who had, therefore, lost every recollection of their divine origin – the great spiritual truths of the transcendental worlds.

The Secret Doctrine, i 267

If, despite this sacred lineage and divine descent which lends to man the sacrificial light of self-consciousness, he nonetheless desecrates the gift of creative imagination through moral turpitude, then there is a tragic loosening or sundering of the vital connection with the immortal Monad. Turpitude means taking pride in what is vile and base and pleasure in what is shameful; it is bravado in the service of Satan. Such terrible misuse of the will and the potency of thought imperils the life-giving connection between the higher Triad and the lower quaternary, and gravely increases the risk of running loose and "astray into the lunar path".

There is enormous moral danger in any pseudo-scientific categories of thought or pseudo-religious forms of worship that encourage disguised irresponsibility in the name of pseudo-freedom or pseudo-determinism or pseudo-salvation. Once one goes astray into the lunar path, all manner of unholy alliances are made between the astral form and nefarious swarms of tortured elementals, soulless elementaries and evil sorcerers, as also massive legions of malignant, gangrenous and leprous thought-forms going back to Atlantean times. One becomes the helpless prey of whole classes of images intimately associated with the appalling abuse of spiritual knowledge, creative potency and mental energies. This inevitably attracts a host of soul-ailments and diseases, and those who succumb to them face formidable obstructions to finding a human form or congenial conditions in which one can foster spiritual intuitions. Even if, at one level, one wants to aspire heavenward, the entire system seems to conspire against the promise of progress owing to spinal blockages, mental deposits and astral deformities. To purge oneself of spiritual pollution and to heal the moral scars it leaves in the lunar vesture, one must meditate deeply and continuously, with an intensely devout wish to restore and strengthen the fragile connection with the immortal spirit of *Atma-Buddhi.* One must immerse oneself in the Buddhic current of the healing waters of wisdom, the elixir of *Hermes,* the indestructible spark of divine conscience, which is consubstantial with the fiery essence of the *Dhyanis* (the *Angirasa* descended from Agni). This is like bathing in the luminous stream of Divine Wisdom, the only Jordan whose waters can baptize in the name of the Father in Heaven, the *Mahaguru* on earth, the God in man.

The therapeutic restoration of the right relationship between the reflected ray and its divine parent cannot come by ritual chanting and monotonous mutterings, by what is mistaken for prayer, worship or meditation. Rectification must proceed from intense thought, conscious strengthening of the strongest altruistic feelings in oneself, and by an unconditional vow and irreversible determination. This would be enormously helped by invoking and activating the higher faculties which have their analogues with lower *manas* and with *prana.* The manifest energy of *prana* must reflect something of the continuity and self-luminous, self-created spiritual energy of the invisible *Atman.* The polarity of *kama* must be purified through devotion and directed by that inward tropism and vertical movement towards the Divine Triad which could confer the benediction of gratitude and reverence towards the *Ishtaguru* and the Brotherhood of *Bodhisattvas*. Lower *manas* must be brought into firm alignment with higher *Manas*, especially through the use of silence and conscious control of speech. If there are daily duties to perform, one should take a universal ideal, a potent mantram, dwell upon these and then look upon obligations as sacred, with a joyous recognition of responsibility and choice. It is unwise to spend too much time on only one thing and to evade other duties. It is wiser to keep moving with cheerfulness while blending the elements of refined thinking, feeling and breathing into a single stream of sacrificial ideation. One must even be delighted to discover obstacles, understanding that so-called bad karma is what one unconsciously or unknowingly desired for one's discipline. Karma is not only what one deserves, but also what one really wants, because it offers a golden opportunity for transmuting past errors and persisting obstacles. Even tainted life-atoms must be welcomed and cleansed, or they will take their revenge if their demand for attention is spurned. They must indeed be discouraged from performing their ludicrous devil dances, and can be gently coaxed into the presence of potent thoughts and feelings of pure benevolence.

Wise devotees who make this regenerative programme the basis of spiritual alchemy will combine continuity of daily practice in modest and moderate doses with the Himalayan strength of unconditional and irrevocable, irreversible commitment. The secret doctrine of *Buddhi Yoga* teaches that though it take a long time to perfect this practice, it needs only moral courage, not the mere passage of time, to give it a firm basis. The spiritual will is released through meditation upon *Vach*, nourished through devotion to Krishna, and intensified through the yoga of *tapas*, consecrated to Shiva. Thus, throughout human evolution, wise individuals in all the ancient centres of Initiation took irrevocable vows and made irreversible commitments. In each life they reaffirmed the irreversibility of their striving on the Path because this alone releases the spiritual will that invites the *Atman* to descend into the vestures and assume divine kingship. *Mental and moral courage, constancy of zeal and concentration of purpose are the three talismans of self regeneration.* Herein lies the clue to the strength of unconditional affirmations. A part of the shadowy self always attempts to be conditional and crafty; one has to renounce allegiance to this pretentious enemy through the sovereign act of unconditional affirmation. There is no other way. When a seeker recognizes this psychological truth through life upon life, the length of the process matters little if the philosophical basis is sound and the spiritual resolve is firm and unconditional. It is a high tragedy that many people for whom access to the sacred teachings was made easy never truly chose the Path because they never really initiated the heroic and sacrificial resolve of *Manas.*

Every seeker must freely choose the Path sometime, choose it wholly, unequivocally and completely. Each must choose it whole-heartedly and single-mindedly, without introducing those seemingly small qualifications which are tiny apertures through which the vermin rush in from the region of spiritual vampires and intellectual vultures. And when the vermin come, they breed fast and make short work of the contaminated structure. To seal off every mental reservation, egotistic escape-route and moral evasion, one must make a supreme, unconditional and absolute affirmation on the *Bodhisattva* Path, renouncing all possible concessions to conditionality and cowardice. Herein lies the dignity of the sacred and the divinity of a Vow or *Vrata,* sanctified by *Rta* or cosmic rightness and its ceaseless rhythm in the *anahata,* the immortal centre of incarnated *Manas.* A person who invokes *Vach* takes a mighty step towards Enlightenment because his or her spiritual energy-field is enormously intensified by the immaculate light of *Atma-Buddhi.* The Lanoo must be calm and patient, moving step by step along the Path, day by day, week by week, month by month. After a point it becomes wholly natural to stay firmly within the noetic current of life-giving wisdom and compassion which streams forth from Krishna and the Lodge of *Mahatmas.*

Hermes, February 1981
Raghavan Iyer

THE FIRE OF PURGATION

Make a difference between Aether and Ether, the former being divine, the latter physical and infernal. Ether is the lowest of the septenate division of Akasa-Padhana, primordial Fire-Substance. Aether-Akasa is the fifth and sixth principles of the body of Kosmos – thus corresponding to Buddhi-Manas, in Man; Ether is its Kosmic sediment mingling with the root-race, it will develop fully only at the beginning of the fifth round. Aether is Akasa in its higher aspect, and Ether Akasa, in its lowest.

H. P. Blavatsky

The mirroring of absolute reality in the triadic heart of the unmanifest *Logos* on the abstract plane of Divine Thought is the archetypal origin of successive births of worlds and men on the noumenal and phenomenal planes of matter. It is the primordial basis of all derivative modes of cognition and causation, and thus the root of relative knowledge and existence in the region of *maya* under the rule of the *nidanas.* Every atom of Monadic life is imbued with an inherent will to self-manifestation, and each is subject to delusion through identification with the illusory forms of the diffused potency of self-ideation. The human Monad, having arrived at the stage of incipient consciousness of its identity with the *Logos*, is in effect a psychic embryo still trapped in the matrix of astral matter, but capable of a new birth into noetic awareness through the arousal of its Buddhic capacity of intuitive apprehension.

The inward stirrings of higher life within human consciousness presage a golden future for the race as a whole, but under the strictures of universal law this prospect will not be realized by its units until they gain some comprehension of *Buddhi Yoga,* the science of spirituality. The essential factors of this arcane science are securely hidden within the Mysteries of Divine Wisdom, but they may be sought through fidelity to the inner voice of conscience and the guiding light of intuition. Above all, one must learn the elements of the mathematics of the soul, the art of impersonal computation of karmic causes rooted in relaxed detachment towards personal likes and dislikes on the astral-physical plane.

Philosophical concepts like "universal unity", "human solidarity" and "global interdependence" cannot be grasped through the inverted imagery of the astral light and the imitative ratiocinative responses of *Kama Manas*. Their hidden meanings must be progressively apprehended by elevating the horizon of one's awareness and the centre of cognition above the limits and inversions of the fourth plane of Spirit-Matter. This is learnt by recognizing that one must replace phenomenal fantasy and concrete images with noumenal awareness and creative imagination through the activation of *Buddhi-Manas*. The noetic science of the generation, transmission and application of thought-energies is exceedingly precise and meta-mathematical. Humanity as a whole is only now becoming prepared to learn this science, but almost every human being has some sense of these immense possibilities through the minor accomplishments of the micro-electronic revolution. In the Victorian age, most people understood neither the telephone nor the telegraph, much less the wireless radio. Today, however, there is no excuse for people not to understand these devices at some elementary level. A growing number of people grasp the logic of these methods because they are involved through micro-electronics in the daily use of complex equipment which enables them to see how instantaneous communication and interaction is possible.

As a beginner, one must discern that all energies, including those of thought, are accompanied by vibrations, whose causal nature is virtually unknown to the individuals who engender them. Those unaware of the potencies and properties of thought-images can at least catch up with those who recognize intuitively that physical modes of electro-magnetic communication are but a material reflection of capabilities and laws inherent in consciousness. This is still easier in simpler societies and more natural cultures than in regions rich in the resources of the earth but poor and backward in the arts of self-discipline. For centuries now the world's peasantry has migrated from farm to town, and from traditional cultures to industrial societies. Hoping to partake of the material prosperity they thought was already there, these restless proletarians soon found themselves mired in the middle class and began to take on bourgeois pretensions. There is nothing new or particularly nefarious in these shared delusions, but many people are trapped by them and squander their spiritual potential. In order to reverse this process, they must be willing to make a fresh start, free from social and economic pretence, free from any false sense of separation from the great masses of the globe, and consecrated to the proper use of the Manasic faculties of concentrated thought, the sacred and priceless, if generally unclaimed, prerogative of every human being.

The effortless mastery of the Adept over manifold energies of potent thought, together with his complete control of the lesser sheaths on the lower planes, is the fruition of an unbroken series of lifetimes of unrelenting discipline and unwavering devotion. The capacity to release the creative light and spiritual genius of the higher Ego as an irresistible impulse for the good of all depends upon the quality and refinement of its instruments. Whilst each Ego is identical to all others in its pristine essence, and each is capable of resonating with the Soundless Sound, no Ego can draw out the harmony of the spheres or transmit noetic energies through an opaque human vesture.

> . . . physical man is the musical instrument, and the Ego, the performing artist. The potentiality of perfect melody of sound, is in the former – the instrument – and no skill of the latter can awaken a faultless harmony out of a broken or badly made instrument. This harmony depends on the fidelity of transmission, by word or act, to the objective plane, of the unspoken divine thought in the very depths of man's subjective or inner nature. Physical man may – to follow our simile – be a priceless

Stradivarius or a cheap and cracked fiddle, or again a mediocrity between the two, in the hands of the Paganini who ensouls him.

Lucifer
H.P. Blavatsky

Most people can roughly imagine the enormous discipline involved in becoming a musical genius of the magnitude of Paganini or Caruso. Very few can even remotely imagine the degree of difficulty involved in mastering the transmission of Divine Wisdom, the eternal Harmony of the Pythagoreans, the Self of *Alaya* in the teaching of *The Voice of the Silence.* Though it has always been a vital part of the vast work of the Theosophical Movement to encourage each human being to enquire earnestly into these sacred matters, it has ever been the case that though many are called, few are chosen. And of these, even fewer are chosen for self-training extending over septenates of seven years from the moment of choice to the moment of death. Amongst these, exceptionally few are able to arouse and sustain inner awakening over a lifetime of meditation. Nevertheless, there are such, and the deeper work of the Movement proceeds unostentatiously. The ratios now are better than at any time in recorded history and much better than in the eighteenth and nineteenth centuries. But they are still marginal, though even three out of a hundred is a good ratio in these matters. Where there are more than three, this is unusually good, and if there are thirteen, this is excellent.

Given these ratios, individuals could become neophytes at some level if they would come into proper magnetic alignment with those true disciples hidden in their midst. This cannot happen externally; only on the causal plane of the noetic mind. Through deep meditation one must overcome the illusion of the near and the far on the physical plane, and recognize that if through daily meditation one could genuinely use more of the Sacred Teaching, help will be given infallibly. The Avatar has, all over the globe, the aid of many Adepts and *yogins,* any of whom can instantly help anyone who deserves it. This transmission works too subtly to explain or elaborate, but the Adepts are not here to explain that which can only be comprehended within the sanctuaries of Initiation. They are here to let everyone know that each honest effort helps, that every sincere resolve to do good is invaluable, because the world is in great pain and can use every good impulse that may be generated.

All that is good and true and beautiful can be enhanced because there is hardly enough of it. Wherever it is active in individuals, it can be linked magnetically with the potential good in others, thereby creating living bonds of brotherhood. None of this can be grasped through materialistic psychology and its corrupt handmaiden, the pseudo-science of psychiatry. Apart from the rarefied intuitions of a few constructive psychologists, the contemporary practice of the science of mind is inherently incapable of conceiving the higher noetic function of the Monad or *Manas*. Where psychology has degenerated into nefarious image-mongering and nebulous manipulation through psychiatry, it is worse than worthless. This is recognized in mature cultures, and it is only in adolescent circles obsessed with personal concerns that this shallow rubbish is taken seriously. One drop of the wisdom of the *Bhagavad Gita* is worth more than all such pedantry. Fortunately, psychiatry is pricing itself out of the market, and more and more people are discovering that they can, with little investment in money or pretension, obtain any one of a number of ancient texts in almost any bookshop. Much to the benefit of all, the swarms of ignorant hypnotists and merchants of pathological pessimism are fading away. This itself is part of a larger and more auspicious pattern of events in which exploiters of human need and misery, of human sickness and conflict, are losing their grip upon popular awareness.

It is still true that many middle-class people remain captive to a desperate desire to improve themselves. Nonetheless, many are finding that their former modes of fantasy and compensation are simply unsupportable. They have become tired of the illusion of upward social mobility and dubious of the overblown claims of the supposed virtues of modern life. They are quite happy to become more natural, and relieved to feel free to be simple. They have begun to discover that the purer ideals of youthful innocence, far from having become irrelevant, are relevant and far more fulfilling than the decaying stereotypes of propriety disseminated by self-interested elites. For increasing numbers of individuals one-dimensionality in consciousness is obsolete. People are progressively learning to use what they need and to do what they are able, without worrying about what others are doing. They are learning to live their own lives, not based upon borrowed, bought or rented images and options, but centered upon their own fundamental convictions and intuitions of what is ultimately natural to mankind.

The more one can remain modest and become a true learner the more the burden of false imagery will fall away from one's consciousness. A mark of becoming a lighter human being is to be able to gaze at the stars with gratitude. When one can look up into the night sky with gladness and realize the infinitude of noumenal abundance behind the veil of shimmering lights, one is beginning to prepare oneself to become a citizen of the cosmos. Without worrying unduly about one's allegiance to any temporal city, one can greet the stars and galaxies that irradiate the canopy of the heavens, but at the same time one should not forget the creatures of the earth. Whilst smiling at the stars one should feel compassion for the ant, because it is the human's privilege to be able to feel the same compassion for the ant that the heavens reflect upon mankind. Whilst raising one's head to the starry vault, bend low and notice the cricket, the frog and the toad, humble creatures that share the earth with man. Learn to show love for all the beings that creep upon the ground whilst one watches the skies. Do not dislike any of the evolving creatures of the earth, neither the scorpion nor the tarantula, neither the mouse nor the mountain lion. To stand as a free citizen of the cosmos, one must first recognize that each and every sentient being in all the seven kingdoms has as much right to exist as oneself. Then one may study and master the obligations and duties of human existence in the cosmic perspective of universal enlightenment.

Out of this renewed and deepened sense of kinship with all the creatures of the earth, one can prepare oneself to go forth and greet with humility all that lives and breathes. To be worthy of the grand human estate one must display a profound respect for and gratitude towards all the lower kingdoms of nature from which the vestures of incarnation must be drawn. Restoring a pure and healthy relationship with the psychic planes of existence, and becoming a co-worker with Nature in the evolutionary task, one can attempt the removal of every trace and taint of selfishness from one's motivation and conduct. To the extent that this is done, one will no more fall prey to various types of mediumship through karmic involvement with (unconsciously produced) forms in the astral light.

Manasic self-awareness is the potential for cognition of the essential identity of the *sutratman* with the universal *Hiranyagarbha*, but this cognitive capacity has its inverted reflection in ahankaric identification with the projected ray of lower *Manas*. Rather than assimilating the reflection of mind upon the astral planes to a growing Buddhic awareness of noumenal realities, which is the proper use of the *antaskarana* bridge, the Ego under the sway of ignorance diminishes the potency of the Manasic principle in a quixotic attempt to perpetuate ephemeral forms. Philosophically, this can be understood as the confusion of cause with its instrumentality and field of multiple effects. Psychologically, it amounts to a failure to realize that the multivalent term "self" in human self-consciousness and self-reference is ultimately the *Atman.* Mystically, this error involves the misappropriation of the triadic fire of the *Logos*, the source of the Spirit, Soul and Body of the cosmos and man, on behalf of its inverted materialized image on the physical plane.

Without noetic discrimination and courageous self-correction, guided by the illumination of selfless meditation, involvement in the astral regions presents a constant danger of dishonesty and self-deception. The astral light has become polluted by the selfish emanations of the pseudo-spiritual, and, whether at death or before, all these matrices of separative consciousness are doomed to be burnt out by the disintegrating fires of karmic retribution. To learn to cooperate self-consciously with Nature one must first learn to cooperate with Karma. Refusing to do so, through attachment to astral forms and images, implies, at this point in evolution, abnormal selfishness and self-annihilation. The universe is sustained by spiritual fire; the world, as the Buddha taught, is a burning house in which all beings are engulfed in a continual conflagration. Impermanence of form is the eternal law of evolution. Identification with shifting shapes in the astral light and attempts to warm oneself by the astral flames can only lead to destruction.

There is nothing inherently wrong with the astral and psychic planes of existence, nor with the various creatures and kingdoms of nature which are the appropriate evolutionary denizens of those planes. But there is a vital difference between *Akasha* and the astral light, which from the standpoint of the Higher Self is the shadow of a shadow. This difference does not in itself account for the corruption of human consciousness. It is the perverse and unnatural obscuration of noetic awareness through ignorant selfishness and egotism that has made the natural faculties of brain-consciousness and personality productive of evil.

> This brain-consciousness or personality is mortal, being but a distorted reflection through a physical basis of the manasic self. It is an instrument for harvesting experience for the Buddhi-Manas or monad, and saturating it with the aroma of consciously-acquired experience. But for all that the "brain-self" is real while it lasts, and weaves its Karma as a responsible entity.

> H. P. Blavatsky

The complex karma created by the brain-minds of human beings returns to them again and again. At certain moments, it cumulatively comes back to them, whether as individuals or as an entire race, in a tremendous mass so that they will be able to confront it and see beyond. To receive such a precipitation of karma is to experience a climactic moment. It is an opportunity for calmness and renunciation, such as one might experience in the mountains when a large boulder falls down. If calm, one would be prepared to accept either the boulder's blessing upon one's head (if this is one's karma), or its passing by (if that is one's karma). One must learn to renounce the will to live, but not out of an escapist wish to die. With calmness, one can be ready to accept and learn from everything, provided one does not exaggerate the importance of one's own survival. Life may be tedious for long stretches of time, but this is no excuse for exaggeration and pretentious self-images. If one cannot accept ordinariness, then nothing will ever seem good enough for more than a brief moment. From a spiritual standpoint, the worst of all delusions is to suppose that one has some exclusive privilege or exalted status through having come into the presence of the Teacher and the Teachings.

What does it mean in consciousness to come closer to the Guru? It is one thing to come closer on the illusory plane of sense-perceptions. It is quite another thing to come closer in noetic consciousness. Pure consciousness has nothing to do with particular desires, wishes and thoughts because it is itself absolute thought, desire and will. Every human being, according to his consciousness of time, emits a certain mental vibration. The degree of awareness of eternity in one's consciousness of time determines the tone, the intensity, the colour and the force of this vibration. Most human beings, preoccupied with today and tomorrow, with this year and the next, are very restricted and fragmented in consciousness. They become prisoners of the external, shifting panorama of human existence, and thereby become victims of history. When they die, they discover they had hardly lived, and in many cases what they called life is what is known to Adepts as living death. But those who are able to transcend the imagery of their immediate perceptions, the narrow horizon of their conceptions of space, time and motion, can think causally in terms of the cosmos and humanity. They resonate with and reflect That which ever was, ever is and ever shall be, for whom the hour shall never strike, the immortal soul within every human being, the *Atman* that overbroods each and all. Typically, the *Atman* comes closer to the fontanelle only once in the lifetime of the average human being, at the moment of death. For it to come closer at any other time requires tremendous self-training and effortless self-mastery earned over many lives. Without this self-discipline it is idle to imagine that one has come close to the *Atman* seated in the hearts of all beings.

If it is not part of one's destiny to do this – and there is no room for self-deception or self-dejection here – then it can be a part of one's destiny to serve those who have done so. More beings on earth today have done this very thing than ever before. Largely unknown, many have waited decades for the right moment to receive the call. The world today is in an unusually fortunate position; not only *Nirmanakayas*, but also numerous disguised Adepts have taken birth in many parts of the world. They are thoroughly prepared in consciousness for the Mysteries, for the City of Man and for the Temple of the Future. And so, the ordinary person who has done none of these things should nevertheless aspire to become part of the future and to find a fitting place in the evolutionary march of humanity. To become part of the solution and not of the problem, to join the future instead of clinging to the past, each must begin by shaving off pretensions and cutting away the obscurations hitherto entertained through ignorance. By becoming natural, straightforward and simple, individuals can enjoy developing a taste for meditation upon pure, unbounded and eternal consciousness. The key is to do *in life* that which one can scarcely do after death (except in an extremely limited sense) and to prepare oneself for future lives of learning.

The sacred, secret mysteries of consciousness which underlie the meta-psychological evolution of mankind will remain unspoken to the vast majority of human beings for ages to come. But every man and woman who wishes to make himself or herself worthy of inclusion in that glorious future is invited to engage in philosophic meditation upon the metaphysical propositions of the *Gupta Vidya.* Therein it is taught that all things in the universe are associated with either spirit or matter, one of these being taken as the permanent element of both. Pure Matter is pure Spirit, and neither can be understood by the finite discursive intellect. All pairs of opposites – light and darkness, heat and cold, fullness and the void – are at once pure Matter and pure Spirit. All are manifestations of Spirit-Matter – *Aether-Akasha. Aether-Akasha* is consubstantial with the plane of substance constituting *Buddhi-Manas,* the jewel in every heart and the diamond light in every soul. That light is one with the fiery ground of the entire cosmos. It is the origin of the three and seven invisible fires in nature and the forty-nine fires in human consciousness tapped at will by Adepts. These noumenal fires can be invoked infallibly through concentrated thought that reaches to universal good.

Any human being who hungers for universal good and truly wishes that the earth be a better world, out of the intensity of thought and will, draws closer to the sacred fires in the inmost essence of being. It is only in those Akashic fires that there is true rejuvenation. Though they are known to Adepts by other and secret names, they may be viewed by the neophyte as the fires of purification, purgation and resolve. By the sustained ideation of *Mahatmas,* they are made accessible to all human beings so that each can emit a powerful vibration in consonance with the global current of Aquarian humanity. Anyone willing to take the Teachings of *Gupta Vidya* as a true talisman can enter the stream of the great endeavour, which is consubstantial with the electric ocean of Life.

Anyone willing to start afresh, without illusions or expectations, but with a new and growing maturity, can forego the compensations of the shadowy past and rediscover a rightful place in the school of universal human evolution. One of the marks of spiritual maturity is a calm recognition that ethical responsibility is self-compelling. Once the resolve is made to grow up, one will recognize that Krishna is on the side of every Arjuna and against none. Then, like Arjuna, one may stand up and be counted amongst heroic souls worthy of the human heritage. Seeing beyond roles and forms, one may learn to breathe the Sacred Sound and the sacred speech – *Om Mani Padme Hum* – the Jewel in the Lotus, the God in man. In this spirit the future will draw out and weave together the best, so that all may be on the side of the finest in the human race, allied with the future, under the all-protecting Shield of the Avatar and his luminous Host of Hierophants.

Hermes, April 1982
Raghavan Iyer

GESTATION AND GROWTH

In the Sankhya philosophy, Purusha *(spirit) is spoken of as something impotent unless he mounts on the shoulders of* Prakriti *(matter), which, left alone, is – senseless. But in the secret philosophy they are viewed as graduated. Though one and the same thing in their origin, Spirit and Matter, when once they are on the plane of differentiation, begin each of them their evolutionary progress in contrary directions – Spirit falling gradually into matter, and the latter ascending to its original condition, that of a pure spiritual substance. Both are inseparable, yet ever separated. In polarity, on the physical plane, two like poles will always repel each other, while the negative and the positive are mutually attracted, so do Spirit and Matter stand to each other – the two poles of the same homogeneous substance, the root-principle of the universe.*

The Secret Doctrine, i 247
H.P. Blavatsky

Outside Divine Darkness, sensed though not seen by the opened eye of Shiva, the graduated polarities of Spirit-Matter pervade all manifestation. The light vitalizing and illuminating each plane of manifestation is the shadow of supersensuous matter in motion upon a more noumenal plane. From above below, from within without, the *Verbum* stirs the entire gamut of rhythmic resonances in the responsive centres of life, causing them to shine forth from the darkness in the myriad rainbow hues of their differentiated existence. The timeless symmetries of sound and silence, motion and rest, darkness and light, upon the *arupa* planes are dimly echoed in the consciousness and conduct of beings caught in the cyclic round of birth and death upon the *rupa* planes. Whatever their partial perceptions of good and evil, of merit and demerit, nothing in manifest nature is so good that it casts no shadow, nor so evil that it does not have its bright side.

The awakening of Divine Wisdom through the Aquarian potency of noetic discrimination is not aided by crude Manichaean distinctions which vainly seek to relegate complex factors in nature to one side or the other of a concretized moral dichotomy. Students of the *Gupta Vidya* are initially vulnerable to just this sort of moralistic over-simplification, especially when they mistakenly surmise that the arcane Teachings suggest that the sun is good and that the moon is bad. This confusion has many roots. First and foremost, it stems from hastiness of thought which itself is the karmic consequence of entrenched error inherited from past lives. Impatience makes the cool comprehension of the elusive and subtle interaction between the solar and the lunar more arduous than necessary. When this facile misconception is perpetuated, it further restricts the range of thought to the merely literal and physical parameters of the problem. Given the vastness and grandeur of even the physical universe, with its circling systems of galaxies, stars and planets, it is foolish to give undue importance to the visible sun and physical moon and thereby compress lofty philosophic conceptions of darkness and light into these two familiar orbs.

Nonetheless, so long as the earth revolves around the sun, so long as there are days and nights, so long as there are four seasons, there is a distinct value in the twelve signs of the zodiac and in the division of the lunar month into twenty-eight days. There is a deeper significance to the broad division of the lunar month into the waxing and waning phases, and in the arrangement of its twenty-eight days in four sets of seven, each of which has its intrinsic logic. This has been sensed in mature cultures, and the simplest calendars and almanacs available to people everywhere provide basic information to make practical use of these intervals. The deeper mysteries of the archetypal divisions of the lunar month are not readily accessible, and would be of little use to most people without an intensive period of preparation involving even the more superficial aspects of this cycle.

Essentially, the new moon is a time for purification and gestation, whereas the full moon is for abnegation and *tapas*. The greater the purification through mystic meditation during the phase of the new moon, the greater can be the silent ripening of spiritual insight during the two weeks of the waxing moon. The waning half of the moon, far from being bad, finds its value in the intensification of self-study, the letting go of illusions. The aim of those who would wisely work with the cycles and rhythms of nature should be to make this period of renunciation a preparation for entry into a broadened and deepened cycle of learning and letting go. Thus, throughout the world, men and women observe the onset of the new moon and the full moon with fasting and deep meditation, seeking a self-conscious connection with the supple forces in nature that foster inward growth. At this point in human evolution, and especially in the so-called developed societies of the West, individuals are fortunate if they find they can make use of the ever-recurrent succession of the seasons and months. It would be well-nigh impossible to find many persons with sufficient spiritual awareness to be ready to make use of the mystical potentials of the lunar month – for example, those marked by its eleventh day.

During the present Impulsion of the New Cycle (1967-2006), every seeker can make use of the simplest facts of *Gupta Vidya* in daily life. Each aspirant can exchange psychic delusions for spiritual facts, so that the name of Theosophy does not become synonymous with self-deception, but rather with honest study, deep meditation and self-regenerating ethics. The degradation of the term "Theosophy" early in this century must be corrected and reversed, so that the Theosophist becomes one who is known for true knowledge based upon authentic experience and self-testing. The sorting out of cumulative confusion concerning the solar and the lunar is an essential part of this painful process of self-correction. The removal of mental confusion requires some grasp of the subtle connection between the lunar and the solar and the suggestive ways in which the solar light works through lunar substance. One must first recognize that all the human Monads of the present earth chain participated in the moon chain, which ended over three and a half Rounds ago. Before this vast period of terrestrial evolution, the hosts of Monads in their various stages of evolutionary advance that are now part of the earth chain were then active, at different levels, on the sevenfold moon chain.

Any meaningful reference to the lunar necessarily involves a reference to a previous field of evolution as complex and differentiated, as full of potential refinement and growth, as the present earth chain. The physical moon that is seen in the sky is a reflection of the disintegrating corpse of the lowest globe of that chain. It is a shadowy remnant of a once vast and vital arena of Monadic evolution. Beyond the peculiar relevance of this particular moon to the present earth, a more general meaning and metaphysical function are associated with the indispensable role of lunar predecessors when involution and evolution are viewed from the broader standpoint of an endless series of planetary chains, each linked with its successor in unbroken continuity.

> Within the strict terms of Simultaneity Theory, succession is not considered as a physically objective phenomenon, but as a subjective one . . . It is only in consciousness, it seems, that we experience time at all . . . In a dream there is no time, and succession is all changed about, and cause and effect are all mixed together. In myth and legend there is no time . . . When the mystic makes the reconnection of his reason and his unconscious, he sees all becoming as one being, and understands the eternal return . . .Our model of the cosmos must be as inexhaustible as the cosmos, [with] a complexity that includes not only duration but creation, not only being but becoming, not only geometry but ethics.
>
> _The Dispossessed_
> Ursula Le Guin

Individual integrity is damaged if one falls prey to an undue fascination with the physical corpse of the moon chain. Such a fascination and even obsession, associated with the Witches of Thessaly and similar coteries elsewhere, is the unwholesome consequence of those human beings millions of years ago who used the dark half of the moon for nefarious practices. Even now, the mere mention of such malodorous practices provokes a quickening of attention. But it is this strangely perverse if fear-ridden fascination with evil which is the prolific source of evil. There should, rather, be a fearlessness in looking at the excreted dregs of human life, but only in the light of a genuine desire to develop a secure taste for the best spiritual food for the soul. One will find no such compulsive fascination with evil amongst high souls. There is only a deeply felt pain that such tragic phenomena have taken place or persist in the present, coupled with the compassionate desire and will to alleviate the immense suffering attendant upon such maleficent practices. High souls are magnetically drawn to the ineffable Light of the Spiritual Sun *(Savitur)*. Those who, alas, find themselves unconsciously drawn to the shadowy side of human life should expel once and for all this degrading and polluting fascination from their lunar minds. Anyone who has widely travelled and witnessed repellent scenes of human depravity through the stern eyes of universal compassion – whether it be in Place Pigalle, Macao or the Sunset Strip – can only be saddened that such sordid places exist and also recognize that there is nothing novel or exciting about them. Heliopolis may be sought even in the midst of the necropolis; there is *Shamballa* in *Myalba*, *Nirvana* within *Samsara*.

Whilst everything emanating from the misuse of human faculties is indeed depressing, this can hardly be blamed upon the moon, which is also seven-fold. Perhaps it could be blamed upon the lunar corpse, which throws off a pernicious influence. Even this, however, is not all bad, and has its enigmatic effects upon the tides of the ocean, which are immensely helpful to mariners and so essential to life on the shore. Every process in nature is imbued with inexplicable compassion, and even that which is slowly disintegrating has its therapeutic function. People should not be preoccupied with cadavers and corpses; but if seen in the right light with the right motive, even these ghoulish concerns may result in some good. Many people are insanely afraid of their own deaths; and their horror of corpses is partly the outcome of their abject fear of the "living dead". These are, however, no cadavers. They are soulless beings which may have some fascination for the fearful personality. And they are extremely active, though only supposedly alive, human forms which are shown often on television or on other channels of the mass media. The entire subject, like everything connected with the mystery of the pilgrim-soul, is somewhat inscrutable. One must preserve a certain reticence, recognize one's puzzlement, accepting that it will long remain, owing to the complexity of the connection between the solar and the lunar and its important implications in relation to the varied hosts of *Pitris* linked with the evolution of humanity.

Some sense of the enormous difficulty in grasping the complex Teachings of the *Gupta Vidya* concerning the hosts of solar and lunar *Pitris* may be gained through an analogy with the awesome developments in modern science. Over the past one hundred years there has been such an untidy expansion of theoretical understanding in fields like physics and chemistry, biology and medicine, that scarcely half a dozen individuals in the world in any of these fields can claim to have a coherent perspective on the complex pattern of development taking place in his or her respective specialty. The scope of investigation and discovery has become so vast, even in a sub-field such as particle physics, that the leading experts in these fields are dismayed by the proliferation and lack of synthesis. If this is true for the best minds of the century, it is even more so for ordinary individuals attempting to understand the trends of thought at the present time. Even though the conceptual complexity in these realms of empirical enquiry overtaxes the foremost theorists, so that none can safely predict even the broad course of subsequent developments over the coming century, very little in this vast expansion of knowledge is anything more than a hit-and-miss approach to the *ABCs* of the *Gupta Vidya.*

There is an immense and immeasurable gap between the Divine Wisdom of the *Mahatmas* and the progressive formulations of modern man. One of the many purposes of *Isis Unveiled* and *The Secret Doctrine* was to put modern man in his proper place, to teach him humility before the stars, and before the Himalayan heights of Spiritual Knowledge *(Brahma Vidya).* The hollow presumption of modern man has unfortunately produced hosts of bewildered victims, the foremost of which is himself. Through taking pride in what amounts to bleak ignorance, modern man blunts the higher faculties of the soul, blocking the Third Eye and rendering the spinal cord incapable of restoring the flow of the divine *afflatus*. These are profoundly serious maladies, but if there is a recognition of the fundamental direction and flow of human evolution, there can be a constructive healing which will have its therapeutic effects in future incarnations. In a world where numerous people are spiritually and astrally deformed, one must recognize one's own ignorance and resolve to take up the ethical challenge offered by the Teachings to stand erect as a *Manasa*, a thinking being.

One must come to see that one's inner posture is improved through mental prostration before the spiritual benefactors of mankind. Far from shrinking from outward physical deformity, high souls may even take birth in deformed bodies so as to help those deformed outwardly and inwardly through their own ignorance, inversion and perversity. It is nearly impossible to tell the spiritual degree of a human being from outward signs. No empirical observation of physical deformity or mental disturbance is an everyday guide to the inner nature of the Ego inhabiting a mortal vesture. It is the height of delusion for anyone inhabiting a seemingly healthy physical form, which may only be the veil over a virtually moribund inner nature, to make judgements, based upon a harsh sense of separateness, of other human souls from their external appearance. It is precisely this persistent sense of separateness which characterizes the lunar Monad, whilst an authentic sense of universality is the recognizable mark of the solar Monad. This important distinction parallels the essential difference between the derivative light of the lunar and the self-generated nature of the light of the solar. In terms of the human principles, this corresponds to the crucial difference between the higher individuality – the *nous*, or matter-moving mind – and the personality or *psyche*, which is reactive or passive in relation to a field of derivative light.

The capacities for self-determination, creative initiative and noetic choice implicit in the concept of ethical responsibility are the insignia of the immortal individuality in man. Hence, as ancient seers and modern sages have taught, the assumption of full responsibility is the beginning of selflessness, true participation in universality. Whilst it is the hope of the *Mahatmas* that a few pioneering souls will become selfless servants of the human race at this point in human evolution, any would-be aspirants must first prepare themselves by becoming fully responsible under karma. In a spineless culture there may be some passing merit in packaged programmes to bolster self-confidence and self-assertion, but these are commonly vitiated by the greed of both sponsors and participants, and in any event can never substitute for true self-reliance and moral courage based upon deep meditation and honest self-study. Unlike costly weekend workshops, meditation and self-study can be embarked upon at any time by anyone; they are not only less taxing on one's pocketbook, but also more challenging psychologically.

By inserting oneself into a programme of regular meditation and proper self-study, one can insulate oneself from the nefarious influences of the moon, enter the Light of the Spiritual Sun, and in time, take advantage of that lunar element which corresponds to the elixir deposited by the sun in the moon. This is channelled through the *sushumna* ray in the spinal column.

> One of the names of the moon in Sanskrit is Soma.... A "soma-drinker" attains the power of placing himself in direct rapport with the bright side of the moon, thus deriving inspiration from the concentrated intellectual energy of the blessed ancestors . . .This which seems one stream (to the ignorant) is of a dual nature – one giving life and wisdom, the other being lethal. He who can separate the former from the latter, as Kalahamsa separated the milk from the water, which was mixed with it, thus showing great wisdom – will have his reward.
>
> H.P. Blavatsky

Something of the meaning of this mysterious alchemical process can be glimpsed by contemplating the threefold nature of *ahankara,* which at its highest level is universal I-am-I consciousness. At its lowest level, the *ahankara* associated with the lunar self or the illusory personality should be made to serve as the necessary focal point of the magnetic field within which the manasic self-consciousness gains proficiency in the exercise of moral responsibility. As the overbrooding individuality learns to master its projected rays, the ephemeral astral forms of its successive incarnations are gradually replaced by a purified and permanent astral vesture. The integration of the immortal individuality into the Universal Self involves still greater mysteries.

In conveying the contributions of the various classes of *Pitris* to the sevenfold constitution of Manu, the Thinker, the *Stanzas of Dzyan* touch upon the mystical side of the moon.

> WHO FORMS HIM? THE SEVEN LIVES; AND THE ONE LIFE. WHO COMPLETES HIM? THE FIVEFOLD LHA. AND WHO PERFECTS THE LAST BODY? FISH, SIN, AND SOMA.
>
> *The Secret Doctrine,* i 238

Commenting upon this passage, H.P. Blavatsky points both to its meaning in terms of arcane symbolism and its vital importance for the future evolution of humanity.

> "Who forms Manu (the Man) and who forms his body? The LIFE and the LIVES. Sin and the MOON." Here Manu stands for the spiritual, heavenly man, the real and non-dying EGO in us, which is the direct emanation of the "One Life" or the Absolute Deity. As to our outward physical bodies, the house of the tabernacle of the Soul, the Doctrine teaches a strange lesson; so strange that unless thoroughly explained and as rightly comprehended, it is only the exact Science of the future that is destined to vindicate the theory fully.
>
> *The Secret Doctrine,* i 248

Here the term "sin" does not mean what it currently connotes in the English language, but is a Chaldean conception having a precise if hidden relation to the moon, as well as being its symbolic equivalent. "Sin" does not merely refer to the physical moon, but rather to the Chaldean moon-god who was the lord of wisdom and of the calendar. The ancient Hindus and Chaldeans understood the vital relationship between the moon and the principles of gestation and growth. They comprehended something of the spiritual aspect of the moon symbolized in the lunar crescent found on the forehead of true *yogins* and on the mighty brow of the Mahayogin Shiva. Manu represents the Heavenly Man, the Father of the human race, who through his mystic meditation gives of the very essence of his divine vesture that which becomes the real and non-dying Ego of every human being. The indestructible spark of the indestructible fire is the deathless Self in every human being. After the Monad-Jiva, the meta-spiritual ray and breath of the Absolute Homogeneity, has been shot down into the very depths of differentiation, and gradually worked its way up through the regions of form aided by the ethereal prototypes provided by the lunar *Pitris*, the divine self-conscious intelligence of the Heavenly Man enters the waiting tabernacle and lights therein the sacred fire. This divine descent can take place only in coordination with the completion of the work of the lunar *Pitris*.

> Whilst the Monad-Jiva spirals downward into the depths of differentiated matter, the lower Dhyan-Chohans . . . are evolving pari passu with it on a higher and more spiritual plane, descending also relatively into matter on their own plane of consciousness, when, after having reached a certain point, they will meet the incarnating senseless monad, encased in the lowest matter, and blending the two potencies, Spirit and Matter, the union will produce that terrestrial symbol of the "Heavenly Man" in space – PERFECT MAN.

The Secret Doctrine, i 247

When from a potential androgyne man has become separated into male and female, then he is endowed with the principle of manasic self-consciousness. Thus, the creation of the animal-man and the creation of Divine Man are joined, Perfect Man in terrestrial space and time becoming the living symbol of the Heavenly Man, the transcendental archetype.

The complete and correct understanding of these mysteries can be acquired only through a mastery of the one exact science, the mathematics of the soul, which is exclusively in the custody of the Lodge of *Mahatmas*. This evidently cannot be taught to all and sundry, but glimpses of it may be shared with the most awakened souls of the age who can use it to help human evolution. This is very much an integral part of the programme of the Theosophical Movement, but like any other factor in spiritual life, can never be understood from outside. In order to begin to participate in this work, one must change one's very idea of the ratio between the invisible and the visible and increase the ratio of the unmanifest to the manifest, thereby creating an intense inner life through meditation. When the inner life becomes rich and replete in contrast to outer life (which only represents a small portion of oneself), true asceticism begins. Even if the vibrant sense of an inner life can only be maintained briefly each day, and needs to be sustained through participation with others also consecrated to the cause of universal enlightenment, one can, by working with others who are helping themselves, learn to work with natural cycles. In this it does not matter if one is a beginner, as long as one is starting in the right direction. It is indeed possible to gain the benediction of the presiding regents of different days – of Mercury-Hermes on Wednesday, of *Surya* the Sun on Sunday, of Shiva, Saturn-Kronos, on Saturday – and use this to strengthen the inner life. One could learn to use the benediction of Venus-Shukra on Friday, consecrated to higher thought, in order to learn to concentrate all one's energies around a still centre in mystic meditation. Becoming motionless within that mystic centre, remaining apart and aloof, one may begin to sense what is meant by standing aside from all the worlds that emanate out of the Divine Vesture, the invisible form of the *Logos*.

What the unmanifest *Logos* provides ceaselessly through the manifestation of the seven *Logoi* is re-enacted again and again in Monadic evolution. It may be re-enacted by each ray of the *Logos* in every human life. Even though extremely difficult, during any incarnation in which there is an awakening to the divine immortal nature – with the body as a temple and the vesture as an energy-field – the Triad above the head can come closer to the fontanelle and evoke from the light in the heart, *anahata,* a continuous current of light-energy which may refine and elevate all one's life-atoms. Such a current could not ceaselessly flow without strenuous training and wise guidance over many lives. Indeed, nothing worthwhile is ever possible without the Grace of the Guru. That help is ever available to every human being on earth in deep sleep. No being on earth is neglected. Every being in the depths of deep sleep, if even for only a moment, comes into that hinterland of the Gods, the Sages, the *Rishis* and the Initiator of Initiates, Dakshinamurti. The Light of the *Logos* is ever available in every life-atom to every being on earth throughout its seven kingdoms. There is no point in all of space beyond the purview of the flashing gaze of the Eye of *Dangma.*

To honour this most precious Teaching is to be propelled forward in evolution and to receive immortal life-energy, or, if one receives it and does not use it, to be thrown backwards. In either case, the consequence is dependent upon the power of choice of *Manas,* the self-conscious freedom exercised by the individual, on behalf of what is strong or of what is weak. The strong must lift the weak, whilst the sick and the perverse must be let go. Every human being must choose between the baser, pathological and paranoid elements in the psyche, and the finer, purer and more selfless elements in his nature. The two are as incompatible as terrestrial fire and water. The cosmic fire of Agni is, however, correlated with the luminous waters of space called *Akasha.* All the physical elements are mere visible representations of the true spiritual essences existing on the higher noumenal planes.

None of the terrestrial elements is good or bad in itself, but each has its place in the formation, nourishment and disintegration of mortal forms. This much is owed to modern science; it has gone farther in the past ninety years than in the preceding three centuries in dispelling rigid and concretized conceptions of material nature and its elements. Such knowledge still lies beyond the mental capacity of many human beings, and even then, it remains worlds away from a full understanding of Spirit-Matter – the One Life. Life pervades the entire universe, whether slumbering in the atoms of dust or awakened to divine consciousness in a perfected *Bodhisattva*. Gradually, over the ensuing centuries and millennia, humanity will awaken to an Aquarian awareness of the fire of the One Life burning within its every unit. Meta-biology and meta-chemistry will flourish when particle physics is ensouled by unitary metaphysics and enriched by the ontological logic of integration and differentiation.

The perception and comprehension of mankind will be progressively transformed by the power of Buddhic intuition, vivifying and brightening the sight of the now dormant Eye of the Soul. This cannot take place without the deliberate use of the powers of thought and self-consciousness to create new matrices of ideation and to break up and discard the calcified accretions of past ignorance which blind the soul. As H.P. Blavatsky noted, Louis Pasteur was wise in his time to observe that microbic life can sustain itself by both aerobic and anaerobic processes, thus indicating the independence of the vital potency from external environments. Through each of its distributive units life builds and unbuilds, creates and destroys, every organic form from the most minute to the most macrocosmic. Integration and disintegration of form proceed hand-in-hand with the differentiation and synthesis of consciousness throughout all the octaves of manifestation from the formless worlds built up out of the divine elements to the shadowy realm of physical existence. All alike are impelled from within by the *Shabdabrahman*, the Divine Sound surrounded by the supernal light of the *Gayatri*, the immortal pulse in the secret heart – the Sound in the Light and the Light in the Sound.

Hermes, June 1982
Raghavan Iyer

INTEGRATION AND RECURRENCE

If, on the one hand, a great portion of the educated public is running into atheism and scepticism, on the other hand, we find an evident current of mysticism forcing its way into science. It is the sign of an irrepressible need in humanity to assure itself that there is a Power Paramount over matter; an occult and mysterious law which governs the world, and which we should rather study and closely watch, trying to adapt ourselves to it, than blindly deny, and break our heads against the rock of destiny. More than one thoughtful mind, while studying the fortunes and reverses of nations and great empires, has been deeply struck by one identical feature in their history, namely, the inevitable recurrence of similar historical events reaching in turn every one of them, and after the same lapse of time. This analogy is found between the events to be substantially the same on the whole, though there may be more or less difference as to the outward form of details.

The Theosophist, July 1880
H.P. Blavatsky

Cyclic causation or the eternal law of periodicity stands midway between the affirmation of the Absolute and the postulate of progressive enlightenment in the set of fundamental axioms of *Gupta Vidya*. Pointing to the inexorable alternation of day and night, of birth and death, of *manvantara* and *pralaya*, cyclic law ensures that all events along with their participants, great or small, are comprehended within the archetypal logic of the *Logos* in the cosmos. *Gupta Vidya* indicates the mayavic nature of all manifestation in relation to the Absolute, whilst at the same time stressing that karmic responsibility is the pivot of all spiritual growth. The essential significance of the complex doctrine of cycles sometimes seems difficult to grasp in theory or to apply in practice. If the mind misconceives the metaphysical distinction between *TAT* and *maya*, then the dignity of spiritual striving through cycles under karma will be minimized. Self-examination and self-correction may be neglected owing to a false and merely intellectualist theory of transcendence. Conversely, the mind which embraces a too literalized conception of the immanence of the Absolute will find itself mired in experience with no accessible power of transcendence. It will tend to acquiesce in a sanguine or despairing doctrine of mechanical destiny which is psychological fatalism resulting from a mistaken conflation of causality with the ephemeral forms of outward events.

The true teaching of cyclic causation implies neither a trivialization nor a mechanization of life in a vesture in terrestrial time. Instead, it intimates the mysterious power of harmony, the irresistible force of necessity, which resides in the eternal balance of the manifest and the unmanifest in every living form and phase of the One Life. The ceaseless vibratory motion of the unmanifest *Logos* is the stimulus of the complex sets and subsets of hierarchies of beings constituting the universe, and of the intricate and interlocking cycles and subcycles of events that measure out its existence. The intimate relationship between temporal identity and cyclic existence is symbolized in the identification of the lifetime of Brahmâ with the existence of the universe, a teaching which also conveys the true meaning of immortality in *Hiranyagarbha.*

From the standpoint of universal unity and causation, the universe is a virtual image of the eternal motion or vibration of the unmanifest Word, scintillating around a set of points of nodal resonance within that Word itself. From the standpoint of individual beings involved in action, the universe is an aggregation of interlocking periodic processes susceptible to reasoned explanation in terms of laws. Understanding the nature of cycles and what initiates them, together with apprehending the mystery of cyclic causation itself, requires a progressive fusion of these two standpoints. The exalted paradigm of the union of Eternity and Time is *Adhiyajna,* seated near the circle of infinite eternal light and radiating compassionate guidance to all beings who toil in the coils of Time. Established in Boundless Duration, all times past, present and future lie before his eye like an open book. He is Shiva, the *Mahayogin,* the leader of the hosts of *Kumaras,* and also Kronos-Saturn, the lord of sidereal time and the ruler of Aquarius. If humanity is the child of cyclic destiny, Shiva is the spur to the spiritual regeneration of humanity. And, if the *Mahatmas* and *Bodhisattvas*, the supreme devotees of Shiva, live to regenerate the world, then it is the sacred privilege and responsibility of those who receive their Teachings to learn to live and breathe for the sake of service to all beings.

It is in this spirit that H.P. Blavatsky, in her essay entitled "The Theory of Cycles", suggested several keys to the interpretation of cyclical phenomena. We can readily discern the vast variety of periodic phenomena which has already been noticed in history, in geology, in meteorology and in virtually every other arena of human experience. We can also recognize the statistical recurrence of certain elements in reference to economics, to wars and peace, to the rise and fall of empires, to epidemics and revolutions, and also to natural cataclysms, periods of extraordinary cold and heat. H.P. Blavatsky's intent was not merely to persuade the reader of the pervasiveness of periodic phenomena through the multiplication of examples, but rather to convey the immanent influence of the power of number and of mathematics within all cyclic phenomena. She reviewed the original analysis of certain historical cycles made by Dr. F. Zasse and published in the *Prussian Journal of Statistics.* Dr. Zasse presented an account of a series of historical waves, each consisting of five segments of two hundred and fifty years, which have swept over the Eurasian land mass from east to west.

According to Dr. Zasse's chronology, which began at approximately 2000 B.C., the year 2000 of the present era should mark the conclusion of the fourth such wave, and the inception of yet another wave from the east. Commenting briefly upon the importance of one-hundred-year cycles within the longer cycles indicated by Dr. Zasse, H.P. Blavatsky cited his analysis of ten-year and fifty-year cycles of war and revolution affecting European nations. In order to draw attention away from external events and to direct it towards deeper psychological causes, she pointed out:

> The periods of the strengthening and weakening of the warlike excitement of the European nations represent a wave strikingly

regular in its periodicity, flowing incessantly, as if propelled onward by some invisible fixed law. This same mysterious law seems at the same time to make these events coincide with astronomical wave or cycle, which, at every new revolution, is accompanied by the very marked appearance of spots in the sun.

"The Theory of Cycles"
H. P. Blavatsky

Elsewhere, both in *Isis Unveiled* and *The Secret Doctrine*, she made reference to the eleven-year sunspot cycle, suggesting something of its occult significance in the respiration and heartbeat of the solar system.

During the nineteenth century a number of scientists speculated about the relationship of sidereal and terrestrial events. Dr. Stanley Jevons, one of the founders of econometrics, saw a correlation between sunspot cycles and the rises and falls of economic output and productivity. Jevons went so far as to speculate that "the commercial world might be a body so mentally constituted . . . as to be capable of vibrating in a period of ten years". In *The Secret Doctrine*, H.P. Blavatsky observed:

> Drs. Jevons and Babbage believe that every thought, displacing the particles of the brain and setting them in motion, scatters them throughout the Universe, and they think that "each particle of the existing matter must be a register of all that has happened".

The Secret Doctrine, i 104

Correlating this idea to the occult conception of the enduring impress of thought upon the subtle matter of the invisible human vestures, H.P. Blavatsky intimated the vital relationship between the impress of sidereal influences upon the *psyche* and the cyclic destiny of human souls.

> The Hindu Chitra-Gupta who reads out the account of every Soul's life from his register, called Agra-Sandhani; the "Assessors" who read theirs from the heart of the defunct, which becomes an open book before (whether) Yama, Minos, Osiris, or Karma – are

all so many copies of, and variants from the Lipika, and their Astral Records. Nevertheless, the Lipika are not deities connected with Death, but with Life Eternal.

Connected as the Lipika are with the destiny of every man and the birth of every child, whose life is already traced in the Astral Light – not fatalistically, but only because the future, like the PAST, is ever alive in the PRESENT – they may also be said to exercise an influence on the Science of Horoscopy.

The Secret Doctrine, i 105

From such considerations a complex picture emerges of myriad overlapping cycles and subcycles on several planes of existence. Whilst the enormous breadth and depth of cyclic phenomena would render elusive any exacting analysis of cycles for the neophyte in *Gupta Vidya,* one should attempt to nurture a cool apprehension of the regular periodicity in the excitement of mental and physical forces affecting both collective and distributive karma. It may help to begin with a relatively simple example. Consider the case of a single family living within a larger household and a local community. Each member of the family is born at a different moment. Each, therefore, has a different constellation in the ascendant at the moment of birth, and each has different cycles determined by the positions of the moon, the planets and the stars in the heavens at the moment of birth. For each, the angular relationships between these sidereal bodies – and their placement relative to the zenith and horizon in the place of the individual's birth – will vary. Already, even at the simplest level, one can see an inherent complexity to the cyclic destiny of every individual.

Within the lifetime of the individual a variety of cycles and subcycles will operate, some marked off by septenates of years and having to do with the incarnation of the higher principles, and others governed by a cycle slightly more than eighteen years having to do with the revolution of the nodes of the moon. Each of these cycles will have its own subcycles, and these in turn will be comprised of still smaller cycles, down to those which may last only a few weeks, a few days, even a few hours. Although this kind of mathematics can be most readily handled with the help of a minicomputer, it is not beyond the capacity of the human brain. Nor should it be forgotten that several people live together in families, and that there is a close interaction between what is happening in the orbit of the father, the mother, the children and all the ancestors of each. Owing to the complex overlapping and intersecting of the mathematics applying to each individual and to a specific group of individuals, one might think of constellations of energy-fields wherein many people produce an immense clustering of elements, all of which obey the laws of cycles. If one passes from the limits of a single family to the scope of a mini-commune or even a small community, it is evident that the degree of complexity involved in comprehending the cycles at work will become very great.

In order to understand the activity and overlapping of cycles on any broad scale, one must adopt a set of categories that has nothing to do with the perceptions and propensities of the personal nature. To the integrative and synthetic vision of the Adept, the interplay and interaction of human beings on the terrestrial plane are resolved into the occult correspondences of sounds, colours and numbers. Individual human beings are seen as having manvantaric stars, or rays of individuality, which pertain to them throughout the vast cycle of their incarnations. Within each incarnation that individuality takes up a personal existence connected with a personal star or ray. Whilst the tone, coloration and number associated even with the latter is generally unknown to most human beings in incarnation, and only crudely guessed at by contemporary theories of personality, the still more fundamental elements of individual identity as a Monad are scarcely even conceived. Yet, for the Adept the world of human interaction consists of a series of mathematically governed octaves of colour and sound beyond the comprehension of even the most speculative forms of modern painting and music. Nonetheless, if an individual is privileged to have received spiritual instruction regarding the nature of colour, sound and number, then he may begin to make experiments. By taking one of the simple colour charts available, he could discover how, out of the primary colours, complex shades and hues may be derived. Also he could gain some insight into what the developed artist means by a pure colour – an extremely pure blue or a luminous gold.

All such experiments are clearly relative to perception and to circumstance, because the pigments used will inevitably introduce a tincture which is part of the physical chemistry of what is called colour. And, whilst discrimination of colours on the physical plane can be heightened to an extraordinary degree – as exemplified by silk dyers, for instance – this skill represents only the most mundane aspect of the conscious refinement of colour vision. There is a tremendous difference between what is ordinarily perceived as colour and what is potentially perceptible on the subtler planes. Many are aware of the possibilities of subtle hearing or melodious colouring in music, whether it be through Indian music, with its refined system of quarter tones and complex rhythms, or through classical European music, with its intricate system of voices and use of silences. By playing a raga or a symphony, one can transform the entire elemental field of one's room. When one listens to such music, cycles overlap and the *psyche* fluctuates, in ways intensified by the collective nature of these forces. By noetically imposing upon the field some elevating spiritual note, one can gain the benefit of the fluidic nature of the field without being drawn into or absorbed by the psychical atmosphere.

If colour, sound and number can work such soothing charms, they can also work destructively. Great deliberation and intelligent sifting are, therefore, paramount in the use of alchemical knowledge. There are secrets locked within the spectrum, within the octave and within the series of numbers from 1 through 7, which can kill as well as heal. Without discrimination based upon purity of motive, any attempt to manipulate these *Fohatic* factors of cyclic destiny is likely to result in either unconscious grey or even black magic. In the realm of unconscious motivation, this will emerge through impulsiveness, particularly in speech, and a tragically misplaced sense of timing. Despite these dangers, inherent to a universe in which Manasic beings have free choice, persistently shines the ever-present possibility open to each human being to help Nature and harmonize with her through cycles, striving for the elevation of the human condition. Neither the ideas of Pythagoras on the mysterious influence of colours, numbers and sound, nor the theories of the ancient world-religions and philosophies, are so bizarre or so irrelevant as sectarian dogmatists and secular empiricists would pretend.

H.P. Blavatsky's aim in hinting at the occult foundations of the law of cycles was to restore the rights of ancient wisdom, and she recognized that nine out of ten human beings are somewhat open to the Teachings of *Gupta Vidya*. There is, alas, always the tenth person who has a problem – whether it be materialism, soul-blindness or suggestibility – and therefore goes around proclaiming some sort of superstitious humbug or general nihilism out of nervousness and a lack of courage, traceable to previous lives. And as long as some people talk shallow nonsense about sacred matters without real knowledge, this will tend to reinforce the sceptic. Hence, there exists a kind of see-saw action between people who talk about the sacred but do not really know it, and those who hear about it but refuse to consider it because their survival depends upon their illusions. All this waste provides a negative example of the cyclic reinforcement of social attitudes. As the Upanishadic and Socratic traditions demonstrate, the dialectics of speech and silence can convey as well as obscure the highest knowledge.

H.P. Blavatsky knew that the time was fast approaching when more and more people would emerge who have the courage both to examine ancient wisdom and to correlate it with the discoveries of science. It was for those who would ask questions, and make their own investigations by looking at the heavens and looking within themselves through meditation, that she partially unveiled the Teachings of *Gupta Vidya*. Those who use these Teachings – and daily consult *The Voice of the Silence* – in order to understand the profounder visions and longings of their hearts will progressively gain confidence in charting the seas of the psychic unconscious. With steadiness and persistence, they will become more skilled in handling the take-off and landing, the vertical ascent and descent in consciousness, so critical to the Aquarian Age. The ability to sustain oneself in any state of consciousness or meditation and the related ability to move deliberately from one plane or state of consciousness to another with relaxed control depend upon one's access to a fixed point of reference or vibration within consciousness. If the sevenfold human constitution were likened to a miniature solar system, the centre of consciousness would reside on one of the planets of that system.

Despite all the variations and fluctuations of cyclic existence affecting states of consciousness, all points of view within the system revolve in complex orbits around the central sun of the *Atman.* The motions of attention from one point to another are regulated by that central sun in accordance with its breath and heartbeat. As in the macrocosm of the universe, so too in the microcosm of human nature – all the oscillating motions and emanations of the MONAD and the Monad are comprised in an original fundamental vibration.

All are contained within the *Maha-Yug,* the "Great Age" or Cycle of the Manu calculation, which itself revolves between two eternities – the "*Pralayas*" or *Nights of Brahma.* As, in the objective world of matter, or the system of effects, the minor constellations and planets gravitate each and all around the sun, so in the world of the subjective, or the system of causes, these innumerable cycles all gravitate between that which the finite intellect of the ordinary mortal regards as eternity, and the still finite, but more profound, intuition of the sage and philosopher views as but an eternity within THE ETERNITY. "As above, so it is below", runs the old Hermetic maxim.

Insofar as individuals can assimilate this radical perspective within themselves, they will not be so dependent upon transient fashion and fickle opinion, nor will they be so susceptible to volatile psychic influences. In a society where many have scarcely any conception of self-magnetization and magnetic purity, they perpetually throw off negative emanations through speech and the eyes – and thought. Through the natural rhythms of daily life – the cycle of waking and sleeping, of going to work and returning home, of interacting with family and friends – strong focal points are established for the aggregation of psychic impressions. If one has not prepared oneself through proper meditation to use these focal points for the strengthening of positive vibrations, then they will by default turn into rats' nests of negativity. Through identification with the personal nature, one may tend to take every one of these disturbances literally and personally, and thereby make it the hooking-point for further infestation of the *psyche*. If, instead, one strengthens a meditative awareness of the manvantaric vibration of the Avatar, then these inevitable collecting-points in terrestrial consciousness can become powerful regenerative agents enabling one to meet one's own karmic responsibility and to lighten the burden of others.

Meditation upon the cosmos as a complex hierarchy of interacting cycles radiating from a common source may be aided by simple, yet suggestive, diagrams like the following:

This *yantra* represents a spiral seashell with a lotus at the centre, the outside of which is like the head of a coiling serpent. The diagram is in ceaseless motion. At the same time, because of the harmonizing of different strata – which resemble the skins of the earth, the layers of language and concept, and even the different hierarchies of reality – the *yin-yang* alternation within the different strata harmonizes with the lotus-like sun in the centre. Thus, lines of emanation radiate out from the centre and return to it. Through meditation upon such a *yantra* one can break the fixity of the static geometry and the limited algebra governing one's responses to the world, and move on to a more dynamic and topological post-Newtonian conception of space, a more fluidic and flexible post-Euclidian geometry, and a more interactive conception of a post-Cartesian algebra founded upon matrices and groups. As one gains a sense of Aquarian meta-mathematics and meta-geometry, founded upon the triadic meta-logic of *Gupta Vidya*, one will prepare oneself to participate self-consciously in the dialectical calculus of the cosmos. Daily meditation can provide the basis for dynamic integration of distilled perceptions.

Cycles are not mechanical recurrences of events, but living curves of dynamic causation. Every individual has a karmic curve, and at each point has potential access to the sum total of karmic energies generating that curve. Through noetic conceptions of maxima and minima, of curvature and inflexion, one can self-consciously generate a line of life's meditation. Through the Buddhic powers of correlation and discrimination, of integration and differentiation, one can penetrate the deceptive surface of events and reach towards the underlying planes of causation. Most individuals, alas, fail to maximize their opportunities because their notions of cause and effect are mistaken. This may be discerned by comparing the concepts of explanation and definition. If told that the term "lion" is defined as "a large carnivorous feline mammal found most often in Africa and Asia, with a tawny body, a tufted tail and a shaggy mane", one will not think that the phrase defining "lion" is actually a lion in any way. One will understand that the term being defined and the phrase doing the defining both have the same meaning. Similarly, if one is told that a certain event is to be explained by the occurrence of certain other events, one should not think that the events constituting the explanation are the cause of the given event, but rather that both the explained event and the explaining events are manifestations of the same cause.

To the eye of Shiva the entire universe and all its cyclic phenomena comprise a single harmonious consequence of one Causeless Cause, the Karmic Sum Total symbolized by the lifetime of Brahmâ. Most human beings are unable to maximize their opportunities even under the lesser, though still vast, sum totals and karmic curves of individual Monadic existence, prefigured by the manvantaric star. They die hardly having used one percent of their potential brain-power, and hardly having tapped one-tenth of one percent of their far more powerful heart-energy. If the spiritual and mystical heart is not exercised, it begins to atrophy. If, however, it is strengthened through the exercise of dispassion and devotion, it gains strength, firing the synapses of the nervous system and stimulating the cells in the centres of the brain. Through heart-energy, through an abundant love of one's fellow men, of their children and their families, one begins to break down the false boundary of the *persona* and its limited view of family and friendship. As this barrier is dissolved, other human beings, and the world at large, seem less alien and less hostile. Life becomes more meaningful and challenging through the perception that all other human beings are immortal souls, like oneself, capable of reciprocity in spiritual aspiration. One can tap more and more of one's heart-energy, and thus quicken the Buddhic mind and even release the spiritual will.

Then, passing beyond the narrow horizon of personal existence, one may naturally insert oneself into the broader evolutionary development of humanity. One will learn to discard that which is perverse, whilst turning that in oneself which is unique and individual to the good of others, all the while strengthening an inward sense of that which is common to all and confined by none. As Mahatma K.H. taught in the last century:

> Whenever any question of evolution or development in any Kingdom presents itself to you bear constantly in mind that everything comes under the Septenary rule of series in their correspondences and mutual relation through nature.

In the evolution of man there is a topmost point, a bottom point, a descending arc, and an ascending arc. As it is "Spirit" which transforms itself into "matter" and (not "matter" which ascends – but) matter which *resolves once more into spirit*, of course the first race evolution and the last on a planet (as in each round) must be more ethereal, more spiritual, the fourth or lowermost one most physical (progressively of course in each round) and at the same time – *as physical intelligence is the masked manifestation of spiritual intelligence* – each evoluted race in the downward arc must be more physically intelligent than its predecessor, and each in the upward arc have a more refined form of mentality commingled with spiritual intuitiveness.

One must not forget for even a moment that there are seven colours, seven sounds, seven days of the week, seven principles in the cosmos and in man, that the physical body has seven layers of skin and that every seven years one experiences important and irreversible changes in the mortal vestures. It will thus become possible to draw those kinds of Buddhic analogies and correspondences which are essential to the comprehension of cycles and the alchemical task of noetic integration. Disabused of any false dichotomy between spirit and matter, one will come to understand that if spirit transforms itself into matter and matter resolves itself once more into spirit, then matter is nothing but a passive lower expression of spirit, whilst spirit is, through ideation, an intensification of the energy-field in matter with a transforming power. How much one can bring this power to bear will depend upon one's degree of constancy in remembering the septenary rule. Without comprehending the entire series, it is not possible to enjoy the entire spectrum or to employ the seven notes with accuracy and timing.

To do the right thing at the right time depends upon a lively awareness of the subtle phases and stable conditions of prevailing cycles. In the Aquarian Age it is helpful to acknowledge that human beings, having begun in the First Root Race as extremely ethereal and spiritual beings, have now completed their arc of descent into matter and are engaged in a progressive process of etherealization and spiritualization. In the Fifth Root Race, going from the Fifth Sub-Race to the Sixth Sub-Race, this process is giving birth to a profound spiritual sensitization of intelligence through the elevation of life-atoms. This is connected with the cosmic electricity of *Daiviprakriti,* the Light of the *Logos.* All the modes of physical and astral intelligence throughout the various kingdoms of nature are nothing but masked manifestations of the synthesizing spiritual intelligence of *Mahat.* Along the upward involutionary arc of growth and spirituality, each human being, each individuated ray of *Mahat* in *Manas,* must self-consciously cultivate what Mahatma K.H. calls a "refined form of mentality commingled with spiritual intuitiveness". Refined mentality is *Manas-Taijasi,* and spiritual intuitiveness *Buddhi.* Thus, *Buddhi-Manas-Taijasi* is the colouring, the tonality and the number of the Avataric impulse in the present cycle. It is the spiritual essence of secular monasticism which, from its present *bija* or seed state, will flourish as a new mode of self-regenerating civilization in the maturing phases of the Aquarian Age. Like seeds that lie beneath the protection of mountain snows, every element of spiritual intuition, of mental refinement, and of the heart radiance that comes through compassion out of the mystic marriage – *hieros gamos* – of truth and love is being helped and nourished by Shiva-Shakti *(Ardhanari)* at this sacred moment and hour in the evolutionary history of mankind. Such seeds, sown in trust by courageous pioneers in the chill midnight of outward darkness, will bring forth a rich harvest for mankind in the warmer dawns of the foreseeable future.

Hermes, November 1982
Raghavan Iyer

AQUARIAN HARMONY

"Our old writers said that Vach *is of four kinds....*para, pasyanti, madhyama, vaikhari *(a statement found in the Rig-Veda and the Upanishads).... Vaikhari-Vach is what we utter."* It is sound, speech, *that again which becomes comprehensive and objective to one of our physical senses and may be brought under the laws of perception. Hence: "Every kind of* Vaikhari-Vach *exists in its* Madhyama . . . Pasyanti *and ultimately in its* Para *form . . . The reason why this* Pranava *is called* Vach *is this, that these four principles of the great Kosmos correspond to these four forms of Vach . . . The whole Kosmos in its objective form is* Vaikhari *Vach; the light of the* Logos *is the* madhyama *form; and the* Logos *itself the* pasyanti *form; while* Parabrahmam *is the* para *(beyond the* noumenon *of all* Noumena) *aspect of that Vach."*

The Secret Doctrine, i 432
H.P. Blavatsky

Harmony is the central idea in Aquarian thought. Compassionate sacrifice and intelligent suffering are the necessary means to an understanding of harmony; their eventual fruition is noetic self-knowledge. Spiritual growth is epitomized by the image of the silent, ceaseless construction of the Temple of Truth, precipitated in its crystalline splendour by meditative action out of the Akashic waters of life. True spiritual will, the conscious direction of energy by intelligent ideation and self-conscious volition, is the supreme criterion and sovereign talisman of Aquarian humanity. Opposed to this vision are the irrational and involuntary forces of blind desire, the persistent and obscuring veil cast over human perception and action through lives of thoughtless involvement with the grosser fields of material nature. Aquarians can readily grasp this problem, but they are few and far between. The therapeutic Aquarian standpoint depends upon a fundamental appreciation, through meditation, of the metaphysical structure of all reality and Nature, of God and Man.

The idea of cosmic harmony and human solidarity is as old as the *Vedas* and is vital to every authentic spiritual tradition. Long before the Christian era, at the time of Confucius and Buddha, when the basis for civilization was being laid in different parts of the world, Pythagoras required all his diligent pupils to study arithmetic, geometry, astronomy and music. Musical harmony was considered one of the four branches of mathematics, a reflection of the deeper nature of spiritual harmony. At some instinctive level, all human beings recognize the difference between harmonious and disharmonious movement. In one of the first human rites of initiation, learning to walk, it is necessary to learn, to assimilate and to embody some understanding of the relationship between harmony and self-direction. The art of physical movement is analogous to the mystical process of treading the spiritual Path. Pythagoras said that he could understand the inward nature of a human being by watching the way he or she walked, because he comprehended the continuous embodiment of universal harmony which extends from the highest to the lowest in Nature and Man.

> Pythagoras esteemed the Deity (the Logos) to be the centre of unity and "Source of Harmony." We say this Deity was the Logos, not the MONAD that dwelleth in Solitude and Silence, because Pythagoras taught that UNITY, being indivisible, is no number . . . The Pythagoreans asserted that the doctrine of Numbers – the chief of all in Esotericism – had been revealed to man by the celestial deities; that the world had been called forth out of Chaos by Sound or Harmony, and constructed according to the principles of musical proportion; that the seven planets which rule the destiny of mortals have a harmonious motion "and intervals corresponding to musical diastemes, rendering various sounds, so perfectly consonant, that they produce the sweetest melody, which is inaudible to us, only by reason of the greatness of the sound, which our ears are incapable of receiving."

> *Ibid.,* i 433

To rise above a merely instinctual awareness of harmony and to become a more receptive agent and instrument of cosmic harmony, one must apprehend the idea in reference to the mind and the heart and understand too the rhythms of the invisible vestures. One must reflect upon what it means, first of all, to see oneself as a *source* of harmony, a Logoic being, capable of centering oneself in consciousness at that point in abstract space which is indivisible, unconnected with any form. This point is a focus of concentration, and also a point from which there can be diffused in every direction, as in a sphere, radii reaching out with deliberation and benevolence towards every life-atom. Whether putting on one's clothes, or eating food, or sitting down, one is always dealing with life-atoms. How grateful and gentle is one towards everything that one has the privilege of touching and using? To increase benevolence one must locate oneself correctly through meditation, heightening awareness from a central point of harmony. In the *Bhagavad Gita,* Krishna instructs Arjuna to take the point between the eyes as his starting-point in coming to see himself as a centre of harmony. A being is not his eyes, his ears, his mouth, his head, not any of his organs, nor his entire body. But he can be the mystical point between the eyes.

This meditative exercise to see oneself as a monadic point should be complemented by an effort to see what is at the core of every relationship with other human beings. What gratitude does one owe one's father, who initiated one's physical incarnation by providing not only one's bone structure but also the seminal essence out of which the body was formed? What reverence does one owe to one's mother, who gave not only the flesh and soft tissue of the body, but also the egg itself from which was born the embryo that was gestated for seven months in the womb and then protected for two more months before being delivered? What does one owe one's spouse and children in the present lifetime and one's former spouses and children in all one's former lives? What is crucial in one's relationship to one's friends and neighbours and their families who constitute the community one lives in, and what is at the core of one's relationships in one's sphere of work?

All such questions highlight the crux of one's *Dharma*, that which upholds a human being, linking him or her to the entire fabric of human life. If human beings would only begin to centre themselves through meditation, reflection and preparation, they would realize the great privilege of entering the world. One must prepare oneself inwardly before using one's eyes, if one would see other human beings reverentially as points of light. If one is going to speak compassionately, not compulsively, one must consider before speaking how one's words may be relevant or beneficial to another. "Please" or "Thank you" must be said sincerely, not automatically; favours must be asked kindly, not imperiously. By coming to see life in terms of the primary facts of birth and death, one may learn to act with deliberation and noetic discernment, like an orderly in a hospital who, though always very busy, does not mind being overlooked. By a smile, by a word or by silent exemplification alone, one may remain centered as a monadic point, giving off therapeutic vibrations to all.

Seen in this way, life can be extraordinarily beautiful and simple. Life seems difficult only because so much comes in the way of understanding oneself as a source of harmony. Human beings are continually concerned with the boundaries between themselves as individuals, yet those boundaries exist only in the realm of ephemeral forms, and therefore provide no stable basis for self-centering. Without deep meditation and fundamental metaphysics, it is impossible to learn anything significant about centering oneself in consciousness. Thus, thousands of people who use those terms loosely are looking for disciples and not finding any who will stay with them. That is because they never stayed with anything themselves; they have hence not centered themselves in their own consciousness. Like the dilettantes Plato warned against in his portrayal of democracy, they have no internal sense of priority or proportion, and hence no spiritual will. Yet there exists today an increasing number of Aquarian pioneers, like the scattered droplets presaging the monsoon, who have begun in earnest the difficult task of gradually centering themselves in the *Verbum – Brahma Vach.*

232 SELF-ACTUALIZATION AND SPIRITUAL SELF-REGENERATION

By removing what is excessive and by refining a sense of what is essential, they are learning to radiate benevolence and intelligence. They are learning the constructive use and dissemination of thought, feeling and will-energy. They have become self-consciously engaged in the transformation of the energy-field of the entire earth, that grand project which is the task of the Aquarian Age. The forces of harmony will be progressively strengthened, whilst disharmony will become nothing but a dialectical opportunity for growth. As the Aquarian Age unfolds, there will be a continuous increase in human awareness, a deepening of privacy. Each human being will become more of a solitary person of silence and meditation. In mature Aquarian culture, what is said and done will be meaningful and thoughtful, deliberate and discerning, but rendered with ease, sweetness and even beauty.

Clearly, the transformation from Piscean to Aquarian civilization poses an extraordinary challenge. Yet the resources available to any human being who wishes to assist this transformation are tremendous. The internal reservoirs of Akashic energy and ideation potentially available to the aspiring human soul are virtually infinite. To tap them self-consciously and thereby to contribute to the civilization of the future requires an understanding of metaphysics grounded in meditation as well as a moral self-discipline enlightened by at least some preliminary understanding of the arcane teachings about cosmic hierarchies. The greatest conceptual barrier to a practical increase in the sense of human solidarity is the mistaken notion that human beings must do something to unify the world. It is an ultimate and irreducible metaphysical fact that the world is already one. All beings are one, and all Being is One. Since all beings are one in a primordial invisible state, the true task is to mirror that unity on the lower, manifested planes of differentiated thought and action. This is impossible without first reaching towards that invisible unity, and hence Pythagoras taught his disciples to be extremely humble about That which is No Number. That is not zero, a place-holder in the number continuum. It is, rather, the source of dynamic harmony that lies behind all the spheres and circles of the metaphysical and physical universes. The key to the harmony and Akashic continuity of the One and the many lies concealed within the mystery of the zero and the point.

To convey this to the modern age, the great Rishi masquerading as H.P. Blavatsky set forth before the world the ancient *Stanzas of Dzyan*. During the nineteenth century, the Sixth Century Impulsion in the septenary series initiated by Tsong-Kha-Pa, the term *"Brahma Vidya"* was often used as an equivalent to *Theosophia*. Whilst *Brahma Vidya* refers to the sacred science, spiritual knowledge has not, over a hundred years, been put to intensive use by very many individuals. In that sense, the Theosophical Movement was once again a comparative failure. As it had failed over two thousand years ago in the time of Jesus, it failed again and again throughout the six impulsions of recent centuries. It failed especially, dramatically and poignantly, in the eighteenth century, despite an extremely powerful infusion. It gained a partial success on the secular, social and political planes, but the true import and teaching of the Enlightenment was subverted. "Liberty, equality and fraternity" did not come about in the true spiritual sense in which it was envisaged by the great Adepts of the eighteenth century.

In the present Cycle, wherein the Avatar works mainly with magicians in different parts of the world, no quarter is given either to spiritual pretensions or to paranoid empiricism. The clutter and lumber of the past, whether pseudo-Theosophical, pseudo-religious, pseudo-scientific or pseudo-political, are being wiped out, so that human beings must endure severe testing before they can return to the timeless basics of living. They are being forced to ask themselves what it means to be a human being and how one uses sound and speech. Given the course of human evolution over the last five million years, a situation must be created in which the word "human" cannot any more be applied in the future tense to someone who misuses sound and speech. Nothing can be done about the right use of speech on the plane of appearances without getting to the root of the problem on the plane of thought. There must be a restoration of the Mysteries and an elimination of the worldly worship of secondary and tertiary emanations through religious systems and mindless rituals. New rules must be created for speech, and new criteria must be created for silence, so that meditation can become more widespread and constructive. It must be brought home that *Dzyan* means self-reform through meditation, and that maturity is nothing more than mastery over the power of speech.

For these reasons, *Brahma Vidya* in the present Cycle has been supplanted by the term *"Brahma Vach"*, as a synonym for *Theosophia*. The aim is to get to the root of that which is beyond even the pre-cosmic sidereal gods. Whether it is called the Logos or *Vach* or *Brahma Vach*, it is the primordial latent sound and light in *Parabrahm*. That latent sound and light in *Parabrahm* is *Para Vach*, and that *Para Vach* is beyond both manifestation and non-manifestation. It is the Great Breath beyond the cosmos that vitalizes root matter, the eternally self-existent vibration of eternal motion. It transcends the distinction between *Mahamanvantara* and *Mahapralaya*, and even the creative vibratory light of the *sandhyas* at the dawn of differentiation. In the dawn of manifestation that light exists in its most virginal, luminous and noumenal potential state. Its latency becomes meditated upon and thus draws upon the ideational energy of the Logos. This is *Pashyanti Vach*, coexistent with the Logos and inseparable from its own highest self-awareness. *Para Vach* is like a ray from the primordial ever-darkness of *Parabrahm*, flowing out of the pre-cosmic sources of all as *Kalagni*, dark spiritual fire. It is misleading to think of it as actually emerging from *Parabrahm*, because it is always the ever-concealed potency in *Parabrahm*. There is a stirring within that eternal state from which arises the awareness of latent light and sound, which becomes *Pashyanti Vach*, yielding the Logos, Brahmâ, *Ishwara*, Sanat – the Ancient of Ancients. Simultaneous with the emergence of the androgyne Logos is the emergence of its feminine counterpart which is *Vach*.

Vach thus refers in its *para* form to that which is absolutely latent light and sound. *Vach* also refers to Brahmâ, who, as the Logos, is

Vach, whilst *Vach* as the consort of Brahmâ is the light of the Logos – *Daiviprakriti* – which is *Vach* in its *madhyama* form. In other words, given latent light and sound, and given ideation upon that latent light and sound, that ideation is expressed in a most pristine form in the dawn of manifestation. It is like the dawn of Venus on the terrestrial plane; physically, there is darkness, but a most noumenal light is irradiated on earth. Cats have a psychic awareness of this and wish to be outside at that time; even the glow-worm enjoys the light before dawn. Human beings should understand the analogy between terrestrial dawn-light and the noumenal and causal light of the invisible Sun. On the plane of *Buddhi-Manas* intellectual light is consubstantial with the essential light-energy of *Suddhasattva*, the substance of the gods. In this sense, *Vach*, as the consort of Brahmâ and the Light of the Logos, is also the mother of the gods. She is Sarasvati, the goddess of wisdom and beauty, and Aditi, out of whose noumenal form emanate the seven primordial rays, each of which carries a luminous vesture.

The substance of these vestures is not matter in any sense that can be understood by terrestrial criteria, but rather rays so luminous and radiant that they are called the sons of *Daiviprakriti*. These sons are preconditions to a cosmos, and it is from these primordial seven that there is a rapid multiplication in sevens and fourteens, in tens and twelves, producing *en masse* the array of the hierarchies. It is these in turn that produce the objective manifested universe, or *Vaikhari Vach*. Thus, H.P. Blavatsky speaks of *Vach* as

> the most mysterious of all the Brahmanical goddesses, she who is termed "the melodious cow who milked forth sustenance and water" (the Earth with all her mystic powers); and again she "who yields us nourishment and sustenance (physical Earth). Isis is also mystic Nature and also Earth; and her cow's horns identify her with *Vach*. The latter, after having been recognised in her highest form as *para*, becomes at the lower or material end of creation – Vaikhari. Hence she is mystic, though physical, Nature, with all her magic ways and properties.

Ibid., i 434

The conception of *Vach* as mystic Nature points to the continuity of the entire field linking *Para* to *Vaikhari Vach*. The two opposite poles, the one beyond all manifestation and the other representing the maximum degree of differentiation, the most transcendental and the most immanent, are held together by *Akasba*. It is a supersensuous, fiery, fluidic ether surrounding the earth and the solar system, but also pervading the brain, the heart and the entire human body, which is largely composed of water and empty space.

> "Waters" and "water" stand as the symbol for Akasa, the "primordial Ocean of Space," on which Narayana, the self-born Spirit, moves; reclining on that which is its progeny.... "Water is the body of Nara"; thus we have heard the name of water explained. Since Brahmâ rests on the water, therefore he is termed Narayana".... "Pure, Purusha created the waters pure..." at the same time Water is the third principle in material Kosmos, and the third in the realm of the Spiritual: Spirit of Fire, Flame, Akasa, Ether, Water, Air, Earth, are the cosmic, sidereal, psychic, spiritual and mystic principles, pre-eminently occult, in every plane of being. "Gods, Demons, Pitris and men," are the four orders of beings to whom the term *Ambhamsi* is applied (in the Vedas it is a synonym of gods): because they are all the product of WATERS (mystically), of the Akasic Ocean, and of the Third principle in nature.
>
> *Ibid.,* i 458

Akasha-Vach is mystic Nature pervading the entire cosmos. It is the celestial virgin and alkahest of the alchemists, the "Virgin Mother" of the magician. It is the mother of love, mercy and charity, as well as the waters of grace which can only be tapped by true meditation, total benevolence and selflessness. That is why it is only possible to gain self-knowledge through selfless love. A mother blessed with pure love can, just by a glance, avert impending danger to her child. Through the power of pure love, the mother and child become one, experiencing *Akasha*. This notion of two identities fusing is neither simple in itself nor vague. Although it may be readily observed in the animal kingdom, it cannot be understood through terms like "instinct". Crude notions such as "mother instinct" are worse than useless. In seeking to understand *Akasha*, it is best not to speak. The less one analyses, the better. Too many people analyse too much instead of living and learning from the simplest aspects of life.

Mystic Nature is extremely close to everyone. It flows in and through the human form. This can be seen as soon as one investigates the pressure points in one's hands and feet, gently and lovingly, but also with firmness and courage. Suddenly one will discover that there are many knots throughout the body, causing people to fall ill. The same lesson may be learnt by treating objects gently, using *Brahma Vach* in daily life when washing dishes or walking, when putting on clothes, or touching any object. If one does not learn harmonious and gentle action in the sphere of daily duties, which are the *ABCs* of *Theosophia*, one will never become even remotely able to understand the Mysteries. Above all, one must learn harmony in speech, for sound is the leading attribute of *Akasha-Vach*. When an Adept sees the aura around a human being who has not yet entered the Mysteries, the Adept is interested only in whether that human being will learn before death the *ABCs* of life. Has the person learnt how to be humble, how to learn, how to apologize, how to mentally prostrate before elders and teachers? The degree to which a human being has learnt generosity and gratitude during life will infallibly determine his or her state of consciousness at the moment of death.

If the basics have been learnt in this lifetime, then karma will be kind in the next. The person will find birth in a family where the parents are not much moved by likes and dislikes, and raise their children accordingly. Such parents will give their children few options, and they will also probably be impoverished peasants. The child will have no option but to learn the only arts that its parents have to teach – farming, carpentry, housekeeping. For the fortunate soul life does not consist of menus; there is only one thing to eat. In such an environment the soul can perfect the lesson of the *ABCs* and advance towards self-knowledge. Many people are terrified that they are not learning the *ABCs*, that they are merely repeating formulae and not really learning, and this is indeed a widespread and dangerous condition. But instead of exacerbating it through futile fears, they can begin letting go of the tight, knotting egotistical grip they have on themselves, can begin to renounce the psychic claustrophobia that imprisons them. Many lifetimes may pass before they can hear the Akashic sounds of the mystic heights or before they can feel the flow of the *Akasha* within the heart and brain.

Such persons can still look up at the sky and have their vision healed by it. They can still appreciate the light of the dawn and have their hearts renewed by it. They can still sit quietly in the twilight and sense in the sounds of nature its uninterrupted harmony as day recedes into night. They can behold the midnight sky, thrilling to the sight of stars more numberless than human beings, and gain an inward sense of the spaciousness of the cosmos. Seeing the sky as the great purifier of consciousness, they may touch the veil of mystic Nature as the container of all things *in potentia.* Using the great Teachings in these ways, they may prepare themselves for preliminary exercises in meditation and lay the seeds for the discipline of silence which is ultimately consummated in the full perception and self-conscious embodiment of universal harmony by the sovereign Adept. Every honest effort to follow this alchemical path is irrevocably a step towards the noonday Sun of Aquarian enlightenment.

Hermes, October 1983
Raghavan Iyer

RESONANCE AND VIBRATION

As the aggregate sound of nature is shown to be a single definite tone, a keynote vibrating from and through eternity; having an undeniable existence per se *yet possessing an appreciable pitch but for "the acutely fine ear" so the definite harmony or disharmony of man's external nature is seen by the observant to depend wholly on the character of the keynote struck for the* outer *by* inner *man. It is the spiritual* EGO *or* SELF *that serves as the fundamental base, determining the tone of the whole life of man – that most capricious, uncertain and variable of all instruments, and which more than any other needs constant tuning; it is its voice alone, which like the sub-base of an organ underlies the melody of his whole life.*

The Theosophist, January 1882
H.P. Blavatsky

The entire cosmos is a complex matrix of sound and light vibrations. Every element in our world and every kingdom of beings derives its essential nature from the keynote resonating as the basis of its consciousness. All primary questions concerning origins and destiny turn upon the rate of vibration, the plane of matter and state of consciousness, and corresponding conceptions of space, time and motion. Beyond the planes of manifestation and prior to the primal differentiation of spirit and matter lies the one invariant and all-potential vibration of the *Paramatman*, which through its radiation gives periodic form and substance to the septenary universe. Ultimately, this is a purely transcendental process entirely exempt from rational analysis. It is necessary to discard the false notion that each human being is somewhat like a machine or a self-contained box. As the universal vibration of the One Life is at the core of every living form, no being in the universe is entirely dependent upon any external source of motion. Owing to the transcendental commonality of consciousness, all beings are inevitably involved in a universal system of mutual interdependence.

Whilst mechanistic models of man and nature, popular in the seventeenth century, served to stress the order of nature, they nonetheless contributed to the false notion that each person is separate and identifiable with a body construed as a self-contained mechanical unit. Today, however, no one who is well-informed even at a simple level about electronics can think in this way. To take a contemporary analogy, it is more plausible to think of oneself as a collection of receiving and transmitting centres, capable of self-attunement to a wide variety of vibrations in the universe. Even the elusive concept of a unified field theory corresponds on the physical plane to the metaphysical idea of the eternal motion of the *Atman.*

The idea of universal vibratory consciousness must be linked to the concept of ethical responsibility if it is to be of help to human beings in daily life. The idea of instantaneous interdependence of all beings must be joined to the ideal of continuity of consciousness through variegated experiences. Memory must be linked to motion. Since the eighteenth century and the development of the mechanical theory of heat, all physical conceptions and models of memory have been circumscribed by the doctrine of entropy. In this view, all motions exist on the same plane and are therefore subject to mutual interference and obscuration, gradually tending to the increase of chaos and confusion. In such a scheme, it is inconceivable that any vibratory motion could be preserved intact over any long period of time. This itself is a consequence of the assumption that all things are moved from outside, and that, being subject to conflicting external influences, no single body can remain in a constant vibratory state of motion. For theories of memory, this implies that any matrix wherein memory resides must be constantly subject to corruption and forgetfulness. As a consequence, ethical responsibility is ephemeral and all learning is inevitably undone by entropy.

In various popularized versions, especially in the social sciences and in psychology, the mechanical theory of heat has come to resemble an *a priori* road-block barring all conceptions of universal responsibility and continuity of consciousness. Conceptually, it is important to recognize that the law of entropy applies only to closed systems having no access to additional sources of energy. Philosophically and psychologically, it is crucial to see that these sources of energy might just as well be internal as external.

The ethical significance of the problem of memory and forgetfulness was stressed by both Plato and Shankara. Plato held that all learning is recollection, whilst Shankara said that the negligence of recollection is death. But unlike contemporary mechanists, they held that learning and life are capable of enormous conscious extension. These abundant possibilities are connected with the Vedic conception of fire, the pristine symbol of wisdom and the immortality of spirit, as well as with the primal heat of Kamadeva associated with the manvantaric awakening of the manifested universe. According to *Gupta Vidya*, the universe is not a closed system but is instead pervaded by the immanence of its purely transcendental radiation. This immanence, which is realized in the fullest enlightenment, is reflected within the universe in an ordered series of planes and sub-planes of consciousness and matter. On each of these planes, objective existence and subjective relationship correlate with characteristics of space, time and motion defining that plane. Each plane, however, stands as the effect of a more noumenal plane whilst at the same time serving as the causal basis of a yet more differentiated plane, all within the overall limits of a vast gamut of manvantaric manifestation. Life on the highest noumenal plane is consciousness of the illimitable ground of all possible differentiated existence.

As the highest noumenal vibrations in the cosmos are themselves constantly sustained by the unmanifest eternal motion of the *Atman,* human beings can strengthen and maintain fidelity to those vibrations through self-transcendence and self-purification. Each vibratory state of consciousness on every plane is a reflected resonance of the highest noumenal states of consciousness and hence of *Atma Vidya.* This is the meaning of the occult axiom: *The highest sees through the eyes of the lowest.* Yet to realize this self-consciously, it is necessary to work with secondary and tertiary vibrations. The term "self-reference" actually refers to a process in consciousness whereby a vibratory matrix of long or short duration is established on a plane or sub-plane that is subjective when compared to the apparent content or basis of the reference. In this way, all self-conscious activity on an objective plane has a tendency to establish or reinforce subjective matrices on relatively subjective planes. These matrices, which do not decay through the mere passage of time on more objective planes, form the basis of memory – and hence of continuity of consciousness and ethical responsibility. As H.P. Blavatsky explains:

> Nothing that takes place, no manifestation however rapid or weak, can ever be lost from the Skandhic record of a man's life. Not the smallest sensation, the most trifling action, impulse, thought, impression, or deed, can fade or go out from, or in the Universe. We may think it unregistered by our memory, unperceived by our consciousness, yet it will still be recorded on the tablets of the astral light.

> *Lucifer,* October 1891
> H.P. Blavatsky

This implies that every feeling and every thought, however guilty or courageous, everything that one has known within the privacy of one's own solitude, has been recorded in a universal computer. Every visible and invisible manifestation is somewhere recorded. Manifestation itself is a process of unfoldment from within without; but insofar as human beings operate from without within, they do not grasp the nature of the inward matrices of their own manifestation. Nothing that is recorded may be lost or erased. No angel or saviour can alter or edit the karmic record. No sensation or act is too trifling to be registered. This is a staggering fact. Normally, in their egocentricity, most people see every occurrence in relation to their own likes and dislikes.

Gupta Vidya, however, affirms that the most trivial element of experience of any single being, and particularly human beings, is permanently retained in a kind of universal brain. But whereas mechanistic information resides on media that are external to the being generating and deploying that information, karmic information resides within the subtle vestures of the being itself. It consists of conscious vibrations, feeling-tones, colorations of attitudes, flavours of actions, aromas of characters, all of which are elements of one's conscious existence. Every vibration in manifestation, from the last vibration of the Seventh Eternity at the end of *pralaya* and the first flutter of manvantaric dawn, to the supple creative light witnessed in the final *sandhya* before *pralaya*, is alive and suffused with the consciousness of the One Life. Every field of objective sensation springs from the differentiated Dhyani-energies of that One Life in manifestation intimated by those mystics who speak of the aroma of lifetimes being preserved in the *sutratman*. For human beings, the cycle of incarnation involves a continual disintegration of everything below the fourth plane, and a continual recording of everything in the living *akasha* and astral light. Light itself, as vibration, is life.

Once this is understood, it is clear that there can be no flight from the universe or escape from the past. No agency of vicarious atonement can rewrite the record for any being. One's response to this realization is itself a decisive step in consciousness with immense karmic consequences. To some the very idea may seem sinister. This is the result of an absurd adolescent escapism that has been reinforced by self-appointed external authorities using false dogmas to trade in human weakness. This is not only unscientific and arbitrary, but also dangerous. It is characteristic of all systems which are unphilosophical but employ religious and occasionally pseudo-scientific language, including behaviourism. Anything and everything which tends to erode the sense of ethical responsibility is false. Anything which addresses human beings in terms of their enormous responsibility for all that they have emanated and initiated is true. Yet this still provides only one, though basic, criterion – responsibility and irresponsibility. We need a more complex conception offering an account of the degrees and interactions of responsibilities. Without it, one's conception of individuality will remain truncated, while one's concern with karma will be perverted into an interest in salvation and damnation.

To understand the operation of karma and memory across lifetimes, it will help to consider situations where there is a loss of memory within a single lifetime, and the nature of the opportunities afforded by the recovery of memory. For example,

> There are cases on record of long months and years of insanity, of long days of fever when almost everything done or said, was done and said unconsciously. Yet when the patients recovered they remembered occasionally their words and deeds and very fully. Unconscious cerebration is a phenomenon on this plane and may hold good so far as the personal mind is concerned.

> *Lucifer,* October 1891
> H.P. Blavatsky

Such an abrupt break in personal memory can be prompted by fever, the influence of drugs, psychic spells, madness, infatuation, terror and fear. Similar though less serious lesions in memory occur through impulsive talk, automatic action or daydreaming, through intensity of emotion or confusion of thought. All of these processes involve the spiritual nerve-currents of the subtlest vesture, which affect in turn the intellectual nerve-currents of the mind-vesture, and, ultimately, the astral nerves and the physiological form. All of the vestures resonate and respond to each other ceaselessly, whether one notices it or not. Thus, in comparison with the self-consciousness of an Adept, human beings are behaving thoughtlessly, unself-consciously or semi-consciously most of the time. When they suddenly recall what they have been doing after a spell of oblivion, they are often terrified – terrified of death, of confronting themselves or any honest human being. To meet integrity is to be reminded that one must pay up.

Perhaps, however, one will not be terrified and wish to run away when confronted with the nature of one's past actions. In proportion to one's commitment to the pursuit of integrity before the traumatic episode, one will be relieved to remember what one actually did. Though shamed and shocked to discover one's actions, one can refine moral sensitivity through a chastening experience. Instead of fleeing from memory, one will gladly receive the help needed to prevent recurrences in the future. Like Immanuel Kant, who said that he was grateful to be awakened from the nonage of his dogmatic slumbers, individuals seeking participation in the humanity of the future will make every effort to overcome the unconscious cerebration of the personal mind. This unconscious cerebration – so boring, so inconvenient and so pervasive – is entirely at odds with the quickening of the Race-mind that is taking place in the present cycle. Beings will either become automata or more wide awake, morally and spiritually. The only effective contribution individuals can make to the future is through bringing ethical awareness to the centre of one's consciousness, making it the basis of every act and every attitude. If one fails to do this, one's awareness will become frenetic and manic, and certainly not honourable. Self-respect is only possible through the acquisition of moral self-consciousness, for that is the only basis of the fearlessness required to face alternatives. Only when this is possible can one look at one's accounts and have the courage to change the line of action and thus to rectify them.

Yet if all of this is only applied to the personal mind and to personal memory and consciousness, it will only yield an ego-centered sense of ethics and moral awareness. In becoming concerned with one's motives and moral life, one should not just become more preoccupied with oneself. Meta-psychologically, holding oneself up as a victim of the world is little different from holding oneself up as entirely responsible for the whole world. If one forgets that other people are moral agents, and sees them only as puppets upon the stage of one's moral life, one becomes outwardly permissive, yet inwardly self-righteous. In a position of responsibility, yesterday's libertine becomes today's tyrant. Whilst powerless, the crypto-power maniac is content to play the role of the victim, acting out martyrdom whilst wallowing in judgementalism. But it is rapidly becoming impossible to live unless one truly loves other human beings and lives for them. Unless one can learn to live for children, one cannot live for the future. Nor is this merely a matter of words or exhilarated emotions. It is a function of one's capacity to hold a transcendental vibration in one's consciousness, thereby giving life to what is real and turning away from what is dying with no fear, but with calm compassion. Only thus can the subjective matrix of personal self-reference be dissolved from above below.

Collective humanity is presently undergoing a crisis that is both painful and fortunate. During this psychological Vietnamization of the world, there is no escape. There are corpses, shells, wounded and deformed beings everywhere in the astral light. They may seem to be other people, but they all affect elements in oneself which are distorted and deformed. This is not actually new; a noble seer like H.P. Blavatsky spoke in the nineteenth century of modern civilization being a necropolis. The *Rishi* sees astral forms and auras not in some psychic way but calmly and consistently, everywhere and all the time. Without the slightest disturbance to his or her state of consciousness, everything is known and nothing is hidden. Naturally, the eyes of a seer are eyes of deep wisdom and immense compassion for humanity. And when the seer speaks, it is through *The Voice of the Silence.*

> Behold the Hosts of Souls. Watch how they hover o'er the stormy sea of human life, and how, exhausted, bleeding, broken-winged, they drop one after other on the swelling waves. Tossed by the fierce winds, chased by the gale, they drift into the eddies and disappear within the first great vortex.

The Voice of the Silence

This vision of the spiritual travail of humanity, caught in the darkness of loneliness and despair, of spiritual failure and desperation, is overwhelming. It cannot be either understood or assimilated by personal consciousness, but requires a universal vision of karma and human experience. Authentic impersonality in consciousness must be restored, whether through contemplation of the vastitude of starry nature, through adoration of heroic figures and scenes in distant epochs or through meditation upon universal ideas. To connect oneself to the fathomless resources of the akashic light, one will need a conception of the karmic recording process which goes beyond any analogy to the individual brain or a computer. Instead, one must conceive of every atom in every blade of grass as intimately and eternally involved with every other sentient atom throughout the whole cosmos. This is difficult to conceive of because of the immense thoughtlessness, callousness and insensitivity of much human interaction. Caught up in their self-conceptions, individuals imagine that they are isolated in consciousness from each other, or if they take interaction seriously, they tend to blame each other for the disturbances they experience. To counter this narrow view, one might re-read some of the great plays of Shakespeare: in the great duet between the frightened apprentice Macbeth and the more accomplished black magician, Lady Macbeth, who nonetheless goes mad in terror at the end, we see the agitation of nature consonant with human beings. Not only is there a resonant response to every human emotion on the sounding-board of nature, but one may even, if perceptive, discern in these responses of nature the archetypal processes that envelop the human individual in birth and in death.

Kama loka and *devachan* are objective resonances of human consciousness; as permanent possibilities in nature they are present everywhere and always. If, with all their implications regarding soul-memory and the cycle of reincarnation, they are not perceived continuously, it is because human beings are so isolated in their personal awareness and bodily identification that they are blind to the causal matrices they are continually elaborating Without overcoming this obscuration of consciousness it is not possible to consult the book of memory and the book of judgement at the dawn and twilight of incarnation in a constructive manner. During life, individual karma and memory must be inserted into the vast living fabric of visible and invisible nature, which is conscious and responsive at every point, having nothing to do with any mechanistic conceptions of the recording of information.

Personal memory is a fiction of the physiologist. There are cells in our brain that receive and convey sensations and impressions, but this once done, their mission is accomplished. These cells of the supposed "organ of memory" are the receivers and conveyors of all the pictures and impressions of the past, not their retainers. Under various conditions and stimuli, they can receive instantaneously the reflection of these astral images back again, and this is called memory, recollection, remembrance; but they do not preserve them.... But the Universal Memory preserves every motion, the slightest wave and feeling that ripples the waves of differentiated nature, of man or of the Universe.

Ibid.

Once one understands that in universal memory everything is not only recorded but felt, one can no longer hold to a separative concept of ethics. Instead, one will turn to the perspective of the poets, the seers, the Great Compassionaters who have always taught that every thought affects every plant and every star. Whilst caught up in a separative conception of ethics, one may hold oneself responsible for hurting another person, but not necessarily every leaf and plant on earth. Yet, when human beings generate maleficent vibrations, every element in nature is wounded. Innumerable ripples reach out throughout all differentiated nature, and they are all preserved in the universal memory, not merely as information about individual lives, but as part of the constitutive basis for living beings in general. When this observation is coupled with a consideration of the problem of unconscious cerebration, at the level of the personal mind, the entire nature of the quest for continuity of consciousness is transformed. Instead of simply insisting to oneself that one should be more responsible or more effective, that one should learn from past failures so as to acquire virtue in an egocentric sense, such personal conceptions are supplanted by a sensitivity to universal responsibility, universal causation and the operation of karmic law within the framework of universal unity.

The Wheel of the Good Law revolves for all at all times. If individuals are not aware of everything that is emanating out of them and creating effects throughout the whole of nature, this is because they are indulging in their own vibrations in a self-protective or egotistic manner. Whether positive or negative, one's feelings nonetheless affect the overall vibratory field of life in which all living beings live, move and have their being. Unlike mechanical means of recording, which make a frozen image of the motion that produced them, the karmic preservation of vibrations preserves the actual motion itself. Because karma works regardless of whether one knows about it or not, everything produces irreversible consequences that return upon oneself quite independently of whether one remembers producing the causes or not. Since one is ceaselessly interacting with everything else and constantly sending out and receiving back karmic vibrations, human life on the objective plane is perilous. Depending upon one's past thoughts, feelings and actions, the universe can be a hazardous place. To conceive of all this in terms of a limited and egotistical notion of security, particularly on the outer physical plane, is simply to reflect an ignorant fear of karma grounded in lack of self-consciousness. Measures of self-protection, locking oneself behind doors, are only hopeless and delusive stunts. Because of the integrity of karma and the universal memory, there is no place to hide from the consequences of one's actions.

These fearful and self-righteous responses to the lessons of karma are bound up with the standpoint of a finite differentiated self-limiting personal consciousness. If one could become capable of burning out the sense of separateness of personal identity, and become attuned to universal life and feeling, universal thought and consciousness, with universal memory which receives all action, one could become karmaless. Such is the paradox of karma and memory. *The more limited one's self-reference, the more one feels karma and the more one fears it. The more universal one's sense of self the more one becomes all karma and even karmaless.* To resonate to the universal naturally implies that whenever there is a quiver of pain anywhere in the world, which is constantly witnessing birth and death, that pain is going to be felt. The pain of every being is relevant to the universal memory, and in meditation the greater height and breadth of one's perspective is going to draw one into contact with all this pain. It is not possible to draw the tremendous range of manifestation self-consciously into awareness without at the same time experiencing all karma, without learning to respond compassionately to every sigh of everything that lives and breathes. At the same time, one becomes karmaless because the conception of a personal karma associated with the limited self no longer has any meaning. One is no longer subject to personal reaction in terms of likes and dislikes, but instead lets go of everything personal and lives only in the universal. Therefore, there are no residues to sustain the matrix of personal self-identity.

To become karmaless is to become an Adept, fulfilling every single responsibility completely whilst having no debt to discharge. At any given time, becoming aware of something undone, of something not returned, one is able to amend and redress the balance. Desiring nothing for oneself, the plenitude and bounty of boundless being may be given away to others. Unconcerned about the accrual of merit, one is free from the insidious separateness of moral self-satisfaction and complacency connected with the idea of being virtuous. All of this is burnt out, and one needs no thanks from others, oneself or the universe itself. Instead, one creates spontaneous rhythms of breathing which keep one moving with full attention from one duty to the next without residues and with no inherence in the *linga shariram.* This is what it means to reduce the lunar form to a zero at will, to attenuate the coil in the spleen, reducing it to ashes and leaving only the seed for the makers of your vesture.

All of this is far removed from the sort of egotistical self-absorption that many people believe is equivalent to spiritual life. Many people recognize at some level that they are going in the opposite direction, but they do not know what to do about it. Instead of moving in the direction of serene joyous self-transcendence combined with courageous acceptance of karma and human pain, they are becoming more and more preoccupied with success and failure. They re-enact everything to do with personal likes and dislikes but do so on a more subtle plane bound up with individuality. They walk backwards. No one, at this point in evolution, is doing this for the first time. If people are in this position, it is because they have been there before in other lives. Possessing knowledge, they made mistakes, but they do not now remember what they did because their consciousness is obscured by the consolidated ego. This creates a hardening of the apertures of the soul, as if a stone were blocking the free flow of energies from above the head down through the spine to the toes. As a consequence, their consciousness and their memory are bound in a sphere of small radius. The only way to cut these bonds is to determine to learn from all karma, and then to treat everyone as a teacher.

Every experience of pain should be taken as an opportunity for learning. A preoccupation with salvation should be converted into a dedication to the endless process of learning. This cannot be done with a frenetic violence that only reinstantiates egotism. Instead, it is better to sit back sometimes and reflect upon what has happened. When it does not interfere with evident duties, it is good to take time to ask oneself, "Which way am I going? What kind of person am I becoming? Why did this happen? Why did I do these things? Why didn't I have more control over my speech? Why do I have such egotistic reactions and such hostility towards innocent people? What do I ultimately value and what do I ultimately want to become? Who am I?" This self-questioning should not be undertaken in a self-accusatory mood, but rather with a meta-psychological calmness rooted in the contemplation of metaphysical ideas. It aims to get to root causes through *dianoia* and to prepare the questioner for authentic learning.

As all consciousness on every sub-plane of the seven planes of the universe derives from the *Atman,* even if one's efforts to learn originate on the plane of personal existence, they invoke a sacred and universal vibration. The earnest desire to learn inevitably strengthens the *antaskarana* bridge. It is not possible to become altruistic overnight and very few can master karma, but all can become true learners and experience the joy of continuous learning. The more one learns, the humbler one will be in coming to judgements about other human beings or in issuing indictments of nations, races and institutions. Whilst sensing a great deal that is wrong, one will be moved to find out where one can do those little things that add up to something that is clean and right. One will become more of an observer and learner, suddenly finding the world to be a vast and generous school. Then one will become more attentive to the invisible layers of this cosmic university, noticing its invisible classrooms with invisible textbooks and invisible beings involved in teaching and learning. One will notice that people cannot say what is keeping them alive, because they do not remember when awake what they experienced in deep sleep. One will realize that it is impossible to understand, and therefore to judge any human being from the outside. Only when one learns to look upon others with love and compassion rooted in a sense of the mystery of the Ego is it possible to learn from all.

What applies to others applies to oneself. While becoming humble towards other beings, one can become fearless in one's own quest for the truth, rejecting all evasions and excuses. As one becomes rooted in a life dedicated to learning, one's whole conception of memory and of what it is important to remember will change. When the primary concern is to do justice, there can be no fear to remember anything, but at the same time there will be no tendency to indulge in a great deal of memory which is useless. Above all, it will be important to keep green and fresh the memory of the moment of spiritual birth, the moment of spiritual awakening and initiation at the most minor level. Pride in one's soul-memory is not a matter of detail and information, but rather of a vibratory current of consciousness. Whether this is put in terms of the posture of the *shravaka*, the *lanoo* disciple, the devotee and searcher after truth, or the pilgrim-soul, self-conscious fidelity to this vibration is crucial to soul-memory. By maintaining this vibration intact, it is possible to begin to shift the emphasis in the fields of one's karma.

These fields are not related to each other like the rooms of a house, but rather as the butter, the milk and the water before the churning. They are the interwoven resonances of the one primal vibration of the invisible Word, and the science of karma is the discovery of their hidden correspondences in oneself and throughout the visible and invisible cosmos.

As soon as one constitutes oneself an apprentice to this science, even in the most probationary way, one naturally becomes a silent adorer of the mighty peaks in human evolution, beings of boundless love and compassion, who are not sitting somewhere else, and who are not merely appearing at certain times as Teachers, but who are always present and working in subtle ways. Suddenly one becomes aware that there is a great deal hidden which one did not fully understand, and that at various moments in one's life one has been spoken to by human beings overbrooded by their *Dhyanis*. To have received such profound help from any other human being and to realize the meaning of the event is at once to begin to revere the ceaseless relevance of karmaless beings in a world of painful learning, of extremely slow but real progress, where, by modest increments, humanity moves in ways that are authentic, unseen and unmanifest.

Through strengthening thought, memory and choice, one will become relaxed in reference to likes and dislikes, but in extreme earnest in relation to truth. That is why one enjoys the privilege of human existence. Like Ivan in Dostoevsky's *The Brothers Karamazov*, one will seek to know the meaning of life and the cause of the persistence of pain and sorrow. By inserting the purpose of one's life and the sweet aroma of one's spiritual striving into the universal stream of spiritual evolution, one may earn in time the privilege of coming into the presence of the *Guru*. Having established within oneself a firm standpoint of authentic human responsibility, one will be ready to commence the study of universal compassionate action.

Hermes, May 1983
Raghavan Iyer

SPECTATOR AND PARTICIPANT

. . . those who 'ascend and descend' are the 'Hosts' of what we loosely call 'celestial Beings.' But they are, in fact, nothing of the kind. They are Entities of the higher worlds in the hierarchy of Being, so immeasurably high that, to us, they must appear as Gods, and collectively – GOD.... there may be a certain limited communication between some of those worlds and our own. To the highest, we are taught, belong the seven orders of the purely divine Spirits; to the six lower ones belong hierarchies that can occasionally be seen and heard by men, and who do communicate with their progeny of the Earth; which progeny is indissolubly linked with them, each principle in man having its direct source in the nature of those great Beings, who furnish us with the respective invisible elements in us.

The Secret Doctrine, i 132-133
H.P. Blavatsky

In the mystical language of *The Voice of the Silence,* every human being is both agent and witness, both radiator and radiation. As an immortal *Atma-Buddhi* Monad, each human being is a spectator in eternal Duration. As a ray of the ever Unmanifest, each Monad can see what all other Monads can see, through the eyes of the highest *Anupadaka,* the *Mahatmas* and silent watchers during the night of *pralaya.* Each human being can witness the deaths of civilizations, of beings, even of his own body, just as *Mahatmas* observe the deaths of worlds, galaxies and all that is at *Maha Pralaya.* Every human being is also a participant, a *Manasa,* a pristine ray capable of pure self-conscious awareness and creative thought, authentic individuation as an 'I am I' consciousness. This active individuality, the *sutratman* that threads the soul's incarnations like jewelled beads upon a string, affords endless opportunities for learning and service. At the same time, each human being is also a spectator and participant in a more immediate spatial and temporal sense.

As a projected ray of *Manas* caught up in *kama* and involved with the astral plane, each human being is also a cerebrating animal ensnared in expectations and excuses, rationalizations and regrets, fantasies and frustrations. On the planes of the lower quaternary, every human being is immersed in vast fields of elementals and *devas,* all the hosts of secondary forces that are under the control of the four *Maharajas* spoken of in Hindu mythology. These Regents of the four cardinal points of the compass are the channels through which *karma* is transmitted magnetically, forming and affecting the organs of perception and action of the incarnated human being.

Given the archetypal logic of the involution of spirit into form, it is truly vital that the boundless potential of the Monad must be awakened through the trials of incarnation on the lower planes. The depth and complexity of the lessons to be learnt ensure that each human being will pass many lives of apprenticeship before realizing the ideals of universality in consciousness and freedom from *karma.* The inherent integrity of the Monad and its consubstantiality with cosmic truth guarantee that it will not rest content until it has wrought this task through to the end, however long it takes. Owing to the integrity of the innumerable intelligences constituting the planes of the lower quaternary, which are themselves ultimately derived from the same Monadic plane of existence as humanity, and which constitute the incipient human kingdoms of future evolution, every self-conscious abuse or misuse of human capacities is exactly mirrored in the lower human vestures. If incarnated human beings find themselves passive and drowsy participants, dim-sighted and dull-witted observers, caught in a seemingly chaotic and confusing world, that is the result of their own past self-neglect. The forces of *tamas* and *rajas* predominate in the *linga sharira* and its vital energy, rendering the temple of the physical form mostly unused and even useless.

The emphasis in incarnated consciousness is almost entirely upon the lower centres. Because the spleen, the liver and the stomach are over-active, most people are caught up to the point of emotional exhaustion. This condition reacts upon the solar plexus, creating a congestion that interferes with both physical and mental digestion, assimilation and elimination. In effect, human beings have handed over their instruments to myriads of entities that execute a kind of a devil dance through a human body. Very few human beings are noetically involved in the processes that ordinarily pass for eating, sleeping, bathing, speaking or making love. A pathetically large proportion of what passes for human life is simply a shadow-play of elementals resulting from human resignation of responsibility. Yet, people are deceived into supposing that they are engaged in meaningful human activity because they have manufactured particular elementals drawn around the *namarupa*, the name and form, which mimic authentic action.

If, through suffering and solicitude for others, one begins to gain a sense of the magnitude of this dismal delusion, it is natural to want to restore dignity to one's own life through a search for knowledge and for the means of making a genuine contribution to the lives of others. Having thus raised one's sights, one may be prepared to read the *Stanzas of Dzyan* and resonate to the ancient accent and self-validating summons of *Gupta Vidya.*

> LEARN WHAT WE, WHO DESCEND FROM THE PRIMORDIAL SEVEN, WE, WHO ARE BORN FROM THE PRIMORDIAL FLAME, HAVE LEARNED FROM OUR FATHERS.

Ibid., i 88

Here speaks the voice of the primordial Mysteries, the voice of all the self-shining Initiates who speak by thinking and think by ideating. Arrayed around a common ineffable centre, like the *Buddhas* and *Bodhisattvas* in Tibetan *tankas,* they are ceaselessly engaged in fathomless meditation. Through their adoration and compassion they continually point to Amitabha, to Avalokiteshwara, the one Source and the primordial Flame. This is the divine *Tetraktys*, the sacred four, the eternal self-existent One called the concealed Lord and also known as the androgyne Father-Mother, the direct emanation from the primordial Flame. From this emanate the primordial seven, the highest *Ah-Hi*, the divine breaths; from those emanate the *Manasaputras* as well as the builders of form. The primordial seven, the highest beings on the scale of existence, latent during *pralaya* and active during *manvantara*, constitute the ray of the *Tetraktys*, which is eternal in essence and periodic in manifestation.

The same Teaching is given in terms of the seven *Kumaras*, the eldest mind-born sons of Brahmâ sprung from the fourfold mystery. Brahmâ is *Hiranyagarbha,* the resplendent Spiritual Sun, the effulgent golden egg which is like the aura of the entire cosmos.

> In the *Rig Veda* it is said: 'THAT, the one Lord of all beings...the one animating principle of gods and man,' arose, in the beginning, in the Golden Womb, *Hiranyagarbha* – which is the Mundane Egg or sphere of our Universe.

Ibid., I 89

From that One and the egg, the inseparable and androgyne *Hiranyagarbha-Prajapati,* emanate the Three-in-One, the *Tetraktys* or sacred Four. The original triune rays in the *Tetraktys* are the primeval Vedic *Trimurti* of Agni, Vayu and Surya – spiritual fire, spiritual air and spiritual sun. From these emanate the other seven. Together they constitute either the seven or the ten, depending upon how one counts the original Three-in-One. However reckoned, one must not emphasize any separation between Agni, Vayu and Surya or between these three and the primordial seven, the *Ah-Hi.*

It is best to think of them as one while meditating at dawn, at sunset, at midday and midnight. Whether one employs a sacred *mantram* or invocation to draw one's entire attention to the great Mystery, or whether one has the idea of it so impacted in the consciousness that it may be linked to anything before the mind's eye, this is the path of those who are serious about living a life of constant gratitude. Once a taste for it is developed, it is pure bliss. It is better to spend time in gratitude than in brooding over the shadow. At the highest level of maintaining a current of ideation, where one becomes a true man of meditation in silence, the One, the egg, the Three-in-One, the seven and the ten are all comprehended within the supreme *Paramatman,* called *guhya* or secret. Even in thinking of it one must exercise reticence, never thinking about it carelessly or mechanically. It must be assimilated, enjoyed and allowed to cohere in secret.

This indivisible unity of *Sarvatma,* the Supreme Soul, has been portrayed in many mystic images – such as that of Vishnu seated upon Adishesha amidst the great ocean of space with Brahmâ springing forth from his navel. The symbol of the Spiritual Sun riding a chariot drawn by seven steeds has the same meaning. Hence it is said: "*The seven Lords of Being lie concealed in* Sarvatma *like thoughts in one brain.*" This is the basis of the highest meditation and the highest magic, giving strength to the continuous maintenance of one's consciousness as a monadic spectator. Constant adoration of the *Ah-Hi,* the Seven-in-One, the *Trimurti* of Agni, Vayu and Surya, is the inherent and essential activity of the Monad. Owing to its constant adoration of the primordial One, the primordial Three, the primordial Seven, the Monad is able to maintain ceaseless awareness in eternal Duration. Hence, it can understand Krishna speaking in his highest aspect when he states: "*I established this whole universe with a single portion of myself, and remain separate.*" This is Krishna as Narayana, the first *Logos.* He is also *Ishwara,* the second *Logos* and the *Avatar.* He is all these simultaneously, and, as he reveals to Arjuna, he is the Supreme Self – *Sarvatman* – dwelling in secret within every human heart.

The fundamental question facing human beings as obligatory participants in incarnated life is how to sustain this mystical awareness. Owing to the very nature of the vestures of incarnation, one will have to cope with multiples, with matter and with sense-experience. Differentiated, fragmented patterns of thought will arise in the lower mind as the sense-organs prompt comparisons and contrasts. To reaffirm the One in the many and to benefit, as a participant, from the standpoint of the spectator, one may, therefore, meditate upon the Soundless Sound of *Nada Brahman* in its unmanifest essence and in its multiple differentiations as the Army of the Voice. One may meditate upon the OM as the ceaseless eternal sound and also as the great affirmation of the Army of the Voice symbolized by *Oeaohoo.*

> The 'Army of the Voice,' is the prototype of the 'Host of the Logos,' or the 'WORD' of the Sepher Jezirah, called in the Secret Doctrine 'the One Number issued from No-Number' – the One Eternal Principle.

> *Ibid.,* i 94

Here, in the arcane code language of *Gupta Vidya,* fully accessible only to hierophants but amenable to contemplation by any earnest seeker at any level, is a clue to the relationship of sound and number. From zero comes one; that one, when taken together with the zero, makes ten. These are the one from the egg, which are followed by the six and the five, yielding 1065, the value of the first-born who answers to the numbers 7, 14 and 21. This particular sequence of numbers, connected with *Hiranyagarbha,* Brahmâ and *Vach,* intimates the archetypal logic of the pre-cosmic and the logic of the cosmic.

> The esoteric theogony begins with the One, manifested, therefore not eternal in its presence and being, if eternal in its essence; the number of the numbers and numbered – the latter proceeding from the Voice, the feminine *Vach,* Satarupa 'of the hundred forms,' or Nature. It is from this number 10, or creative nature, the Mother (the occult cypher, or 'nought,' ever procreating and multiplying in union with the Unit '1,' one, or the spirit of Life), that the whole Universe proceeded.

> *Ibid.,* i 94

Guided by *Vach,* Sarasvati, Isis, the Army of the Voice is ceaselessly at work as the conscious intelligent host in invisible mystic nature.

Acting with mathematical precision through the fiery force of the *Fohatic* whirlwind, *Vach* establishes the Army of the Voice in abstract space reflecting divine Thought. First, the germs of wheels are established in the six directions of space, which represent the junction of pure spirit and matter, the *arupa* and the *rupa*, symbolized by the interlaced triangles or Vishnu's *chakra*. At each angle stands an army of the Sons of Light, whilst the Lipika, the recorders of *karma*, stand in the middle. The Dhyanic hosts at the angles are mystic watchers, appointed to watch over each respective region from the beginning to the end of the *manvantara*. This is the Divine World, called the 'first' because the manifestation which precedes it, the world of SAT, is the realm of noumena in their primary manifestation. Coeval and coexistent with the One Life, and with that through which the direct energy radiating from the One Reality reaches all beings,

> this 'World of Truth' can be described only in the words of the Commentary as 'A bright star dropped from the heart of Eternity; the beacon of hope on whose Seven Rays hang the Seven Worlds of Being.' Truly so; since those are the Seven Lights whose reflections are the human immortal Monads – the Atma, or the irradiating Spirit of every creature of the human family.

Ibid., i 120

From this septenary light proceeds the Divine World, the countless candles lit at the primeval source, the *Buddhas* or formless divine Souls of the last *arupa* world, the world of the Lipikas and their mystic watchers. *Fohat* as divine love seeks to unite the pure Spirit, the ray inseparable from the one Absolute, with the divine Soul, the two constituting in man the Monad, and in Nature the first link between the ever-unconditioned and the manifested. Next in the series of developments concerning the cosmic and human principles comes the building of a set of four winged wheels at the corners of a great square. At each of the four cardinal points stands a Regent, one of the four Maharajas, and his host. These guardians of the world are the *Lokapalas*, including Indra in the east, Yama in the south, Varuna in the west, and Kubera in the north. By analogy and correspondence, what applies to the entire cosmos may also be applied to this tiny globe that we call the earth. Even though it is but a speck of dust in the vast sidereal cosmos, there is that on earth which corresponds to the four Regents and their hosts at the four cardinal points of the compass.

Each of the four Regents who rule over the cosmical forces of the four directions and the four primitive elements leads a host of spiritual beings, acting as the protectors of mankind throughout its evolution. Whenever human beings make pilgrimages to the icy northern lands of the midnight sun, whenever they greet the sun rising in the east, or turn with reverence to any direction of the compass, they may salute the spiritual heritage of humanity, and invoke the protection of its guardians, guides and mystic watchers. Anyone who even remotely begins to apprehend this will readily appreciate that the universe, the earth and humanity are fully protected. Human anxiety, individually or collectively, does not reflect any chaotic uncertainty in the cosmos, but only a fear of not being able to acquire a suitable vesture and environment in the future.

If one recognizes that the universe is fully protected through the Army of the Voice, then the question becomes simple: Is one on the side of the universe, or is one, owing to an inability to control breathing and thought, a slavish fascination with foolish opinions, against life? It is better to train in silence to become a silent servant, attentive to the inner voice. One may not hear the voice until the moment of death, the time of which is uncertain, but not distant in any event. If one earnestly listens to the voice in waking, in meditation and in sleep, one will certainly receive intimations. One will learn how to become a silent server of the human race. As each human being has set in motion certain causes through the potency of thought, magnetically awakening and attracting the reaction of the corresponding powers in the sidereal world, the destiny of each human being is connected with one or other of the constellations and their presiding planetary spirits, the *Lokapalas* of the four cardinal and four intermediate points of the compass. These beings rule the forces that direct the physical and material agents required to carry out the decrees of *karma*. Through them and through the *Lipika*, the recorders of *karma*, the destiny of every human being is intimately interwoven with the hosts of the Army of the Voice.

To see oneself as a part of mankind acting under the benevolent protection and karmic discipline of the Army of the Voice is to bid goodbye to identification with one's compulsive, competitive, raucous animal nature. It means becoming a true human being, with a deep inner strength and an enormous willingness to learn, to heighten retention and wakefulness, and to develop a continual reverence for the human race and its invisible guardians. In practice, this means withdrawing attention from external relations, and focussing upon that which is on top of the head of every human being. By seeing oneself and others only as the light that is above the head, one may learn how to move from morn to night, acting towards other human beings with dignity and silence.

Through a growing awareness of one's assured place amidst the Army of the Voice, one may gain a stronger, sharper and more refined sense of *Dharma.* At the same time, one will bring a sweeter gentleness and subtle fragrance to the performance of duty, nurtured in meditation and harvested through sacrificial action. One's tone of voice will improve, attaining a clarity and a kindness that does not hurt or exclude others. But this venture requires a constant, patient redefinition of oneself. Each day and every week one should refine one's tone of voice, one's attitude towards duty, and one's actions towards one's fellowmen. If one has been the source of pollution through fascination with shadows, then one should restore a higher awareness, physically and mentally. One should ask how, through self-correction, one can improve the sphere of duty in the coming days and weeks. This should not be done neurotically out of self-concern, but noetically out of concern for others, through meditation and through invocations that draw one closer to the Voice.

As one grows in this discipline, it will begin to have an irresistible effect upon one's faculties of perception and action. Through one's purified thought one will begin to resonate to the currents of magnetic force on the invisible planes presided over by the four Regents. Were it not for the ceaseless activity of these cosmic agencies, it would not be possible to lend intelligence to sight. The human eye is extremely mysterious. It contains a minute pin-point of eternal light-substance – *suddhasattva* – the substance of the *Dhyani Buddhas* and of *Ishwara*. This pin-point of light in the centre of the eye is the gift of the divine Fathers of the human race, the Light-Bringers who illuminated the minds of human beings over eighteen million years ago. One must treat the eyes as sacred, taking care over their spiritual cleansing. One must look intelligently and benevolently, as an immortal soul gazing upon other immortal souls. One does not want the wandering eye, the fixated eye or the day-dreamy eye. Instead, while using both eyes, one should try to think of the Third Eye, the invisible eye of compassion, negation and transcendence. Great souls sometimes choose to take incarnation as blind persons so that they can avoid the distractions of sight. The physical eyes must be used with scrupulous care. Likewise, one must use the ears to become a good listener, catching not only what is on the physical plane but also the inaudible sounds of nature. Through the sounds of the ocean, the forests and even noisy cities, one may train the ear, tuning in to the resonances of the Soundless Sound.

> It is through the four high Rulers over the four points and Elements that our five senses may become cognisant of the hidden truths of Nature.

Ibid., i 125

Through the refinement of the senses, one may come to see to the root of the four elements. As one does so, one will become aware of magnetic currents that pass out of oneself and come into oneself whenever one uses the senses. As a constant transmitter of magnetism, one will be concerned with beneficent motives and with sending out strong, healthy vibrations. One will also want to guard against perceiving that which one cannot handle. This is the message of the statue of the three monkeys – see no evil, hear no evil, speak no evil. They are a reminder not to see, to hear or to speak unnecessarily. By taking up this discipline and without having to enter a monastery, one will begin to move in line with Nature's harmony and rhythms. One will participate cooperatively with the twenty-eight-day lunar cycle, the seven-day cycle of the week, the thirty-odd days of the solar month, the seasons of the year, and so on. As a participant in Nature, through mastery of the vestures, one will learn to retain and extend one's awareness of the invisible and universal ground of Nature and man, benefiting and being benefited by the ordered numerical sets of the hosts of the Army of the Voice.

Through expanding and deepening one's awareness and participation in the invisible universe, one will gradually reduce fascination with the shadow. The enemy is not fascinating, but only a pathetic knot of muddled thinking. On the physical plane, neglect of exercise may cause a congestion in the spine, a kind of stiffening of the nerves, which results in backaches and a loss of physical mobility. This is part of ageing and may be met with proper measures. But those suffering from mental arthritis or cerebral congestion experience psychological pain and a lack of mobility that prevents them from doing their duty. They need to heed the advice of *The Voice of the Silence:* "*Mind is like a mirror; it gathers dust while it reflects. It needs the gentle breezes of soul-wisdom to brush away the dust of our illusions.*"

If the mind is tied up in self-made knots, it is because of terrible illusions as a child, perhaps becoming a *chela* of Hollywood, addicted to day-dreaming. The best thing is to see these for what they are, while showing compassion for those enslaved by them. Perhaps one was averse to homework or mathematics or afraid of having to look after oneself without one's parents. In addition to developing such barriers to true self-dependence, one may have deemed oneself a 'sensitive' person, when in truth one was weak-willed and afraid. Human beings learn to play these games over a number of lives. In themselves they are uninteresting, but they indicate an unwillingness to be quiet and to take one's place in the human family. They represent diseases of the soul and the mind, as well as of the astral form. There is some one thing about oneself that must be faced; until that is faced, the knot will not unravel. This itself must not, however, be turned into a protracted drama out of pride. The knot will never be loosened by brooding on the shadow.

The oldest and wisest course is to begin to practise altruism. Try to live for others. Try to see beyond the self, by forgetting the self. Everyone is entitled to look earnestly at the sky under which all human beings live and to look lovingly at the earth upon which all human beings walk. Everyone is entitled to think with gratitude of the elements, which offer help from all directions and all departments of Nature. But one must first practise self-forgetfulness, dutifulness and detachment. Through taking an intense interest in humanity and in the possibilities of the human condition, one may develop a deep love for the spiritual family into which one has entered. Seeing this as one's own true family, linked up to the mighty Brotherhood of *Bodhisattvas*, one may let go of the tension of self-concern. Then at the right time, through help in dreamless sleep and in daily meditation, the truly devoted and totally faithful will come to see the knot for what it is and it will loosen up. There is no point in worrying about these things, because that is how the knot was formed in the first place. Anxiety contracts, benevolence expands. Following the *ABCs*, one should move from anxiety to benevolence, and then to contentment. Then one may return to *A*, recognizing that it does not stand for anxiety but rather for the *Atman*, the Absolute and the *Ah-Hi*; that *B* stands for the Brotherhood, for the Builders and for the Great Breath. When one learns to see life with childlike simplicity, one can begin to get ready to receive the ancient Catechism:

"Lift thy head, oh Lanoo; dost thou see one, or countless lights above thee, burning in the dark midnight sky?"

"I sense one Flame, oh Gurudeva, I see countless undetached sparks shining in it."

"Thou sayest well. And now look around and into thyself. That light which burns inside thee, dost thou feel it different in anywise from the light that shines in thy Brother-men?"

"It is in no way different, though the prisoner is held in bondage by Karma, and though its outer garments delude the ignorant into saying, 'Thy Soul and My Soul'."

Ibid., i 120

Hermes, July 1983
Raghavan Iyer

JIVA AND SELF-GENERATION

THE ONE RAY MULTIPLIES THE SMALLER RAYS. LIFE PRECEDES FORM, AND LIFE SURVIVES THE LAST ATOM (of Form, Sthula-sarira, external body). *THROUGH THE COUNTLESS RAYS THE LIFE-RAY, THE ONE, LIKE A THREAD THROUGH MANY BEADS* (pearls).

The Secret Doctrine, i 222
H.P. Blavatsky

The archaic *Stanzas of Dzyan* present a symbolic statement of the archetypal process of becoming throughout all planes and in all spheres of manifestation. It is none other than that through which the One becomes the many while remaining the One within the many. At the highest level of abstraction, surpassing both subtle and sensory perceptions, as well as all the conceptions of the materializing mind, the one pure Ray of primordial Light out of the absolute Darkness is said to multiply the smaller rays. This is a symbolic representation of the quintessential logic of differentiation, the logic of divine descent and manvantaric manifestation. There is in this fundamental logic a mirroring of the miraculous nature of birth on every plane. Gestation and growth on every plane is rooted in the universal solidarity of all life. That solidarity is much more than a physical fact or a psychic sentiment. It is a moral and metaphysical framework within which takes place all transformation of form and consciousness.

The symbolic code language of *Gupta Vidya* contains the fundamental challenge of Divine Wisdom to modern thought. Through elaboration and ramification, modern thought has created a vast conceptual structure of explanation and thus unravelled many secondary processes of causation. Yet, at the same time, modern thought cannot explain so basic a phenomenon as how a foetus emerges and develops from a single minute cell. Despite all the popular cliches about the extension of life through genetic engineering, the fundamental mystery of the embryo remains.

Similarly, modern thought has little to say about the metaphysical mystery of the One or the psychological mystery of the Ego. In all three, there is the same challenge. The mystery of the One is a challenge of metaphysics and meditation. In meditating, one gathers within oneself all the many rays, archetypally collected into the primary seven and then merged into one central invisible point. Through repeated effort, one can thus experience something of that state of consciousness which is prior to differentiation. This is an experience of the metaphysical Void, but it is different from the experience of deep sleep because one retains full self-consciousness.

The challenge is to imagine what it would be like in the Divine Darkness, where there is no thing and no forms. Then one must imagine that within the germ of divine thought within the Divine Darkness there may arise one ray of ideational energy which contains the potentiality of the entire cosmos. From that one ray one must imagine an entire ordered array of progressive elaborations and manifestations. This is symbolized in the language of the *Kabbalah* by the phrase "thrones, powers and principalities". These refer to all the subtle hosts of invisible Nature. In meditation one must reach beyond all of them to the One. Then one will be able to accommodate all these thrones and powers and principalities, the manifold hierarchies involved in multiplication of the one ray, within the folds of hebdomadic and unitary life. Although this is a challenge to metaphysics, it can only be met through deep meditation.

The mystery of the one Ego was intimated by Plato, who said that the human soul was a compound of the same and the other. This is the mystery of that which is different from, yet consubstantial with, that which it reflects. This mystery poses a profound challenge to one's deepest sense of "I-am-I" consciousness. At the root, "I-am-I" consciousness involves a total negation of all time and form, and of all identification with memories, sensations, expectations and anticipations. It can also abstract from all that exists in the realm of appearances and thus experience pure being, which is indivisible and universal. How, then, is "I-am-I" consciousness different from

Deity itself? That is, one might say, the ultimate mystery of the Sphinx, the riddle that has to be unravelled by each human soul, not in sleep or dreams and not after death, but through intense reflection in waking consciousness. This abstraction of meaning from experience must be achieved through introspection, through identification with other hearts and minds and souls, and also through the intimate knowledge of all the life-atoms that ceaselessly circulate between all beings. The soul must acquire a working acquaintance with the pantheistic conception of Deity in Nature. To solve the problem of the Ego in its entirety is the fundamental challenge of meta-psychology.

Both of these problems – the problem of the One in relation to the many and the problem of the same and the other in relation to the "I-am-I" consciousness – are replicated and reflected within the mystery of the embryo, the foetus and the germinal cell. H.P. Blavatsky posed the challenge to biological thought by asking

> whether it seems unnatural, least of all "supernatural", to any one of us, when we consider that process known as the growth and development of a foetus into a healthy baby weighing several pounds – evolves from what? From the segmentation of an infinitesimally small ovum and a spermatozoon; and afterwards we see that baby develop into a six-foot man!

> *Ibid.*, i 222

The mysteries of embryology are inseparable from those of cosmology. The philosophy of *Gupta Vidya* is fundamentally based upon the ultimate analogy in every process of manifestation between the most cosmic and the most atomic, between the divine and the human. Hence, the *Stanzas of Dzyan*, in depicting the origin of the cosmos, contain innumerable references to *Hiranyagarbha* – the cosmic egg. They speak of the primeval gestation within the waters of space, and explain how the entire spectrum of worlds emerges from a point in the germ to yield manifestation as we know it. These cosmological processes are truly difficult to comprehend, for they raise fundamental questions which cannot be answered merely through some pious reference to the heavens or through intellectual imagery. Unfortunately, this is all that pseudo-religious and pseudo-philosophic traditions have done, and they have therefore failed to answer the challenges of universal cosmogenesis and anthropogenesis. If one grasped the integrity of the universal processes that give rise both to Nature and Man, then one would understand that these questions are no easier to answer than parallel questions about the human body and physical birth. Since Deity, Man and Nature are philosophically inseparable, one cannot comprehend the origin of the cosmos, the origin of humanity or the birth of a single baby independently of each other. One needs to regain a sense of wonder that something so infinitesimally small as an initial germinal cell can give rise to a full-grown human being.

H.P. Blavatsky proceeded to develop and sharpen the mysteries which embryology poses by crediting modern thought with an approximate understanding of

> the atomic and physical expansion from the microscopically small into something very large, from the – to the naked eye – unseen, into the visible and objective. Science has provided for all this; and, I dare say, her theories, embryological, biological, and physiological, are correct enough so far as exact observation of the material goes. Nevertheless, the two chief difficulties of the science of embryology – namely, what are the forces at work in the formation of the foetus, and the cause of "hereditary transmission" of likeness, physical, moral or mental – have never been properly answered; nor will they ever be solved till the day when scientists condescend to accept the Occult theories.

> *Ibid.,* i 222-223

If, in other words, one wishes to give a systematic account of the process of immense expansion that goes on in the development of the foetus, one must have a knowledge of different planes and subplanes of matter, mind and consciousness. One must also develop an account of the interactions of these agencies and forces during the different stages of the development of the foetus, and give a philosophically coherent account of the processes of transmission of likeness, through which active forces promote actual growth. In commenting upon one of the more intuitive developments of nineteenth century biology, H.P. Blavatsky praised Professor Weissmann and his view of the ancestral germ-cell operating on the physical plane. She made a vital distinction between this physical plasm and a spiritual plasm. If one accepts the notion of an ancestral germinal cell which is through its very substance the agent of transmission over an immense period of time, then one must ask at what point man becomes endowed with that cell. Suggesting the metaphysical mystery of *Jiva* or cosmic life-energy, she stated:

> Complete the physical plasm . . . the "Germinal Cell" of man with all its material potentialities, with the "spiritual plasm", so to say, or the fluid that contains the five lower principles of the six-principled Dhyan – and you have the secret, if you are spiritual enough to understand it.

Ibid., i 224

Such fundamental questions cannot be answered on the basis of inductive methods and within the confining categories of modern thought. No experimental science, however systematic and complicated, can penetrate the ontology of the process of becoming. A poet or mystic, using metaphors, can often come much closer to invoking a sense of the mystery of that process, as, for example, when Rupert Brooke wrote, "Dateless and deathless...the intricate impulse works its will." Poetic intuition intimates something intrinsic and inherent to the life process, something that is extremely fertile, extremely complex and intelligent, yet unerringly precise. The vision of mystics and poets touches that which is beginningless and endless in life, that which eludes all categories, formulas and equations.

The substantial and independent nature of the life principle is one of the fundamental tenets of *Gupta Vidya*. Behind all the myriads upon myriads of phenomena of life in form subsists that which is prior, and also posterior, to all forms. The continuity of this life-essence is expressed in the concept of the *sutratman* or life-thread, the essence of which is like a ray originating or penetrating innumerable embodiments. It is also likened to a drop which is an integral part of a vast indivisible ocean of life-energy or *Jiva*. Universal Life at the macrocosmic level must be understood on its own – independent of function, independent of manifestation and independent of form. This marks a fundamental point of divergence between the methods of modern knowledge and the modes of Divine Wisdom. According to arcane science, life alone can understand life. One must experience through meditation what it is to give birth to an idea, to a current of ideation which can then produce a powerful electrical vibration in the *Akasha*. This process of abstraction in the unseen universe stirs up all that is latent and consubstantial with an authentically universal idea, and which can thereby work over immense periods of time through many minds and in many forms.

To comprehend this brings one closer to the magic of *Bodhisattvas* and *Mahatmas*, as well as to the powers of creation, spontaneous generation and gestation that are inherent to Universal Life. Only in this way can one begin to apprehend something of the inexhaustible ocean of life. In order to begin to understand what it means to give birth to an idea, one might meditate upon the architectonic process of evolution from a minute germ into a foetus. To think deeply and profoundly about this would involve thinking about all the stages through which the foetus passes, by analogy with the cosmic process. Then, though one may not immediately approach the mystery of embryology or cosmology, one will begin to experience something of the logic of that process of becoming which the *Stanzas of Dzyan* put in terms of the one Ray multiplying the smaller rays. This is the universal and archetypal mode of the manifestation of life which precedes form and which survives the last atom of form. For the human being, that process must be intuited and experienced within the noetic mind before it can be understood in its reflected forms.

Once one gains some experience of this inward process of life, then one can understand that seemingly familiar reflections of life on the gross physical plane are in fact profoundly mysterious, unfamiliar and wonderful. From an occult standpoint the gestation of the human physical foetus is almost totally misunderstood by contemporary biology. Since, for example, contemporary biology is completely ignorant of the processes of the involution of spirit into matter through successive rounds and globes of the earth chain, its observation that embryogenesis follows the lines of phylogenesis is inaccurate. *Gupta Vidya* is totally at odds with contemporary evolutionism and particularly with Darwinian and neo-Darwinian ideas. It holds that the human species is much older than all the fauna that have gone through so many transformations on the physical earth plane. Whilst agreeing that there is not a single animal today which exists as it did millions of years ago, it nonetheless holds that the human form is indeed identical to the human form that existed long before all the fauna of the mammalian kingdom came into existence. Further, there is that within the human form which is archetypal in a cosmic and divine sense.

It is, not surprisingly, extremely difficult for contemporary human beings to understand the sanctity of the human form or to recognize the body as a divine temple. They are too engrossed in sense-perceptions and too engaged in the desacralization of the human body, which starts with the abuse of sex even before puberty. Yet the body is in truth the most divine phenomenon in the universe. If humanity knew this during the golden age of the Third Root Race, it certainly lost sight of it a long time ago.

Yet the nature and development of the physical human form is inseparable from the inner growth of man. Pointing to the supercilious attitude of contemporary humanity to its own physical embodiment, H.P. Blavatsky remarked:

> If this physical phenomenon astonishes no one, except in so far as it puzzles the Embryologists, why should our intellectual and

inner growth, the evolution of the human-spiritual to the Divine-Spiritual, be regarded as, or seem, more impossible than the other?

Ibid., i 223-224

If a foetus and eventually a human form can develop from a cell, why cannot human beings develop their subtle spiritual vestures in a similar manner? What is the nature of that spiritual germinal cell which can be energized by meditation and which can unfold to the full glory of human perfection? If one asks how a basis of continuity and transmission of physical life came to exist in man, one can also seek the origin and nature of that spiritual plasm within the universal history of the human race. This is connected with the mysteries of the embodiment in matter of the *Dhyanis.* It is not something which only took place long ago, but a continuing fact of manifested life. H.P. Blavatsky quoted from a work on occult embryology as follows:

> When the seed of the animal man is cast into the soil of the animal woman, the seed cannot germinate unless it has been fructified by the five virtues (the fluid of, or the emanation from the principles) of the six-fold Heavenly man. Wherefore the Microcosm is represented as a Pentagon, within the Hexagon Star, the "Macrocosm".

Ibid., i 224

Thus, there is actually involved in the birth of a physical human being that which is quite independent of physical procreation and physical passion. It involves the cosmic hierarchies, the divine elements within the invisible theogony of the universe that constitute the *Dhyani Buddhas.*

Some of the *Dhyani Buddhas* are involved with the lower principles and hence with the physical processes of gestation and conception. Others have much higher functions in relation to universal life. All are relevant to the life of the microcosm within the macrocosm, the pentagon within the hexagonal star. All are somehow reflected in the process of embryogenesis and involved in the unfoldment of consciousness that takes place throughout the life cycle of the human being. In fact, there is no point in the experience of any human being that does not involve the hosts of *Dhyanis*. This may be understood by grasping the fact that life as an abstract universal essence is present in all its potency in every one of its differentiations. Again quoting from the same source, H.P. Blavatsky continued:

> "The functions of *Jiva* on this Earth are of a five-fold character. In the mineral atom it is connected with the lowest principles of the Spirits of the Earth (the six-fold *Dhyanis*); in the vegetable particle, with their second – the *Prana* (life); in the animal, with all these plus the third and the fourth; in man, the germ must receive the fruition of all the five. Otherwise he will be born no higher than an animal"; namely, a congenital idiot. Thus in man alone the *Jiva* is complete. As to his seventh principle, it is but one of the Beams of the Universal Sun. Each rational creature receives only the temporary loan of that which has to return to its source; while his physical body is shaped by the lowest terrestrial lives, through physical, chemical, and physiological evolution.

> *Ibid.*

It is crucial that *Jiva* not be narrowed down to its aspects on the lower planes of manifestation. It is true that there is life in the infusoria, the bacteria and the minutiae of every atomic point in manifestation. Hence the doctrine that every microscopic form is composed of billions upon billions of "lives". There is also life in each of the seven kingdoms. There is life in the elemental kingdom composed of sylphs, salamanders, undines and gnomes – the elementals connected with the elements below the mineral. There is life in the stone and in rock, and there is life in the vegetable kingdom, marked by the emergence of sensation on a subtler plane than the cohesion characteristic of the mineral kingdom. In what may be thought of as an analogue to vision, there is the osmosis by plants of light. The light that a plant receives from the midnight sky and in the early hours of the dawn, the light it receives from the moon and the sun, are all different aspects of *Jiva* in relation to the vegetable kingdom. The same life process is at work in complex and diverse ways throughout the animal kingdom.

Other aspects of *Jiva* cannot be equated with anything that comes out of the entire process from below, up to and through the animal kingdom. Otherwise, the human form would be nothing more than a Frankenstein monster. There is nothing in contemporary knowledge that can remotely imagine what it is that makes such a fundamental distinction between a living animal form and a living human being. There is nothing, in fact, in contemporary knowledge which can distinguish even between a living body and a robot or automaton, so impoverished are its conceptions of life and motion. The assumption of a vital essence or principle is not, in itself, sufficient for such distinctions, since the life-fluid or Paracelsian *Liquor Vitae* differs between the animal and the human kingdoms. That aspect of *Jiva* which circulates in the human body sustaining its vitality is a gift of the higher *Dhyanis*, a flow of noumenal, self-conscious intelligence. Because this distinctively human vitality is not directly involved in physical manifestation, it is virtually unknown to human beings. Yet it can be recognized through its absence, or when there is a danger of losing it. It is that which vitalizes, brings to birth and releases the spiritual will. It is that which lights up the creative energy of the higher imagination and that which belongs to the power of ideation and intention. It is that power of the human monad capable of impressing desire with a form and with an intelligence. It is that life which is given by the power of ideas, and hence it is connected over the long process of history with what is called education.

It is the central thread of the slow, painful and imperfect process of soul instruction. Though liable to inversion and corruption, it remains the central process of unfoldment through which alone there can be a release of what would otherwise remain a merely latent potential within humanity. Life in this higher sense is inseparable from the power to choose and to reflect, the capacity to concentrate and connect. This power of synthesis is so crucial, even in its physical reflection at the level of the limbic system in the brain, that even a small amount of damage to that part of the physical vesture can result in paranoia or schizophrenia. Millions upon millions of people alive today experience an intense splitting of the thought process. They cannot anymore connect or coordinate; they cannot show full awareness of beginnings, middles and endings. Instead, they are merely involved in an immense proliferation of images without control or coordination.

Paradoxically, awareness of and participation in *Jiva*, or life in this highest sense, can only be increased by non-manifestation. That is why people cannot understand it. On the one hand, without sleep the human body would die. It is only in sleep and the quietude of the sensory apparatus, especially the lower physical senses, that the spiritual senses have any chance at all in the ordinary human being. It is only through sleep that there is a real osmosis, a connection, with the higher vestures. Without sleep there would be death. The physical form is the product of inward vitality or *Jiva*, and not the reverse. Therefore,

> The animal tissues, . . . from the moment of the birth of the Entity, are regulated, strengthened, and fed by it. It descends in a larger supply to vegetation in the Sushumna sun-ray which lights and feeds the moon, and it is through her beams that it pours its light upon, and penetrates man and animal, more during their sleep and rest, than when they are in full activity.

> *Ibid.*, i 537

Without this process of inward nourishment and restoration through sleep, there would be no resistance to the intense excitation of nervous energy, connected with the vital fluid, which ultimately comes from the Spiritual Sun and is therefore, on its lower plane, extremely destructive if uncontained. Where there is no discipline or no shielding of that energy, it gives rise to extreme fatigue and drains all human life.

> This is called nervous excitation, but no one, except Occultists, knows the reason of such nervous perturbation or explains the primary causes of it. The "principle of Life" may kill when too

exuberant, as also when there is too little of it. But this principle on the manifested (or our) plane is but the effect and the result of the intelligent action of the "Host" – collectively, Principle – the manifesting LIFE and LIGHT. It is itself subordinate to, and emanates from the ever-invisible, eternal and Absolute ONE LIFE in a descending and a re-ascending scale of hierarchic degrees – a true septenary ladder, with SOUND (or the Logos) at the upper end and the *Vidyadharas* (the inferior *Pitris*) at the lower.

Ibid., i 539

To be able to release the higher *Jiva*, one must become extremely calm and quiet, capable of sitting for hours doing nothing – not even thinking in any strenuous sense – but receiving. One must be wide awake, attuning oneself to the Spiritual Sun, to the regents of the sacred planets, and to the spirits of the elements – to the spirit of fire, of air, of water and of earth, and above all of Ether-Akasha. Only when one becomes a man of silence, a man of meditation capable of remaining still and wide awake while abstracted from even the subtlest sensations, can one come any closer to experiencing what *The Voice of the Silence* calls ALL-THOUGHT. Only by mastering the mind can one intelligently guide through the fifth principle, or *Manas*, the second principle of the universal soul, the vital force in Nature which circulates through man. When one has mastered these inferior potencies, one can experience the subtle fiery substance of *Akasha*, Nature's infinite library. Through introspection and silence, through oceanic calm, one can increase one's spiritual life-energy, which is the highest *Jiva*. To do this is to emulate those *Vidyadharas* who are esoterically the hierarchy that endows man, in the Third Root Race, with self-consciousness. These *Siddhas* are beings "affluent in devotion" and exemplars of the highest and holiest communion with the Logos.

To intuit and assimilate their presence in oneself, one must learn to sit in the silence of one's own meditation, without projects or pencils, pens or tape recorders, icons or insignia. All apparatus must go. One must simply reflect, beginning with a *bija sutra*, a sacred *mantram*. Then one can commune with all those beings in evolution who are wealthy in the power of adoration. They are those who so rejoice and adore others above and beyond them that through that adoration they release divine *Eros* in the highest sense, the power of divine adoration and worshipful prostration. Through the thrill of that inward adoration and mental prostration, the opposite of the self-made man's crude conceit, it is possible to tap and release spiritual energy. That energy comes out of communion with the collective hosts of light-beings who are involved in endowing human beings with the highest vital energies and powers.

It is in this sense that *Jiva* is complete only in man. And yet even this *Jiva* is independent of the highest Atmic light connected with the seventh principle, which may be likened to one of the rays or beams of the Central Spiritual Sun. The ultimate spiritual origin of life is intimated in the cryptic code language called Sanskrit by *Jivatman*, which suggests the whole of the universe in a single word. If one truly understood the many dimensions of *Jiva* and the many hierarchies to which it is connected, and if one also understood something about spiritual life and the Spiritual Sun, one would be able to understand the *Atman* as perpetual motion, and to grasp the continuity between the radiations of the Central Spiritual Sun and the pulsations at the heart of the solar system.

"The Sun is the heart of the Solar World (System) and its brain is hidden behind the (visible) Sun. From thence, sensation is radiated into every nerve-centre of the great body, and the waves of the life-essence flow into each artery and vein.... The planets are its limbs and pulses . . . . "The Sun *in abscondito* being thus the storehouse of our little *Kosmos*, self-generating its vital fluid, and ever receiving as much as it gives out", and the visible Sun only a window cut into the real Solar palace and presence, which reflects, however, faithfully the interior work.

> Thus, there is a regular circulation of the vital fluid throughout our system, of which the Sun is the heart – the same as the circulation of the blood of the human body – during the manvantaric solar period, or life.

Ibid., i 541

The mystery of the *Jivatman* encompasses the mystery of the cosmos, the Ego and the embryo. It is the most powerful motor of spiritual energy, tapped by *yogins* through the power of vows upheld intact over lifetimes of meditation. It is the essence of immortal life which may be drawn upon through penance, through *tapas*, through true repentance and through compassion. It is the living essence of the Kwan-Yin Pledge, one with the spiritual life-energy and spiritual will, the spiritual plasm of occult cosmology. It is altogether beyond terrestrial perception and the seeming reality of animal existence. It is beyond the ethereality of the lesser gods. It is that which is ever present and primordial, indestructible and omnipotent. It is the fluid in *Akasha*, the very energy that circulates in the highest beings in manifestation, released through renunciation and devotion, sacrifice and meditation. It is, in essence, immortal life in spirit, the mystical Logos permeating the cosmos, and the divine Presence in every human heart.

Hermes, June 1984
Raghavan Iyer

Glossary

> *Let us use with care those living messengers called words.*
>
> W. Q. Judge

JIVA *(Sk.)*. Life, as the Absolute; the Monad also or *Atma-Buddhi*.

JIVANMUKTA *(Sk.)*. An Adept or Yogi who has reached the ultimate state of holiness and separated himself from matter; a *Mahatma*, or *Nirvanee*, a "dweller in bliss" and emancipation. Virtually one who has reached *Nirvana* during life.

JIVATMA *(Sk.)*. The ONE Universal Life, generally; but also the Divine Spirit in man.

WILL. In metaphysics and occult philosophy, Will is that which governs the manifested universes in eternity. Will is the one and sole principle of abstract eternal MOTION, or its ensouling essence. "The will", says Van Helmont, "is the first of all powers.... The will is the property of all spiritual beings and displays itself in them the more actively the more they are freed from matter." And Paracelsus teaches that "determined will is the beginning of all magical operations. It is because men do not perfectly imagine and believe the result, that the (occult) arts are so uncertain, while they might be perfectly certain." Like all the rest, the Will is *septenary* in its degrees of manifestation. Emanating from the one, eternal, abstract and purely quiescent Will *(Atma* in *Layam)*, it becomes *Buddhi* in its *Alaya* state, descends lower as *Mahat (Manas),* and runs down the ladder of degrees until the divine *Eros* becomes, in its lower, animal manifestation, *erotic* desire. Will as an eternal principle is neither spirit nor substance but everlasting ideation. As well expressed by Schopenhauer in his *Parerga,* "In sober reality there is neither *matter* nor *spirit.*"

KRIYASHAKTI

Kama . . . is in the Rig Veda *(x, 129) the personification of that feeling which leads and propels to creation. He was the first movement that stirred the ONE, after its manifestation from the purely abstract principle, to create, "Desire first arose in It, which was the primal germ of mind; and which sages, searching with their intellect, have discovered to be the bond which connects Entity with Non-Entity." A hymn in the* Atharva Veda *exalts* Kama *into a supreme God and Creator, and says: "Kama was born the first. Him, neither gods nor fathers* (Pitara) *nor men have equalled."... The* Atharva Veda *identifies him with Agni, but makes him superior to that god. The* Taittariya Brahmana *makes him allegorically the son of* Dharma *(moral religious duty, piety and justice) and of* Sraddha *(faith). Elsewhere* Kama *is born from the heart of Brahmâ; therefore he is* Atma-Bhu, *"Self-Existent", and* Aja, *the "unborn".*

The Secret Doctrine, ii 176
H.P. Blavatsky

There is a vital connection between *Kriyashakti*, the creative potency of self-conscious thought, and Kamadeva, the Rig Vedic deity of compassion. At the highest metaphysical level, *Kriyashakti* is continuous with the most primal currents of cosmic creativity and impulsion. This supreme potency of self-conscious thought is capable of bodying forth from the most sublime states of transcendental awareness an unbroken stream of emanations that may serve as sources of strength for all aspirants on lower planes of consciousness. Like all the mighty *shakti* powers hidden in the constitution of man, *Kriyashakti* can be fully aroused and made active only out of the most compassionate and universal motives. The divine imagination can be awakened only in the service of universal good. This capacity to enact in manifestation an ideal vision of the *Agathon* is a self-conscious embodiment of the creative compassion of the cosmos symbolized in Kamadeva. Ordinarily, the current of *kama* is a force that makes for human bondage. This impact of *kama,* however, is but a shadowy reflection of the cosmic principle of divine creativity and universal compassion.

The Rig Vedic *Hymn to Creation* highlights the intimate relationship between precosmic desire at the most primordial level and precosmic ideation. Precosmic ideation connotes a great deal more than mere passive contemplation of abstract ideas. Indeed, the very concept of ideation implies active volition. At the most primeval level of the cosmos, on the plane of *Mahat,* this volitional agency is represented as the primal seed or germ of mind. It is the pristine ground and unmanifest matrix of universal self-existence. As the causeless Germ in the Root, it is *Atma-Bhu* and *Aja* – Self-Existent and Unborn. It is the unmanifest Logoic Heart of the cosmos-to-be, the ineffable self-conscious source which radiates through every dimension of space, and the transcendental reflection of the unknowable Absolute. Between the ineffable zero of Be-ness and the infinitude of existing beings, it swells and vibrates with the pure desire to create, the volition of the One to become the many. It is within this mysterious Root of the cosmos that the highest *Rishis* have found and realized "the bond which connects Entity with Non-Entity". Such a *Rishi* has plumbed to its depth the problem of identity and mastered the meaning of universal self-existence in Deity. The fully perfected human being has become one with Deity, one with God. He is therefore able to understand from within his own universal self-consciousness the deific principle of cosmic creation. He has become one of the rays streaming forth from the heart of the Spiritual Sun. He has become one in consciousness and being with the kernel of the mystery of the One and the many.

Apart from this most mysterious and sacred realization, it is logically and psychologically impossible to resolve the impasse between the unconditional and the conditioned. In the arcane metaphysics of *Gupta Vidya,* the One without a second, by its very nature, can have no relationship to the world of differentiated time and space, the realm of manifested subjects and objects. How, then, is it possible to account for the world of differentiation? To the uninitiated mind it would seem that either there must be a god who creates the world out of nothing or that the world and all its life are a godless accident sprung from material chaos. Yet this apparent dilemma – anthropomorphism or atheism – is but a false dichotomy. Through travelling the inward path of meditation *(dhyana),* it is possible to apprehend the bond between that One, which is eternally absolute, and the world of time and of manifestation. To understand is to become and to participate in the mystery. One must merge in consciousness with the *Logos,* become refulgent like the sun with the unconditioned potentiality of Divine Thought and diffuse the rays of unconstrained creativity throughout universal space.

The universal indifference of the *Logos* to all possible modes and forms of manifestation is equivalent to its universal compassion and benevolence. As the mystical mirror of the *Agathon,* it is neither subject to itself nor possessed of any object. It is neither added to nor subtracted from by the appearance or disappearance of the manifested cosmos. To begin to conceive of it, one might think of a realm of the unmanifest causally prior to the region of the manifest. Even this, however, may only confuse minds addicted to thinking in terms of subjects and objects. It is extremely difficult to sunder Deity from its emanations, to distinguish between the subliminal force of abstract terms like *TAT, Daiviprakriti* and *Mulaprakriti* and the unmanifest *Logos.* Ultimately, even these words are themselves emanations from that plane of transcendental self-existence. They are themselves reflections and radiations, focussed out of compassion and for the sake of understanding, of the consciousness of enlightened beings. They are meant to serve as the basis for deep meditation and an inward ascent in noetic consciousness.

Through intensity of devotion in meditation upon such potent ideas, even the neophyte can come to sense some glimmering of the mystery of the relation between Entity and Non-Entity. When one ideates in the realm of pure thought, without reference to objects or temporality, one will in the end experience within oneself the intrinsic continuity extending from one pole of that meditation – which is voidness – to the other pole – which is fullness and plenitude. Through this mystical experience of emptiness and plenitude within the same state of universal consciousness, one experiences something of the mystery of *Fohat*, something of the mystery of the bond connecting Entity with Non-Entity.

Hidden within the folds of this mystery is the ultimate metaphysical basis of all *Kriyashakti*, all creative imagination. At this highest level one must understand the whole universe as the product of the highest *Kriyashakti*. One must therefore recognize the consubstantiality of the essential nature of each human being with the Divine Ground that is prior and unrelated to all manifestation. This recognition can come about only through entering into that realm of pure being which is the Divine Darkness prior to all worlds and to all forms. The highest basis of creativity is, naturally enough, very far removed from worldly notions and tokens of creativity. It has nothing to do with concretized desires for results impelled by an acute sense of deficiency and want. It is completely free from any illusions foisted by an incomplete self-consciousness upon that which is necessarily mutable and mortal. In spanning the poles of pure voidness and pure plenitude, this highest *Kriyashaktic* creativity transcends all limited modes of affirmation and negation, whether in relation to space or time or motion. It is neither tinged with the angularity of self-interest nor trammelled by the distortions of exaggeration and denial.

Something of the supreme self-confidence of self-existence is conveyed in the hymn of the *Atharva Veda* which portrays Kamadeva as the offspring of *Dharma* and *Shraddha*. *Dharma* in this sense refers to supreme necessity, flowing forth from precosmic harmony or *Rta* as its architectonic embodiment in abstract space. On the one side, it is the stern decree of necessity, imposing harmony upon the relations of all manifested beings; on the other side, it is the compassionate fitness of all things and the vital sense of everlasting right. In the primal exercise of pure cosmic *Kriyashakti*, there is an element of seeming involuntariness, of that which is both binding and holy. In this *Dharma* there is a solemnity and sacredness which far transcends all derivative notions of destiny and faith, all earthly promises and prospects. Standing prior to all of these, and serving as the root of all legitimate aspiration, *Dharma* is the unwavering and authentic imperative of the truth of Self-Existence. It is the abstract principle of integrity and the fount of all obligation and its fulfilment.

At the same time, there is in that pure cosmic *Kriyashakti* an element of *Shraddha* or faith. This faith is an unshakeable conviction of the inherent value of the action of *Kriyashakti*, independent of entropy and of the reflection of creativity in the complex processes of change. It is the unbroken assurance of the Divine, which is unborn and undying; it is the full freedom of selflessness, the formless joy and boundless beneficence that gives freely of itself without a shadow or hint of calculation. Thus, the allegorical offspring of *Dharma* and *Shraddha* is the mystical power of divine creation at the heart of the invisible cosmos. It is *Kriyashakti* personified as Kamadeva, the infinite potency of Divine Thought and the Law of laws, Compassion Absolute. It is *Eros* in its most profound philosophical sense, the awesome creative and therapeutic force extolled in the *Banquet* of Plato. Whether one speaks of it as pure love or cosmic creativity, it cannot be understood without reference to a world that is unmanifest and a state of being which is prior to manifestation. Before the dawn of manvantaric manifestation, pure thought and pure creative desire become fused within the primal germ of mind. This spirit of unconditioned self-existence was called by H.P. Blavatsky "Love without an object". As the mystical confluence of *Shraddha* and *Dharma*, it is both the source and the fulfilment of all devotion and discipline, all love and service. It is the one flame burning without wick, fuel or stand amidst the boundless field of the Divine Darkness.

This highest Logoic centre of the cosmos is the primordial source from which all differentiated beings come into existence and to which they return. It is all in all, and the binding force of all. In it the many live, move and have their being. It is the law of growth and the entelechy of all existence. All the manifested processes of cosmic life, with their complex interplay of creation, continuity and change, are crystalline aspects of the meta-biological Logoic life within and beyond the cosmos. As that universal current of life is itself unborn and self-existent, there is that in its reflected modes which cannot be construed in terms of any finite sequence of antecedents or formal set of preconditions. The mystery of life outside the cosmos, yet also at its root, is mirrored in the myriad living beings that people the cosmos on its different planes. Each is a spark of that original creativity, and each is an embodiment of its law. Thus, whilst there is comprehensible transmission and continuity among living forms, there are also sudden changes and creative transmutations of living form that cannot be reduced to finite causes. These changes do not, however, represent randomness or disorder within the cosmos. Rather, instead of being traceable to the action of the parts, they represent the living presence of the whole in each, the presence of the One amidst and within the many.

On the physical plane this is the problem of heredity and variation which has intrigued intrepid thinkers throughout the centuries. Since Pythagoras inserted the idea of evolution into early European thought, many philosophers have ardently sought to account for biological continuity and change. The rich resources of ancient thought have been largely eclipsed since the nineteenth century by empirical science's narrow and obsessive interpretation of Darwin's thought. When one considers Darwinian notions in the light of a broader stream of thought in world culture, their exclusive respectability can hardly be defended. For though there is evidently something plausible in Darwinian explanations of speciation and variation, there is also something grossly inadequate. What it accomplishes by way of concrete explanation, it achieves at the cost of mechanistic assumptions. By insisting upon the mechanical efficacy of transmission of characteristics at the level of individual instances, it renders collective evolution utterly random and chaotic. Whilst freeing biological thought from the arbitrary anthropomorphism and hazy teleologies of the Middle Ages, it leaves life to languish as a statistical accident, a blind offspring of a philosophy that is itself blind to the potency of ideation.

The price of this shallow materialism and narrow empiricism is a persistent inability to conceive of the nature of the creative potential inherent within human beings. Without taking into account the logic of the *Logos* on the plane of *Akasha,* it is impossible to form any adequate conception of the nature of the modes of transmission of life on the physiological plane. Genetic transmission can only account for some of the variations within patterns that themselves cannot be explained by physical heredity. In order to understand the conception, gestation and birth of even a single human form, one must allow for the invisible progenitors such as the *Lunar Pitris.* Certainly, to gain some grasp of the elusive logic of human procreation, as it applies to the entire race, one must see the present mode of procreation in relation to a series of different modes in the past and the future. One must consider the complex history of anthropogenesis, recognizing the diverse roles played by differing hosts of creators and *Pitris* in the formation and ensoulment of human vestures on the earth. At the very least, one must attempt to abstract one's *idea* of human procreation from its present *means* of accomplishment. Hence, one is helped by mythic accounts of the mysterious modes of birth that characterized the earlier human races – the *chhaya* birth, the sweat-born, the egg-born and the androgynous. Citing a telling example from zoology, H.P. Blavatsky pleaded for a more open-minded approach to the nature of human reproduction.

> The very interesting polyp *Stauridium* passes alternately from gemmation into the sex method of reproduction. Curiously enough, though it grows merely as a polyp on a stalk, it produces gemmules, which ultimately develop into a sea-nettle or Medusa. The Medusa is utterly dissimilar to its parent-organism, the *Stauridium*. It also reproduces itself differently, by sexual method, and from the resulting eggs, *Stauridia* once more put in an appearance. This striking fact may assist many to understand that a form may be evolved – as in the sexual Lemurians from Hermaphrodite parentage – quite unlike its immediate

progenitors. It is, moreover, unquestionable that in the case of human incarnations the law of Karma, racial or individual, overrides the subordinate tendencies of "Heredity", its servant.

The Secret Doctrine, ii 177-178

The cosmic law of Karma, which works through all race evolution, is involved in the descent of the *Kumaras*, the solar ancestors who endowed nascent humanity with the power of *Manas* over eighteen million years ago during the Third Root Race. That same law of inherited Karma is also involved in the procrastination of some of that host, as in their eventual retribution whereby they were projected into senseless forms. Similarly, the law of Karma comprehends the vast scope of the hosts of the Lunar *Pitris* working up the materials of the living lower kingdoms throughout the preceding Rounds. This complex karma of all humanity over millions upon millions of years is involved in the changes and continuities affecting the human race. That karma involves the activity of beings of surpassing wisdom and power as well as myriads upon myriads of elementals, the living atoms of Nature's sounding-board. It should not be surprising, therefore, that it is impossible to explain or anticipate everything that is transmitted through human beings merely through some theory of physical heredity, however complicated in terms of modern biochemistry and microbiology. Whilst it is possible to gain helpful lessons through a microscopic study of its physical manifestations, there are far more important insights to be gained by rising in consciousness to a more global awareness of human life. It is in the multi-dimensional life of humanity as a whole that the deepest mysteries are to be discerned regarding the Logoic processes of creation, continuity and change.

Similarly, abstracting from the present human condition and attempting to recover in consciousness some awareness of the earlier androgynous condition of humanity can help in coming to understand *Kriyashaktic* creativity. Before the separation of the sexes took place over eighteen million years ago, human beings in the

Third Root Race were hermaphroditic or androgynous. Subsequently, the familiar form of division into male and female has prevailed. Insofar as human beings generate in consciousness an exaggerated sense of specialization or polarization through being male or female, they will experience either a false sense of insufficiency or a false sense of self-sufficiency on the lunar plane, which acts as an obstacle to creativity. Once polarization has taken place, there is an intrinsic incompleteness in the male principle and a corresponding if deceptive wholeness or self-sufficiency in the female principle. Each of these could inhibit that potent force of fearlessness and detachment in the realm of imagination which is required to release the higher creative will. Until one overcomes the lower psychic sense of completeness or incompleteness that accompanies the astral form, one cannot tap that authentic fearlessness which enables one to enter the Divine Darkness prior to all worlds and all forms. One must readily transcend the polarity of the astral form that refers to being male or female if one seeks to recover an inner sense of the stern necessity and divine compassion of mental and spiritual creation, and if one is to root oneself in the supreme faith and abiding self-existence of the immortal Triad.

The wings of ideation are typically weighted down through identification with the astral and physical form. One's capacities for meditation and creativity are clipped through attachment to that which is merely a mutable projection. The force of this attachment is increased by the activity of *kamamanas,* particularly through speech and cerebration. All of these causes the astral to bloat until it becomes quite heavy. It is significant that in hinting about the after-death states of consciousness, Plato in the *Phaedo* uses as the primary pair of opposites the heavy and the light. Those whose souls were weighted down in life are weighted down even in death. In contrast, those who lightened themselves in life experience, effortlessly, a degree of lightness after death. They are able to ascend to the higher planes of consciousness. To experience the ultimate in lightness and effortlessness combined with fearlessness, detachment and faith in creativity, one must transcend altogether the astral plane. One must develop an inward sense of being that can function freely through the *karana sharira*, the permanent vesture which is the basis of the permanent astral body.

A developed disciple of *Brahma Vach* can gestate such an astral body in any life, and continue to do so over succeeding lives. Thus he, like an Adept, will eventually be able to exercise some volitional control over incarnation and to conceive and contemplate a voluntary incarnation. This process, continuing through many lifetimes, involves the hatching out of astral matter of a particular kind of permanent astral vesture, which itself is emanated out of the *karana sharira*, out of the purest vesture which might be called "the meditation body". It is what is sometimes called in Buddhist literature the Buddha-nature or Buddha-body. Only through profound meditation can one gain a sense of the potential reality of that subtle vesture of meditation. And only then can one transcend without effort the seeming insufficiency and false sufficiency that belongs to the astral plane through the separation of the sexes.

Long before an individual attains to this advanced and deliberate state of self-evolution, he can gain a provisional and theoretical understanding of *Kriyashakti* arising out of meditation as the paradigm of creativity. Citing the mysterious role played by *Kriyashakti* in the evolution of humanity and the presence of this power as latent in every human being, H.P. Blavatsky characterized *Kriyashakti* as

> the mysterious power of thought which enables it to produce external, perceptible, phenomenal results by its own inherent energy. The ancients held that any idea will manifest itself externally if one's attention (and Will) is deeply concentrated upon it; similarly, an intense volition will be followed by the desired result. A Yogi generally performs his wonders by means of *Itchasakti* (Will-power) and *Kriyasakti*.

The Secret Doctrine, ii 173

Human beings in every walk of life have had intimations of the reality of such powers, and even realized that what the Inner Self truly wishes is what ultimately is handed down through justice.

This is *Kriyashakti* at the simplest level. This relationship of intense volition to tangible result cannot be understood inductively or in terms of likes and dislikes. One cannot even begin to ponder the idea of what one's inner Self – the *Ishwara* within – chooses without attaining a high degree of detachment. According to Patanjali, *vairagya*, or detachment, is indifference to everything but the Supreme Soul, rooted in a sense of supreme fitness and inner moral necessity. To act for and as the Supreme Self is to embody both *Dharma* and *Shraddha*, moral necessity and spiritual conviction. Paradoxically, when the mind and heart are concentrated deeply upon that which is totally right, one no longer desires anything for oneself. Then one will reach one's goal. This process of mental and spiritual creativity through and on behalf of universal good is experienced through mystic meditation. In the perfected human being, permanently rooted in consciousness on the plane of *Akasha*, *Kriyashakti* unfolds as the ceaseless capacity of compassionate ideation extended in protective benevolence over all beings.

This divine capacity of the perfected human being is derived from the creative heart of the *Logos*. Its exercise by *Buddhas* and *Mahatmas* is inseparable from the creative compassion in the primal germ of mind at the origin of the cosmos. All phenomenal matter is only a kind of appearance which, at the root, is in essence inseparable from Root Matter or *Mulaprakriti*. In that primordial matter, which is the invisible essence behind all phenomenal matter, there is *Daiviprakriti*, the primordial Divine Light which is also Life in the highest sense. That eternal Life is also Light and Electricity at the earliest precosmic level. All of these are reflected at the dawn of manifestation in cosmic electricity or in the Light of the *Logos* in manifestation. They are reflected in the life that then becomes the *Fohatic* energy, which maintains an entire set of worlds in manifestation. At the primordial level, Light and Life can be summoned out of the *Mulaprakriti* which is hidden in phenomenal matter. Kamadeva is this highest energy of the purest ideation awakened in the primal germ of mind through *Kriyashakti* on the plane of the *Logos*. It is through *Kriyashakti* that the Lords of Wisdom, the *Kumaras*, the eldest sons of Brahma born of the body of night, created progeny in the Third Root Race of humanity. That progeny was and is both a single wondrous Being and a radiant Host of beings,

> the so-called SONS OF WILL AND YOGA, or the "ancestors" (the spiritual forefathers) of all the subsequent and present Arhats, or *Mahatmas*, [created] in a truly immaculate way. They were indeed created, not begotten, as were their brethren of the Fourth Race, who were generated sexually after the separation of sexes, the Fall of man. For creation is but the result of will acting on phenomenal matter, the calling forth out of it the primordial divine Light and eternal Life. They were the "holy seed-grain" of the future Saviours of Humanity.

> *The Secret Doctrine*, ii 173

The gestation and emanation of a new nucleus of *Mahatmas* and Adepts set apart for the coming races of humanity arose out of the original meditation of the highest divine beings in the Third Root Race. This is *Kriyashakti* in its most exalted sense. It is intimately connected with the mysteries of initiation, whereby a *Bodhisattva* can, out of the light of the *Dhyani Buddha* which is within himself, project a *Manushya Buddha* and a *Nirmanakaya*. It is also possible, through *Kriyashakti*, to project a certain type of human being which becomes a model and a redemptive saviour for races to come. This, associated with *Padmapani Bodhisattva*, is the highest and most sacred form of creativity. Every human being has within himself the principle of *Christos*, *Chenresi*, *Avalokiteshvara* or *Padmapani Buddha*. Every human being has within the spiritual essence of the universal light of the universal *Logos* which is eternal Life, and which encompasses each and every form of divine creativity.

> Attempt, I entreat you, to mark what I say with as keen an observation as you can. He who has been disciplined to this point in Love, by contemplating beautiful objects gradually, and in their order, now arriving at the end of all that concerns Love, on a sudden beholds a beauty wonderful in its nature. This is it, O Socrates, for the sake of which all the former labours were endured. It is eternal, unproduced, indestructible; neither subject

to increase nor decay; not, like other things, partly beautiful and partly deformed; not at one time beautiful and at another time not; not beautiful in relation to one thing and deformed in relation to another; not here beautiful and there deformed; not beautiful in the estimation of one person and deformed in that of another; nor can this supreme beauty be figured to the imagination like a beautiful face, or beautiful hands, or any portion of the body, nor like any discourse, nor any science. Nor does it subsist in any other that lives or is, either in earth, or in heaven, or in any other place; but it is eternally uniform and consistent, and monoeidic with itself. All other things are beautiful through a participation of it, with this condition, that although they are subject to production and decay, it never becomes more or less, or endures any change. When anyone, ascending from a correct system of Love, begins to contemplate this supreme beauty, he already touches the consummation of his labour.

The Banquet
Plato

Hermes, August 1984
Raghavan Iyer

THEURGY AND TRANSMUTATION

To those who knew that there was more than one key to theogonic symbolism, it was a mistake to have expressed it in a language so crude and misleading. For if the educated and learned philosopher could discern the kernel of wisdom under the coarse rind of the fruit, and knew that the latter concealed the greatest laws and truths of psychic and physical nature, as well as the origin of all things – not so with the uninitiated profane. For him the dead letter was religion; the interpretation – sacrilege. And this dead letter could neither edify nor make him more perfect. seeing that such an example was given him by his gods.... Now all the gods of Olympus, as well as those of the Hindu Pantheon and the Rishis, were the septiform personations (1) of the noumena of the intelligent Powers of nature; (2) of Cosmic Forces; (3) of celestial bodies; (4) of gods or Dhyan Chohans; (5) of psychic and spiritual powers; (6) of divine kings on earth (or the incarnations of the gods); and (7) of terrestrial heroes or men. The knowledge how to discern among these seven forms the one that is meant, belonged at all times to the Initiates, whose earliest predecessors had created this symbolical and allegorical system.

The Secret Doctrine, ii 764-765
H.P. Blavatsky

It is, according to Gautama Buddha, a greater feat to govern oneself than to command all the elements in Nature. All Nature and its powers bend heavenwards before the gentle, irresistible theurgy of the perfected *Bodhisattva*, the pilgrim-soul who has reached the summit of the Path and become the son of the *Dhyanis*, compassionator of the triple worlds, greater than all gods. The potential of pure *swaraj*, latent in every Monad, is quickened by the fiery ray of the *Manasa Dhyanis*. When first the dark fire of their formless intelligence ignited self-consciousness in the evolved forms of terrestrial humanity over eighteen million years ago, man became a living link between heaven and earth. Conscious of the divine presence within his preceptors, his companions and himself, he was governed by a natural impulse towards gratitude, devotion and benevolence. He lived in effortless sympathy with the hosts of bright *devas* and *devatas* that he found in and around himself and throughout the entire realm of Nature. Reflecting the Akashic ideation infused into him by the *Manasa*, his actions radiated a benign and spontaneous magic.

Although the impress of that primordial time is ineradicable, human beings have descended so low in consciousness that they can scarcely believe, much less recall, their original estate. Emerson's charitable characterization of man as God playing the fool cannot account for the awful process by which man has become spiritually self-orphaned and blinded, becoming a burden to himself and a parasite on Nature. What, one might ask, are the strange gods and alien altars towards which human beings have directed their pristine powers in degrading themselves? Since there is no power greater than that which made Monads self-conscious, one need not look beyond oneself to find the cause of one's own impoverishment. Nor need one look anywhere but within to find the means whereby one may embody the divine impulsion towards its transcendent end. The regeneration and restoration of humanity requires individuals to heed the wisdom of Krishna's teaching that all beings go to the gods they worship, and thereby awaken to self-conscious immortality in unison with the unmanifest godhead.

Such an awakening can be neither metaphysically cheap nor psychologically simple; one must skilfully navigate between the Scylla of desperate salvationism and the Charybdis of cynical materialism. If man is potentially a self-conscious link between heaven and earth, one might ask how man is specifically connected with the earth and with heaven. The elements constituting the human vestures are indeed consubstantial with the fabric of Nature outside the human form. Thus, man is linked to the earth through the five sense-organs, each of which has its astral analogue, and also through a variety of classes of elementals. Through each of the astro-physical senses, and especially the sense of inner touch, man is continuously involved in complex processes of interaction with the elemental kingdoms. On the other side, he is connected with the

THEURGY AND TRANSMUTATION   297

Dhyanis and the *devas* through *daimons*, which are the invisible essences of the elements, elastic, ethereal and semi-corporeal, in Nature. These *daimons* are made up of a much more subtle matter than that which composes the astral form of the average human being. By consciously drawing upon them, one can bring about the progressive etherealization of one's vestures. Just as the crucifixion of Jesus symbolizes the bondage of spirit on the cross of matter, so too the Eucharist signifies the spiritualization of material vestures and the liberation of the spirit. This process must be initiated through meditation, intensified through refinement in consciousness, through reverence, renunciation and compassion. If one can suffuse one's whole being with benevolent and elevated thoughts and feelings, it is possible, over a period of seven years, to reform the life-atoms that constitute the astro-physical form. Such a radical renewal will be apparent in one's hands, face, toes and tongue – indeed at every point in the body.

This in itself is only one small application of the vast body of arcane and exact knowledge regarding the hosts and hierarchies of beings involved in human evolution. In neo-Platonic thought these beings were divided into three broad classes:

> According to the doctrine of Proclus, the uppermost regions from the Zenith of the Universe to the Moon belonged to the Gods or Planetary Spirits, according to their hierarchies and classes. The highest among them were the twelve *Huperouranioi*, or Supercelestial Gods, with whole legions of subordinate *Daimons* at their command. They are followed next in rank and power by the *Egkosmioi*, the Inter-cosmic Gods, each of these presiding over a great number of *Daimons*, to whom they impart their power and change it from one to another at will. These are evidently the personified forces of nature in their mutual correlation, the latter being represented by the third class, or the Elementals.

H. P. Blavatsky

In every aspect of life, human beings are intimately and immediately engaged with these ordered ranks and legions of *daimons* or elementals. The elementals are neither immortal spirits nor tangible bodies; they are merely astral forms of the celestial and supercelestial ideas that move them. They are a combination of sublimated matter and rudimentary mind, centres of force with instinctive desires but no consciousness in the human sense. Acting collectively, they are the nature-spirits – the gnomes and sylphs, salamanders and undines of alchemical tradition.

All these *daimons*, together with the higher gods, are connected with the seven sacred elements. At the highest metaphysical level, these elements have nothing to do with what we call fire, air earth and water. For, in essence, these elements are not material, nor may they be understood in terms of visible functions on the physical plane. Just as the hosts of celestial and supercelestial gods are guided from within by the power of formless spiritual essences, and act outwardly in their dominion over the *daimons* of the elements, so these *daimons* themselves preside directly over the elements of the four kingdoms of organic life, ensouling them and giving them their outward capacities of action. Thus, when human beings arouse *Buddhi* in *kama,* the reflection of the sixth principle in the fourth, *Buddhi* will transmute the lower *manas.* In the *antaskarana,* in the channel of aspiration, the force of *Buddhi* in *Manas* will actually become manifest in the fingers, nostrils and lungs. *Buddhi* will be aroused in all the centres of the brain and the heart. It will then be possible to invite or invoke the chief controllers of the many classes of *daimons.* When this takes place, the teaching that man is a living link between heaven and earth takes on a concrete meaning in benevolent magic based upon arcane science.

Unless, however, one draws a basic distinction between the spirit and the soul of man, any effort to practise theurgy will be inverted and turn into psychism or even sorcery. Despite the Pauline classification of spirit, soul and body, Christian theology obscured the distinction between spirit and soul. Even the philosophic doctrines of the medieval Kabbalists, though they paralleled the teachings of the neo-Platonists, were not fully in accord with ancient wisdom. The neo-Platonists were, however, well aware of the dangers and seductions of all theurgy; they knew that would-be neophytes could be caught in the clutches of treacherous *daimons*. Those who cannot clearly distinguish between spirit and soul, cannot firmly distinguish between higher and lower *daimons* and theurgy will drift into thaumaturgy. As a result, they are likely to form alliances with lower hosts, worship secondary or even tertiary emanations.

> The most substantial difference consisted in the location of the immortal or divine spirit of man. While the ancient Neoplatonists held that the Augoeides never descends hypostatically into the living man, but only more or less sheds its radiance on the inner man – the astral soul – the Kabalists of the middle ages maintained that the spirit, detaching itself from the ocean of light and spirit, entered into man's soul, where it remained through life imprisoned in the astral capsule. This difference was the result of the belief of Christian Kabalists, more or less, in the dead letter of the allegory of the fall of man.
>
> H. P. Blavatsky

The sad consequence of this concretized view of the Fall of man was twofold. First, by ontologically drawing spirit down to the level of soul, it made possible a dependence of spirit upon a third-degree anthropomorphic deity, Jehovah. Secondly, by repudiating the body as representing the Fall through intrinsic sinfulness, one was left with a passive conception of the soul, concerned only with salvation and damnation. The neo-Platonists, however, who viewed the soul as quite distinct from the transcendental spirit, saw no grounds for such an ontological or devotional subordination to lower *daimons*. They took an active view of the process whereby the soul seeks to link itself to the transcendent spirit. With regard to the spirit,

> they allowed its presence in the astral capsule only so far as the spiritual emanations or rays of the "shining one" were concerned. Man and his spiritual soul or the monad – i.e., spirit and its vehicle had to conquer their immortality by ascending toward the unity with which, if successful, they were finally linked, and into which

they were absorbed, so to say. The individualization of man after death depended on the spirit, not on his astral or human soul – Manas and its vehicle Kama Rupa – and body.

H. P. Blavatsky

From this one may see the central importance of the connection between *Atma-Buddhi* and *Manas.* One may also grasp the fundamental importance of devotion to the Brotherhood of *Bodhisattva*s, for without devotion it is impossible to tap the energies of *Atma-Buddhi. Manas* is only as luminous as its capacity to focus consciously and radiate the *Atma-Buddhic* light. If it can do that, then *Manas* can displace and control *Kama Manas,* disengaging the lower *manas* from *kama,* which means freeing the mind from excesses, excuses and evasions. All such errors arise out of the lower *manas* through its fearful attachment to the body and identification with class, status and property. All of these taints erode the confidence of the soul through the inherent capriciousness of the *daimons* and elementals within the lower vestures. They are based upon a misguided belief in some entity which holds together all these elementals; in truth, there is only a derived or borrowed sense of entitativeness which is appropriated by the quaternary. This temporary coherence is due to its link with *Manas.* The lower quaternary is like an image or reflection of the light occurring through an appropriate medium. If the reflective principle of the mind confuses its own image with the authentic source of its illumination, then the polarity of self- consciousness is inverted and the powers of the soul subverted. Fragmentation precludes integration.

All efforts towards spiritual self-regeneration depend upon strengthening awareness of the shining thread which connects *Atma-Buddhi* to *Manas,* and by reflection, *Atma-Buddhi-Manas* to the quaternary. If this thread is not nurtured in meditation, one will not be able to alter the quality of sleep and so gain continuity of consciousness between day and night and through different states of consciousness. If one cannot do that, one will not be able to generate a strong sense of individuality and "I-am-I" consciousness. One will not realize one's *Self-Being* as a reflected ray of the overbrooding *Dhyani*, linked to the Spiritual Sun. If one cannot do this, one will always identify with one's name and form, and spiralling downwards, fall into the midst of hosts of secondary and tertiary *daimons*. When the vision of the soul is deflected downward, it will look only upon that which is dark relative to the invisible radiance of spirit. Fixed by the immortal soul's energy, this false identification with *namarupa* will be accompanied by a continuous exaggeration and intensification. As this misuse of divine energy is indefinitely prolonged, the immortal soul will, in time, be estranged from its ray. By assigning an exaggerated sense of reality to that which belongs to physical life, to eating, drinking, working at a job – one is generating a false sense of life, limiting both time and consciousness. This remains essentially true even if one generates a strong attachment to the concept of moral probity in connection with this incarnation. Owing to the diversion of divine energies, all identification with name and form ultimately produces dark emanations which accumulate in *kamaloka*, where they must be confronted soon after death.

It is possible, however, to cooperate with the processes of individualization after death. It is possible to live in a manner that dispenses altogether with *kamaloka* and dispels the karmic accumulations of past attachments. But such a life requires a recognition of total responsibility. It means learning to live with no attachment to name or form. One must ask oneself who is responsible for one's personality and body, who is responsible for one's every thought and feeling? Who is responsible for the condition of every life-atom that enters into and emanates from one's visible and invisible vestures? In asking these questions, one begins to withdraw identification from the instruments, to see oneself as a Monad, and to approach the state of total responsibility from above below. This responsibility extends to the entire field of one's manifest and unmanifest interactions with all life-atoms. It extends far beyond face and form, to one's ultimate status as a true Pythagorean spectator. Only by generating a profound sense of critical distance from all names and forms may one learn to exemplify the entirety of one's *dharma* in this world.

Forswearing all anxiety and attachment, all immodesty and false pride, one must learn to put to work in the best possible manner all the instruments and all the energies affecting all the hosts of *daimons* and *devas* involved in the human sphere. This can only be done if one develops, retains and strengthens a sense of being changeless and immortal, as Krishna taught Arjuna in the second chapter of the *Bhagavad Gita.* One must withdraw from all false ideas of vicarious atonement and salvation which are, as Plato taught in *Laws,* extremely harmful to the vigilant life of the spirit. Every temptation to cut corners through selfish propitiations and degrading rituals is indeed expensive karmically. The very attempt blinds the eye of wisdom, cuts the soul off from its source of light and leaves the wandering pilgrim a wretched and ridiculed victim of its false gods.

This, in epitome, is the odyssey of the fall of the human soul since its pristine golden age in the Third Root Race. Just as the divine spiritual instruction of that period retains its impress upon the imperishable centres of the soul to this day, so too does this long karmic history lie like a series of encrustations around humanity and the earth. Because man is linked with hosts of elementals within his vestures and with hosts of *daimons* without, this karmic inheritance is inscribed in the spatial arena of collective human evolution. It may be discerned in the mystical and sacred geography of the globe itself. *Gupta Vidya* suggests that when the sevenfold host of divine preceptors descended upon earth to initiate and instruct infant humanity, they descended from *Sveta Dwipa,* a division of Mount Meru. They established seven divine dynasties reigning over seven divisions of the earth or globe. During the Lemurian and Atlantean ages, some of these divisions changed; others have not.

The eternal and transcendental geography of Mount Meru is partially mirrored in divisions of the earth connected with the polar regions. Hence, northern Asia is termed the eternal or perpetual land and the Antarctic is called the ever-living and the concealed. The freedom of the polar regions from the vicissitudes of racial evolution and geological change is a reflection of the permanence of the *axis mundi* of Mount Meru. The association of the North Pole with *Sveta Dwipa*, however, should not be thought of merely in terms of a terrestrial region. It would be more helpful to think of a *Fohatic* magnetic field associated with ice and snow. It is to be found both in snow-capped mountains and in desert oases, such as the Gobi Desert of Central Asia. The poles of the earth are likened in *Gupta Vidya* to valves regulating the ingress and egress of the solar-selenic radiance affecting the earth. They are intimately connected, through *Fohatic* arteries girdling the globe, with the circulations of *daimons* in the atmosphere. By correspondence, within the human form they are analogous to the circulation of the blood and other fluids with their invisible elemental constituents.

To connect this meta-geography with the inward life of the soul, one must connect the idea of pilgrimage to the idea of the restoration of the obscured flows of spiritual energies within the human temple. As Shankara and others taught, the sacred places of pilgrimage in the world mirror centres within the human body. Thus, there is a deep meaning behind the saying of the *Puranas* that even the incarnated gods themselves rejoiced to be born in the condition of men in *Bharata Varsha* in the Third Root Race. In one sense, *Bharata Varsha* is India, the original chosen land and the best division of *Jambhu Dwipa*. More essentially, *Bharata Varsha* is the land of active spiritual works *par excellence*, the land of initiation and divine knowledge. Hence H.P. Blavatsky's remark that one who visits India in a proper state of mind can find more blessings and more lessons than anywhere else on this earth.

Evidently, this must not be understood in an external mechanistic or physical sense, since there are millions upon millions of souls on the Indian subcontinent who have nothing to do with this eternal current. Just as thousands of people might never show Buddhic perception, even though they saw Sir Richard Attenborough's magnificent film on Gandhi, so too, numerous individuals could either visit or be born in India without developing Buddhic insight. Rather, H.P. Blavatsky's comment must be understood in the light of Christ's statement that whenever two or three are gathered in his name, he was present amongst them. Again, one could think of the meaning of *Dharmakshetra* in *Kurukshetra*, the invisible and omnipresent field of *Dharma* wherein all human beings ceaselessly live and move. Hence the teaching of the eighteenth chapter of the *Gita*: "Wherever Krishna, the supreme Master of devotion, and wherever the son of Pritha, the mighty archer, may be, there with certainty are fortune, victory, wealth, and wise action."

The awakening of *Buddhi* depends upon soul refinement and soul sensitivity, which can only emerge from a noetic understanding of the noumenal language of the soul. That language is experienced by every human being during deep sleep, but it can only be developed when significant connections are made between what transpires in deep sleep and in waking life. One must learn to understand arcane symbols at many levels. One must, for example, become receptive to the idea that the *Sveta Dwipa* of the *Puranas* is one with the *Shamballa* of Buddhist tradition, and that both are identical with the abode of the Builders, the luminous Sons of Manvantaric Dawn. All such mystical names pertain to a plane of consciousness accessible to human beings within. Mount Meru and the mystical descent of the Ganges can be correlated with critical points within the spiritual spinal cord and the invisible brain. Yogic meditation transports one to inner centres, wherein dwell the gods of light. In this *Sveta Dwipa*, the luminous Sons of Manvantaric Dawn are eternally present during the *Maha-Manvantara.* Though they came out of the unknown darkness, according to mythic chronology, they are still ever present on that plane as the root of the world, as timeless spectators in the bliss of non-being. Man links heaven and earth so fully that no mode of incarnation can entirely erase the alchemical signature of one's origin.

The lessons of mythic chronology and mystical geography must be applied by each individual to his or her own incarnation. All human beings are always involved with the cycles of the gods and *daimons*, the *devas, devatas* and elementals. Every child is basically an *Atma-Buddhic* ray with a ray of lower *manas* which becomes active in the seventh month in the mother's womb. Typically, the ray of *Manas* does not become active until the age of seven, around which time it brings with it the power to choose and to take responsibility. In some it may be retarded, in others it may come too soon, before there is adequate moral preparation. But the parent who would follow the wise practices of the oldest cultures will only do the minimum that is needed for the baby. That parent will leave the baby alone to bathe in its own state of consciousness. At the same time, adults should listen to a baby's sounds and address it as an immortal soul, as a human being capable of controlling and commanding the elementals. In so doing, an adult can arouse in the elementals that gather round a child those which are benevolent as well as those which are strong but not possessive. That everything essential to human life is capable of universalization and capable of becoming an object of responsibility may be imparted to a child before it learns to walk, or certainly when it learns to talk. Then it is crucial to draw out a baby's innate intuition in *Atma-Buddhi* by explaining and guiding it through the incarnation of *Manas*.

By the age of seven, the child should have learnt to sit still and to receive wisdom, and be prepared to inhabit *Bharata Varsha*. This is nothing but a recapitulation of human evolution up until the mid-point of the Third Root Race, when the *Manasa Dhyanis* descended into the waiting human forms. Between the ages of seven and fourteen, a child must be very still, calm and deliberate. It can be taught deliberation by deliberate parents; anxious parents find, to their shock, their own neuroses reflected in their children. A child who is given enough basis for self-respect and self-consciousness without verbalization, before the age of seven, can, after *Manas* awakens it, engage in proper dialogue with a respect for alternatives and a freedom of thought. This combination of discernment and discipline is crucial if the child is to resist the chaos of companions in junior high and high school. Here both parents and children alike should closely observe and follow the best examples they can find. They should withdraw attention from negative examples, abstaining from needless analysis. In this way, the parent may help a child overcome the tendency, prevalent since Atlantis, of fascination with evil.

All this preparation encourages a balance between the centrifugal and centripetal forces which engage the incarnated ray more fully by the age of fourteen. The centrifugal power of spirit or *Buddhi* is capable of diffusing from a single point in every direction within a sphere. This omnidirectional diffusion mirrors the ceaseless motion of the *Atman.* In *Manas,* the capacity to hold, to focus and to concentrate these energies is associated with the centripetal energies. A helpful example in the balancing of these energies may be gleaned from those older cultures which never allowed people to speak when they were confused or excited until they had sat down. Adolescents must learn to collect themselves, to draw their energies together in calmness, if they are to avoid the rush, the tension and the anxiety endemic to the cycle between fourteen and twenty-one. Once they have developed some mature calmness, depth and strength, they can release the potential of the higher energies of *Atma-Buddhi-Manas.* In a sense, all humanity is presently engaged in this adolescent phase.

In the Aquarian Age a dynamic principle of balance is needed. Whilst this has its analogues on the physical plane, and even in the astral vesture, it must not be approached on this level, lest there be a degradation of the idea into Hatha Yoga. Instead, one must begin with the *Buddhi-Manasic,* with the emotional and mental nature, and find on the physical plane appropriate means of expressing that creative balance. Thus one can produce a rhythmic flow and a light ease in one's sphere of influence which reflects a life of deep meditation. The ultimate aim is a fusion of love and wisdom, which then becomes Wisdom-Compassion, the fusion of *Buddhi* and *Manas.* The fusion of *Buddhi* and *Manas* at the highest level is inseparable from the path of adeptship.

Because of the inherent pacing and cycle of soul-evolution, and because of the karmic encrustations human beings have produced in themselves through associations with secondary and tertiary hosts of *daimons*, no one can be expected to accomplish all of this in a single lifetime, or indeed in any immediate future series of lives. But each being can make a beginning, and, at some level, fuse *Buddhi* and *Manas*. Although overactive in *Kama Manas*, most human beings are mediumistic, yet in the *antaskarana* there are authentic longings for the higher. Such longings must first be purified and made Manasic through universalization. This requires sifting finer thoughts and higher impulses from the dross of *Kama Manas*, then releasing them for the welfare of humanity as a whole. This means ignoring statistical portraits of humanity given by mass media and developing an inward sense of one's intimate relationship on the plane of ideation and aspiration with millions upon millions of immortal souls.

The more one can change the ratios of one's thought about oneself, one's thought about *Bodhisattva*s, and one's thought about humanity, the better. As these ratios change, the patterns of one's associations of *daimons* and elementals will shift, progressively transmuting one's vestures and refining one's capacity for benevolence. Gradually, as one thinks more and more in the direction of *Bodhisattva*s and of humanity, one will come to see oneself as someone who has the confidence and capacity to control elementals at home, at work and in the world. Thus, one can help oneself and so help others to recover the lost link with the *Manasa Dhyanis*. One may learn to become a being of true meditation and compassion, capable of serving as a self-conscious living link between heaven and earth.

Hermes, January 1984
Raghavan Iyer

TRANSCENDENCE AND TRANSFORMATION

It is argued that "the human mind cannot conceive an indivisible unit short of the annihilation of the idea with its subject". This is an error, as the Pythagoreans have proved, and a number of Seers before them, although there is a special training for it, and although the profane mind can hardly grasp it. But there are such things as metamathematics and metageometry. Even mathematics pure and simple proceed from the Universal to the particular, from the mathematical, hence indivisible Point, to solid figures. The teaching originated in India, and was taught in Europe by Pythagoras, who, throwing a veil over the Circle and the Point – which no living man can define except as incomprehensible abstraction – laid the origin of the differentiated Cosmic matter in the basic or horizontal line of the Triangle. Thus the latter became the earliest of geometrical figures.

The Secret Doctrine, i 616
H.P. Blavatsky

The rigorous discipline of meta-geometry is concerned with the indispensable philosophical ideas required to construct the entire system of the manifested universe out of a single boundless Source. That inexhaustible Source, seen as a pervasive principle in the cosmos, vitalizes all planes and spheres and ceaselessly acts upon all forms, objects and subjects. Metaphysics, when rendered metaphorically and by analogy with the axioms and postulates of geometry, takes on much more than a merely theoretical relationship to the simple points, lines and constructions that are the basic elements of geometry. What at one level may appear to be merely geometrical relations between these elements are, at a metaphysical level, vital elements of the cosmos as a living geometry in repose. This is the deeper meaning of the systematic study of Euclid's elements, and it is a fundamental reality which constitutes the noumenal world. Numbers also interpenetrate the phenomenal world of objects and the complex relationships between them. Numbers, in all their possible combinations, give structure and order in an evolutionary universe to the totality of all that exists. So it is possible, through a highly precise and disciplined consideration of geometrical ideas – in effect, the study of meta-geometry at a preliminary level – to move beyond geometry, as generally understood, towards a true Buddhic insight into the underlying shape of metaphysics. Though a highly difficult discipline, this process is crucial to one who would awaken the metaphysical imagination.

All knowledge arises because of the immense power of visualization. It draws freely upon familiar phenomena from the world of sense-perception, yet alters and modifies the sensory world. This process is exemplified by any artist, whether painter or sculptor, musician or mathematician. Likewise, the creative power of visualization is central to any true science. For this fertile power depends upon precise renderings of formal relations between ever more abstract notions. As an innate capacity of the immortal soul, this enormous power is given exercise and direction through the study of mathematics. It is this which makes the natural scientist capable, at one level, of performing notable and elaborate acts of abstraction. The natural sciences become capable of attaining a seeming stability in their operational concepts through the relationship of thought to number. And through systems of complex equations, theorems and models, some continuity of transmission in this body of knowledge is also achieved.

At the same time, the power of visualization is limited neither by what one may know of objects nor by what one may know of procedures in logic and mathematics. The power of visualization must spring from the deepest core of subjectivity in every human being. Each and every man and woman, every Manasa, privileged to carry the sacred fire of self-consciousness, is necessarily capable of mental creation that transcends the limits not only of the seen but of the known. Thus every human being can, through the power of mental abstraction, ascend into the unknown ground and invisible origin that lies behind the entire phenomenal realm of existence. It is thereby possible through the power of visualization for the individual to transcend significantly all existing knowledge encapsulated in any set of equations, theorems and models.

All human beings are more or less at ease in exercising this power in relation to various subjects and objects. Yet often the very ease with which human beings visualize becomes an actual limitation. Nowhere is this more true than in the twentieth century, when through the natural sciences we have inherited so many extraordinary analogies – linking, for example, the solar system and the atom. This bold insight, coming at the close of the nineteenth century, was both intriguing and confining. In a sense, it was the product of a system of thought which had become fortified and solidified through a narrow interpretation of the ideas of Newton, and so fast becoming an impediment. It took a rare scientist, Werner Heisenberg, to see that it was essential to break with the known ways in which people were visualizing the world, to overturn assumptions confined by an over-simplified view of motion, location and causality. In his attempt to visualize a new way to understand subatomic phenomena, Heisenberg introduced a fresh model of the migration of entities from one point in space to another. He did not mean that subatomic particles literally migrate from one point of space to another as a bird might fly from tree to tree. Instead, he depicted the migration or shift of subatomic particles in terms of certain types of transitions between different possible quantum states. In effect, he introduced a more abstract notion of space than that connected with ordinary Cartesian extension.

Every such remarkable exercise of the enormous power of visualization, whether in the natural sciences or elsewhere, can free the imagination from limiting past patterns. In a society where so much consciousness is concentrated on physical phenomena, virtually any effort to abstract from the phenomenal world will yield some degree of transcendence. What is striking in the case of Heisenberg, and others like him, is that they were able both to transcend the limits of their perceptual models and yet to maintain a continuity with previous thought. So, as soon as his colleagues began to grasp the difficult Uncertainty Principle which Heisenberg had introduced into their science, they began to expand upon it. In Japan, for example, Hideki Yukawa joined the ideas of uncertainty and relativity together to formulate the model of the meson, an entity representing the rest mass of the nuclear binding force.

From the standpoint of meta-psychology, every human being as a subject is capable of drawing from the infinite resources of universal ideation, *Akasha*. What some mathematicians refer to as mind-space is itself only one aspect of the infinite *Akasha*. The capacity of the human being to extend the range of possible thoughts in all sorts of ways not previously imagined is essentially an application of the power of visualization in this mind-space. Far more is indeed possible. Such divine ideas and metaphysical possibilities go well beyond the entire system of visible and invisible manifested relationships.

Since it is precisely this realm of the unmanifest that is the focus and root of *Gupta Vidya*, the true awakening of the spiritual aspects of the power of visualization depends upon the ability to maintain continuity of consciousness completely apart from any perception of differentiated subjects or objects. Hence, H.P. Blavatsky warned:

> Those unable to seize the difference between the monad – the Universal Unit – and the *Monads* or the manifested Unity, as also between the ever-hidden and the revealed **LOGOS** or the *Word*, ought never to meddle in philosophy, let alone the Esoteric Sciences.

And again:

> Draw a deep line in your thought between that ever-incognizable essence, and the, as invisible, yet comprehensible Presence (*Mulaprakriti*), or *Shekinah*, from beyond and through which vibrates the Sound of the *Verbum*, and from which evolve the numberless hierarchies of intelligent Egos, of conscious as of semi-conscious, perceptive and apperceptive Beings, whose essence is spiritual Force, whose Substance is the Elements and whose Bodies (when needed) are the atoms.

Ibid., i 629

The fundamental idea which the student of *Gupta Vidya* must initially grasp is that we can never relate the One to the many unless we first recognize that the One is by its nature unconditioned, without attributes, and so without any relationship to anything else. There is an unbridgeable abyss separating that Unconditioned One or *Parabrahman* from the differentiated world of manifestation. We cannot, therefore, reduce the multiplicity of manifestation to a primordial or primeval unity simply by invoking *TAT* or *Parabrahman* – the absolute, attributeless One. Rather, we can at best, in the dawn of manvantaric manifestation, find that which mirrors the One within a primordial field. This then becomes what is sometimes called the Second One, or more commonly, the Unmanifested *Logos*. The Unmanifested *Logos* is not *Parabrahman*, but it does, in a transcendental way superior to all formulatable conceptions of relationship, mirror *Parabrahman*. Since *Parabrahman* is out of all relation to space and time, not only as they are ordinarily known to finite minds but also in reference to all possible limits known even to the most developed minds, the Unmanifested *Logos* may be treated as the First Cause.

If *Parabrahman* were an infinite ocean consisting of centres of inconceivable potentiality, it is as if one of those centres became the Unmanifested *Logos*, mirroring and reflecting the absolutely inexhaustible nature of the whole in relation to all subsequent stages of manifestation subordinate to that *Logos* understood as a cause. Even here, however, it is crucial not to overlook the abyss between *TAT*, the unconditioned, attributeless Absolute, and the Unmanifested *Logos*. The degree to which an individual appreciates this truth of arcane metaphysics is the degree to which an individual is ready to apprehend a similar analogical relationship between the Unmanifested *Logos* and the manifested *Logos*. There is a conceptual abyss between these two, though it is neither so intense nor so vast, nor can it serve as a model whereby one may reduce the gap between the Unmanifested *Logos* and *Parabrahman*. Abstract though it is, the cognitive leap from the realm of the Unmanifested *Logos* to that of the manifested *Logos* is a less stern test of the power of metaphysical visualization than the "awesome mystery of *Parabrahman* ".

Put in another way, the cornerstone of a real comprehension of the ancient science of spirituality is a proper grasp of the difference between what are called the Universal Unit and the manifested Unity. There is a fundamental difference between the supreme, Cosmic Monad – the Pythagorean *Monas* and the vast aggregated Host of all the monads that spring forth like rays from the original *Logos*. Though this cannot be understood outwardly, it must be made a stimulus to meditation. Between Non-Being and even the vastest concept of Being there is a fundamental difference. Only when a human being is able, through meditation, to create a degree of voidness in relation to all other beings, all subjects and all objects, can the real relationship between the *Logos* and the monads be grasped. It is necessary to negate all finite attributes, even of the subjective self, and come to something like a pure apprehension of "I am" that is consubstantial with, and corresponds to, the cosmic "I am" – the *Logos* in the cosmos. Having attained that preliminary threshold, one must go farther, entering into the realm of Non-Being without any possible reference to any possible concept, thought, form, event or object. This realm, beyond any differentiated field, is, of course, extremely difficult to describe. Mystics, poets and men of meditation have tried by analogy and correspondence to evoke in the minds of those who are drawn in this direction some sense of what it is possible to experience in the way of the ineffable in the realm of Non-Being.

What it even means to speak of experience in this sense is almost impossible to convey. One cannot reduce zero to one, or one to zero. It is impossible to state the relationship between the One without a second, in the phrase of the *Upanishads*, to all that follows from it by multiplication and duplication, by permutation and combination, in the realm of numbers. There is a fundamental incommensurability between No Number and the world of numbers. When the Vedic sages spoke of the mysterious bond of Being in Non-Being, they did not refer to any ascertainable relationship. This truth must be apprehended, even in the early stages of the Path, for it is essential to the development of *Manas* through universalization. It is impossible for the mind to reach the plane of *Mahat* or the universal mind until it is willing to forego its addiction to finitiz ing tendencies . Put more mystically, one must learn to recognize the fundamental difference between the Soundless Sound, the unutterable unmanifested Sound or *Logos*, and that which is partially uttered or revealed and is sometimes characterized by the sacred syllable *AUM*. Without understanding this difference it is impossible to become a true apprentice to Adepts, Magicians and Initiates, and to commence the progressive transmutation of all life-atoms.

Unless a person can to some extent understand this at a preliminary level, making it the basis of abstraction and meditation, he or she should leave *Gupta Vidya* alone. For, a person ill prepared for *Gupta Vidya* will be in constant danger of dragging the Teachings downward, concretizing them either through images of language or of perception. The same point was made by Nicholas of Cusa, in saying that no one would be entitled to have a meaningful conception of God who has not thoroughly mastered the idea of infinity. Human beings do, it is true, have a natural attraction to the unknown – one might even say to the Unknowable – and to the divine. But very few are actually willing to take the trouble to make a fundamental break in cognition with the world of visible things. This is why Socrates said in *Phaedo* that many bear the emblems, but the Initiates are few. Few are ready to enter into the invisible world in which they must progressively ascend towards the realm of the Divine Darkness, the realm of the noumenal Reality.

If the manifested cosmos in its invisible form is difficult for ordinary human beings even to conceive, how much more difficult must it be for them to distinguish that invisible but manifested universe from the absolutely ideal universe of the unmanifest? Where the highest metaphysical discrimination requires the capacity to negate even *Mulaprakriti* if one would not do violence to the mystery of *Parabrahman*, most human beings are not even prepared to cognize, much less negate, those aspects of *prakriti* that lie immediately beyond the physical, visible plane. The visible solar system, for example, is nothing but a superficial appearance upon the waves of space. That space, however, is not a blank abstraction, but rather a sphere pervaded by the *Vaishvanara* fire on the invisible plane of objective consciousness. Though invisible to the naked eye, this magnetic solar fire is the pre-genetic basis in metaphysical substance of the objective solar world. The solar magnetic fire, which is omnipresent throughout the solar system, is itself an emanation from an even more ethereal plane – the realm of the radiant *Hiranyagarbha* or Golden Egg of the solar world. This, in turn, is a differentiation of the eternal germ on the plane of *sutratman* that exists in latency within the bosom of *Mulaprakriti*. The entire range of possibilities inherent in that eternal and all-potent germ gives way to the Golden Egg of the invisible astral realm, itself connected with the objective magnetic fire omnipresent within the solar system. All these gradations of the invisible world lie on what one might call the near side of the unmanifest, forming together the cosmic differentiations of *Mulaprakriti*. *Mulaprakriti* itself is nothing but a veil over *Parabrahman*. Meta-geometry provides a series of powerful aids in comprehending this fundamental distinction upon which so much depends in meditation, mysticism and magic. Meta-geometry is, in effect, an archetypal record of the Mysteries.

> From the very beginning of Aeons – in time and space in our Round and Globe – the Mysteries of Nature (at any rate, those which it is lawful for our races to know) were recorded by the pupils of those same now invisible "heavenly men", in geometrical figures and symbols. The keys thereto passed from one generation of "wise men" to the other. Some of the symbols, thus passed from the east to the west, were brought therefrom by Pythagoras, who was not the inventor of his famous "Triangle". The latter figure, along with the plane cube and circle, are more eloquent and scientific descriptions of the order of the evolution of the Universe, spiritual and psychic, as well as physical, than volumes of descriptive Cosmogonies and revealed "Geneses".

Ibid., i 612

The Pythagorean Triangle was derived from India. In the Pythagorean school it was the basis of understanding something fundamental about the elements of geometry, which are prior to both space and time. They are metaphysical principles, and to grasp them in their pure essence is to understand them in relation to metaphysical space. The first great idea in the series of meta-geometric glyphs is that of the mathematical point within the circle, representing the universal and absolute Deity. The point presupposes the boundless plane of existence, represented by the plane of the boundless circle, which gives rise out of its infinitude and incognizability to that which becomes the pre-genetic basis of all manifestation. That root is the Pythagorean *Monas* or Point, which emerges out of the Divine Darkness, initiates a series of transformations and then withdraws again into the bosom of the Divine Darkness from which it came. Simultaneously with the disappearance of the Point within the Circle of its origin, the Point is transformed into a line or diameter, and then the diameter becomes the cross. Such meta-geometric transformations are not intended to create a logical or empirical relationship between the unconditioned and the conditioned. Rather, they are meant to help individuals reach out in imagination, in consciousness and through meditation, to the unconditioned.

Next in the series of meta-geometric glyphs comes the hierogram, or equilateral triangle, within the circle. Moving from the absolute unity of the Divine Essence, exemplified by the plane of the boundless circle and the point which represents the universal and absolute Deity, one comes to the Pythagorean Triangle.

What it really meant was the triune co-equal Nature of the first differentiated Substance, or the *con-substantiality* of the (manifested) Spirit, matter and the Universe – their "Son", who proceeds from the Point (the real, esoteric **LOGOS**) or the Pythagorean **MONAD.** For the Greek *Monas* signifies "Unity" in its primary sense.

> This Triangle is the unmanifest production of the first Point within the Circle. The Point retires and merges back into the Circle after having emanated the first three points and connected them

with lines, thus forming the first noumenal basis of the Second Triangle in the Manifested World.

Ibid., i 614

Once the primordial Point has radiated its triadic ray to form the equilateral triangle and then disappeared, the apex of that Triangle takes on a Logoic role in relation to the subsequent stages of manifestation.

> The Monad – only the emanation and reflection of the Point (*Logos*) in the phenomenal World – becomes, as the apex of the manifested equilateral triangle, the "Father". The left side or line is the Duad, the "Mother", regarded as the evil, counteracting principle (Plutarch, *De Placitis Placitorum*); the right side represents the Son ("his Mother's husband" in every Cosmogony, as one with the apex); at the basic line is the Universal plane of productive Nature, unifying on the phenomenal plane Father-Mother-Son, as these were unified in the apex, in the supersensuous World. By mystic transmutation they became the Quaternary – the triangle became the **TETRAKTIS.**

> *Ibid.*

Thus, it is the reflection of the original Point within the Circle which becomes, at a later stage, that which generates the Pythagorean Triangle, whose base line serves as the point of emanation for the countless hosts of gods, monads and atoms in the manifested worlds.

> These successive hierarchies of beings are represented within the Pythagorean Triangle by the Pythagorean Decad, the set of one, two, three and four points. It consists of ten points inscribed pyramid-like (from one to the last four) within its three lines, and it symbolizes the Universe in the famous Pythagorean Decad. The upper single dot is a Monad, and represents a Unit-Point, which is the Unity from whence all proceeds, and all is of the same essence with it. While the ten dots within the triangle represent the phenomenal world, the three sides of the equilateral triangle

which enclose the pyramid of dots are the barriers of noumenal Matter, or Substance, that separate it from the world of Thought.

Ibid., 616

Within the Decad, the four points at the base indicate the connection between the Triangle and the world of solid geometry. The Triangle itself may be seen as a tetrahedron or pyramid, transformable into the cube and then into the other five Pythagorean or Platonic solids.

> The Decad within the Triangle is sometimes referred to as the Tetraktys, a mystical term having many meanings. These ten points contain the potential of all manifestation, providing the basis for everything that is possible in the vast multiplicity of the universe. Everything is prefigured within the ten points. The ten points inscribed within that "Pythagorean triangle" are worth all the theogonies and angelologies ever emanated from the theological brain. For he who interprets them – on their very face, and in the order given – will find in these seventeen points (the seven Mathematical Points hidden) the uninterrupted series of the genealogies from the first Heavenly to terrestrial man. And, as they give the order of Beings, so they reveal the order in which were evolved the Kosmos, our earth, and the primordial elements by which the latter was generated. Begotten in the invisible Depths, and in the womb of the same "Mother" as its fellow-globes – he who will master the mysteries of our Earth, will have mastered those of all others.

Ibid., 612-613

To understand the seven hidden points, one should attend to the six small triangles that can be formed within the Decad surrounding its central point. Each of these triangles has a central point of its own, and in addition, the midpoint at the base represents a seventh hidden point. The alchemical significance of these hidden points relates to the creation, through Deity Yoga, of a permanent divine vesture or Buddha-body. Sometimes misleadingly and loosely called the permanent astral, this vesture is an exact replica of the inmost causal body of the perfected man.

Certainly, a conception so central to mystical training cannot have a merely mechanical or external interpretation. Thus, the seven hidden points within the Pythagorean Decad must, like all meta-geometric conceptions, be understood in relation to the concept of metaphysical depth. In addition to length, breadth and thickness, which are accessible in the realm of sensory perception, there is depth. Whatever the objective dimensions of an entity, they can yield no direct sense of the mystical meaning of depth. No merely visual representation, however subtle, can reveal the dimension of depth which has to do with *Mulaprakriti*, primordial root substance, the one element and force in the undifferentiated realm. *Mulaprakriti* is a paradigmatic plane upon which the Logoic constructions of meta-geometry arise. One cannot approach this realm through any kind of inductive process based upon phenomenal conceptions of length, breadth and thickness. Such a below-above approach to meta-geometry can yield only a useless collection of lifeless truisms. The real breadth, depth and points of meta-geometry are living abstractions that embody first on the unmanifest planes and then on the manifest the boundless potential of the Divine Darkness.

The cosmic creativity represented in the glyphs of meta-geometry is inseparable from the *Fohatic* force of the cosmos, the vast reservoir of energy latent in *Mulaprakriti*. Meta-geometric diagrams are capable of endless duplication through transformation, translation and reflection along the axes of metaphysical space. Thus, each of the infinite points in space is capable of becoming and generating all that is displayed in the Pythagorean Triangle. This universally distributed potency is a key to understanding the process of manifestation itself. It must not be conceived in terms of staccato movements or static images, but rather in terms of a series of *Fohatic* unfoldments of pre-cosmic divine ideation within *Mulaprakriti*. Finally, at the third stage this brings about the synthesis of the seven *Logoi*, the seven Sons of Light, and then it becomes the basis of the vast manifestations of the forces at work in invisible and visible Nature. The natural sciences, which seek at once to understand these forces in relation to the phenomenal realm and to transcend them, will never succeed if they remain content in tracing out mere shadows or ghosts of supersensuous matter in motion. Limiting their study to the effects of the activity of that primordial field, they cannot understand very much about perpetual eternal motion. Cut off conceptually from the primordial field of undifferentiated energy, they cannot reveal anything about the infinitudes of latent energy within *Parabrahman*, which have no reference to any period of manifestation.

Nevertheless, each individual human monad in its pilgrimage throughout the seven kingdoms of manifested Nature has an intimate connection to that primordial field. Each and every human being has a living link, through the seven Sons of Light, to the most potent of all realms – that of absolute negativeness. All the scintillas of manifested life emerging through the base line of the Pythagorean Triangle into active manifested existence are ensouled by the divine energies radiating from the noumenon of the seven states of undifferentiated cosmic substance. The divine *Dhyani* energies arise in that zero realm as the differentiated aspects of universal motion, the Great Breath.

> When *Fohat* is said to produce "Seven Laya Centres", it means that for formative or creative purposes, the **GREAT LAW** (Theists may call it God) stops, or rather modifies its perpetual motion on seven invisible points within the area of the manifested Universe. "The great Breath digs through Space seven holes into *Laya* to cause them to circumgyrate during *Manvantara*."

> *Ibid.*, 147

The endless spinning of these seven invisible points in seemingly empty space is supremely potent in relation to the entire manifested realm. This hebdomadic activity of the One *Logos* makes possible, within any manifested system, the capacity to visualize its eventual disintegration and decay. At the same time, within such a manifested system, it is also the basis of the possibility of ultimate transcendence. Krishna, the *Logos* in the cosmos and the God in man, creates all these worlds through the mysterious power of *maya*, causing them to revolve upon the universal wheel of time. Krishna, as the divine Avatar, exists in all the invisible interstices and points hidden in the phenomenal world. Through devotion to Krishna, each pilgrim soul can find the breadth of heart and the depth of understanding needed to realize a relationship with the *Logos* within. Far beyond even the loftiest conceptions of modern thought, this is the true aim of *Gupta Vidya*, the hidden science, and the final goal of meta-geometrical insight, deep meditation and inward transformation.

Hermes, March 1986
Raghavan Iyer

"BY THEIR FRUITS..."

This mergence of the *Jivanmukta* into *Ishwara* may he likened to what may happen in the case of the sun when a comet falls upon it; there is in the case of the Sun an accession of heat and light; so also, whenever any particular individual reaches the highest state of spiritual culture, develops in himself all the virtues that alone entitle him to a union with *Ishwara* and finally unites his soul with *Ishwara*, there is, as it were, a sort of reaction emanating from *Ishwara* for the good of humanity; and in particular cases an impulse is generated in *Ishwara* to incarnate for the good of humanity. This is the highest consummation of human aspiration and endeavour.

Notes on the Bhagavad Gita
T. Subba Row

Shankaracharya, in *Self-Knowledge* and *The Crest Jewel of Wisdom*, provides a wealth of instruction about meditation and particularly the relation between *Viveka* or discrimination and *Vairagya* or detachment. Anyone attempting to apply these teachings will find that it is difficult, but he will also learn that it is extremely enjoyable. If thoughtful, he will conclude that, by definition, there could not be any fixed technique of meditation upon the transcendent. Technique is as particularized a notion as one can imagine, a mechanistic term. A *techne* or skill has rules and can be reproduced. On the other hand, that which is transcendental cannot be reproduced. It does not manifest, and it is beyond everything that exists, so there can be no technique for meditation upon it.

Another way of putting it, an older way and perhaps less misleading, is that of the Dalai Lama in his book *My Land and My People*, where in a few pages he explains that the teaching of the Buddha is both wisdom and method. They go together. Wisdom is meaningless to us unless there is a method. But the method itself cannot be understood unless in relation to wisdom. He says that there is a distinction to be made between absolute truth and relative truth. In other words, wisdom is your relationship to knowledge, and that relationship involves the means you employ. It is skill in the use of what we call knowledge, but skill that is neither rigid nor final in its modes of embodiment. There is a natural allowance for growth in oneself and within others.

In this arena of inner growth, he who really knows does not tell, partly because he knows that what is essential cannot be told, in the Socratic sense in which wisdom and virtue could never be taught. But partly also he chooses not to tell when telling is of no help. The Buddha, the Master of skillful means, said that whichever way you go – telling little, telling much, or keeping quiet – in every case you have created karma. There were times when the Buddha told nothing. There were times when he told a great deal merely by telling a fairy story but saying through it much more than is ordinarily possible. There were times when he said very little, and even this sometimes became a bone of contention among disciples. We are dealing with the karma involved in human encounters, and this karma must not be physicalized and only understood literally and exoterically. That is our whole tragedy. We have a physical conception of telling and of silence, but that is because we still have not understood that the real battle is going on between that subtle and rarefied plane of consciousness where the true suns are, and that boisterous plane of consciousness which is the astral light, where there is an immense array of inverted shadows and images.

Words like "telling," "knowing" and "being silent" have to do with inner postures. As long as we seek *external* representations of the *inner* postures of the spiritual life, the spiritual life is not for us in this incarnation, and perhaps just as well. Maybe this is where humanity has grown up. There is now no need for mollycoddling. There is no need for giving in to the residual and tragic arrogance of those who are on the verge of annihilation, by pandering to them, yielding external tokens, or performing external signs. In this

Aquarian age, spiritual life is in the mind, and people have got to be much more willing to assume full responsibility for all their choices. The reading of the signs requires a deeper knowledge, or a tougher kind of integrity. The only honest position for anyone is that, given whatever one thing he really knows in his life, in terms of that he is entitled, in E.M.Forster's phrase, "to connect" – to connect with what is told and what is not told. People are brought up in India, and indeed all over the East, to know from early on that what the eyes are saying is important, what the physical gestures are saying is important, and that ominous or peaceful silences bear meanings of many kinds. Brought up in the rich and complex poetry of silence, gesture and speech through all the seven apertures of the human face, there is no such problem as between knowing in one particular sense and telling in one particular sense.

A lot of the subtlety has gone out of our lives, probably all over the world, but nonetheless we must recognize that wisdom always implies an immense, incredible flexibility of method. Let us not play games, least of all adopt sick and self-destructive attitudes, where in the name of belittling ourselves we insidiously belittle our Teachers. What this really comes to is blackmail and bargaining and they never helped anyone. On the other hand, let us genuinely be grateful for whatever we receive at all levels. It is part of the meaning of the *Guruparampara* chain that if one were smart enough to be benefitted at some level and to be ever grateful to the person who first taught one the alphabet, then one is more likely to make good use of Teachers in higher realms. We are dealing with something archetypal in which our whole lives are involved, but in which each one will be unique in his or her response.

Conversely, there is nothing predictably easy about the emergence, appearance, decisions, masks and modes of any spiritual Teacher. To assume that would be to limit the Fraternity or to imagine that an organization or some individuals could make captive or bind him. The moment such a being becomes captive, as

Plato pointed out in the *Republic,* his withdrawal or his failure is inevitable. He will be free. And what he is really doing would be known only to him. What is important is to know that existentially he will point beyond himself to the *Tathagatas.* It is a hard lesson for the world – especially in a worn-out West that is still fighting the Middle Ages – that *a true Master is a true servant.* The reason why we find it difficult, even in our everyday language, to understand what is involved in being a Master is because we have ceased to understand what is it to be a true servant. When we can restore the full meaning and the grandeur to the notion of a true and totally reliable servant, only then will we understand what is it to be a Master of Wisdom and Method. Who are the Masters? They are the Servants of mankind. Who, then, must be their agents? Those who exemplify the art of service, who are unquestioning, total, and absolute in their obedience to their *Gurus.*

Apparently, as H.P. Blavatsky stressed, this turns out to be more difficult for many people in the post-Aristotelian age in the modern West than it appears at first sight. Can obedience be combined with a tremendous courage? Can a lion be a lamb as well? Nothing is impossible for human beings when they master the art of acting from within without, from above below. The process could never be successfully reversed. On sacred matters can one say anything definite? If one can, any of us, should he say, or indeed what would be the point of so saying? But all of this must show itself by its fruits. Surely in regard to the latest of Teachers and their servants it would be true, as it was true of the oldest of Teachers who came to what we call the West, but who really came to the whole world from the East: "By their fruits they shall be judged." Surely it could be said of any teacher what was true of the paradigm of all Teachers, the Buddha: he was a spiritual Teacher in that he gave lasting confidence to everyone else. Yet he did it in a way that was inimitable, in a manner that baffles analysis and defies imitation. Or we could even say that every true teacher must have something in common with Krishna, the planetary spirit who overbroods all Teachers, in that Krishna was always an enigma to everyone around him. It took Arjuna ten chapters to put right his relationship with Krishna, to whom he said, "I took you for a friend, I sported with you." In other words, he tried to put him in a box. In the second chapter of the *Bhagavad Gita,* when Arjuna asked him to describe the characteristics of a wise man, Krishna did not say, "Look at me." Krishna gave the most magnificent impersonal portrait. So surely then it is only on the basis of the invisible thirty-two psychological marks of the true Teacher that recognition and direct benefit are possible.

No Teacher can be separated from other Teachers, and when we consider the broader import of spiritual instruction we are really talking about a fundamental renaissance, heralding the civilization of the future. Those who feel they have found clues within themselves should treasure them. Those who want to help should perpetually prepare themselves. Certainly, no one need waste time and energy in speculating about it because this is not a matter which could be a fit subject for opinion or speculation. To put it in a more positive way, anyone's opinion is as good for him as anyone else's, because in the end it is his life; he has to decide. Many are called but few are chosen. But anyone could decide at any point to do the best he can in relation to the best he knows. In the talismanic words of Mahatma K.H., "He who does the best he can and knows how, does enough for us." Anyone who does the best he can and knows how can do enough for the Messenger of the Fraternity, and indeed thereby himself become a messenger, in a sense. He becomes a teacher because he has shown what it is to be a servant.

So then it gets back to oneself. What can one do to prepare oneself? What can one do to be a worthy servant available at the right time to do that which benefits oneself on one's Path, but which has meaning in relation to a much vaster vision and plan that can be seen with the mind's eye? Though it is hidden, it can be seen to be partly manifest, even before it happens. What is there at this very time which is crucial in enabling us to be ready to be at hand in the future? This is the classic *chela*-like attitude that anyone can take, but it does not mean going here or there. It requires that wherever one is, one is willing to be wholly available. There is a protective blindness in regard to the future, a protective blindness in one part of our nature. In another part of our nature we know. It is said in the oldest traditions of humanity that the future is very dangerous knowledge. The future is a closed book at all times through the compassion of the universe, and in another sense through the inability of individuals to be ready to bear the knowledge. A Teacher once said that unless a person is so made up, or so ready in his total makeup, that nothing in the future will frighten him and nothing in the future will make him elated, he will not be ready to know what is in the future. That is surely as true now as always in regard to unveiling the future. Shaw's remark about freemasonry and marriages applies even more to the code-language of Adepts – those who are outside will never know, and those who are within are pledged to eternal secrecy.

Behind all the rhythms of nature that are perceptible to us there are other rhythms that we impose. And behind these there is a kind of chaos in which there is another rhythm that is very mysterious. The Monad of man has no resting place. It is on a pilgrimage where it is ceaselessly changing conditions. There is no refuge, because if there were refuge for the Monad, it would no longer be involved in evolution. In that sense, one might say, surely at the end of evolution there must be a resting place. Whether there is or not, for a Monad that comes voluntarily into the process there is no resting place, in a more poignant sense. Above all, for the Son of Man who comes to bear a certain cross, there is no resting place in that he chooses a destiny within the framework of universal consciousness. We should reflect deeply on that extraordinary passage in *The Secret Doctrine* where we are told that in regard to the great cycle or circle of necessity, in the end the only choice is between being a volunteer in the iniquitous course and being involuntarily propelled into it. As Simone Weil said, you either choose suffering, or suffering chooses you. As Subba Row understood, the *Logos* chooses the *Avatar* who allows himself to be so chosen. This para-historical paradox is pivotal to the destiny of mankind in the culminating decades of this century.

Toronto
October 9, 1971

> Through many millions of world-ages many people hear, when they are born, neither my name nor of Perfect Ones, neither that of the teaching nor that of my community. Thus is the fruit of bad action.
>
> But when gentle and forbearing beings originate here in this world of man, then because of their good actions they see me revealing the teaching as soon as they are born.
>
> Gautama Buddha

Hermes, May 1976
Raghavan Iyer

SHIVA AND SELF-REGENERATION

There is neither teacher nor teaching, learner nor learning, neither thou nor I, nor this empirical universe; I am universal self-consciousness, the reality which is untinctured by any modification. I am the secondless, supreme and attributeless Bliss of Shiva.

The Secret Doctrine, i 616
H.P. Blavatsky

Shiva is the supreme principle of potent ideation and constructive imagination, bridging the unconditioned and the conditioned, the unlimited and the limited, the boundless and what is bounded in the realm of time. Shiva represents a noumenal intelligence ceaselessly at work in the life process through all the elemental, mineral, vegetable and animal kingdoms of Nature. Shiva is also accessible to each and every human being, not only the highest and the holiest, but also the most sinful and depraved whenever they have a flash of true repentance. The mundane realm, of course, is that wherein most human beings encounter a host of difficulties, because they cannot connect disparate elements of fleeting experience or else are victims of false connections that bombard them from outside. Human beings must resolve to stand on their own. They need to wake up to the fact that each is alone in this world, that in the end each is the custodian of his or her own hopes and promises, and that each is the only agent able to make a radical change in his or her own kingdom. This is not a task that can be transferred to any other agent.

A person who comes to understand this is ready to contemplate Shiva as a *yogin*, as the archetypal Man of Renunciation, as the paradigm of the pilgrim soul who has been through every possible experience of every possible human being. But Shiva can also be seen constantly at work destroying the froth of complacent illusion through disintegration. Shiva represents the universal frustration of all the foolish and faulty plans of deluded souls. In other words, Shiva epitomizes the insight that most of human history is based upon a terrible expenditure of emotion, an attempt to force upon this world schemes which must inevitably be frustrated because they are based upon the lie of separateness and cannot be supported by the cosmos. Beyond the lower realms of Nature and beyond the human realm, Shiva is the living metaphysical link between the unmanifest and the manifest *Logos*.

Since most problems arise in the middle or human realm, wherein individuals must learn to take a stand, Shiva is initially most relevant as the archetype of every seeker on earth. There is a specific point at which individuals are ready to take stock of the sum total of their experiences and to cut through the compulsive succession of dreamy, illusionary experiences. For the individual at this crossroad, Shiva becomes the paradigm of the perfect human being who is fully self-conscious. Within all the traumas and tragedies of human beings there lies latent the seed of self-awareness which enables an individual – whether in a future life, or at the moment of death, or many years later in this life – to cut through the froth. Shiva represents the pristine seed of a new beginning rooted in the Truth that makes one fearless. This signifies a new kind of courage – to see all the phases of life together and to cut through the process of *samsara.*

Unfortunately, too many human beings are ready to renounce only after they have been burnt out by their previous refusals to renounce and by the enormous burden of their exaggerated and ever-growing attachments. There is, therefore, a certain sadness in the eyes of a person who starts the climb towards the mountains, often at an advanced age, in the hope that at least his few remaining years may not be wasted in delusion. When one renounces separateness, one's life opens itself up to all human lives, to the enormity and vast Himalayan scope of the human pilgrimage, encompassing not only friends and relatives, but all human beings – strangers in the city, strangers in the streets, millions upon millions of persons who live and toil in extreme conditions of deprivation and desolation. Everywhere human beings are caught up without meaning in a life that is extremely hard economically or enormously wasteful in its focus upon providing for the passing fancies and endless consumption of other human beings. Everywhere there is the pain of emptiness, of fatigue, excess and self-indulgence. But there is also the pain of actual deprivation and the pain of loneliness.

The challenge of Shiva today is to learn to relate to all these beings. What has always been true has now come much more to a head. Many human beings are living lives of utter waste, yet the very impulse that gives one the courage to go back to sleep after a trying day can become something more. It can become the courage to renounce the whole concept of the self bound up with memories and frustrations. It can quicken a sense of a larger self, a sense of involvement in the self of all humanity, and a concern for the wider horizon of human consciousness transcending the visible, the partial and the transitory.

In that fearless willingness to renounce, such a person has not only the actual inspiration of Shiva as an ideal or object – whether as a *linga,* or a statue, or as the author of certain texts, or as the supreme god Maheshvara who presides over and transcends the process of creation – but also as an actual hierophantic *yogin.* In *Gupta Vidya,* Shiva is Dakshinamurti, the Initiator of Initiates, responsible for the Mysteries in the Third, Fourth and Fifth Root-Races. Shiva was involved in all the triumphs and travails of the human race going back to Atlantean times, and Shiva will also be involved in all the heroic struggles of human beings for millions of years into the future, until the emergence of the Sixth Race. It is as if all the knowledge of all human souls in their desperate gropings towards the Mysteries is engraved within his sphinx-like face. He is the silent witness to their terrible failures. At the same time, he also bears shining witness to the vital hint of hope that all may one day begin anew and make a fresher, cleaner, better start.

Shiva, then, has a universal meaning, whether one has explicitly heard or thought much about him or not. No human being who experiences suffering and deep disappointment, no one who is frightened by what lies ahead when death draws near or who deeply reflects upon the suffering of humanity can help but see that something new is needed to understand the human predicament. Something is needed which involves going within, and it comes from silence rather than speech, from brooding rather than verbalizing. It involves thinking deeply and with total honesty about oneself, acknowledging every tendency of prevarication, doubt, procrastination, contradiction, ambivalence, ill will, envy, jealousy, hatred, pride and vulnerability. The willingness to enter into the dungeon within the *psyche* in which these demons exist, and the strength to come out of it courageously, vindicate Shiva. Shiva represents the assured capacity to reduce delusions to ashes. The fire of spiritual perception and objective honesty, the light of pure *manas,* can burn out psychic dross which is powerful only because of a misplaced allegiance to a false *persona.* This is a long and painful process of purification. It takes years and lives to complete. If it is a true beginning, however, it will have the benediction of all those who have made similar beginnings and who have attained to some level of success on the side of that which is strong in the human race.

What characterizes wise men, Initiates, Teachers and *Mahatmas* is the unconditional faith they can place in every single human being, against all odds, despite the past and whatever the record. This is not faith in something merely potential, but faith in that which is omnipresent, sacred and indestructible. It is like a cry to the divine and an affirmation of willingness to persist, to be tested, to sift and select ever more clearly and wisely. Such a faith implies increasing silence, with less propensity to manifest in the coming years, so that one begins to take on the burden of living with more deliberation and more dignity. This resolve and the very desire to make it, as well as the willingness to persist in it, draw upon that which Shiva represents. Rather than being a negative view of human despair, it is a fearless recognition of the myriads of forgotten instances of extraordinary redemption. Something Christ-like and Buddha-like has happened again and again among millions of human beings, and yet it has been accompanied by a colossal sense of waste, suffering and frustration caused by false consolidation of the ego.

All this involves vast magnitudes. To talk of Shiva is thus to get beyond a narrow focus upon one's own horizon and to take one's own place within the larger whole. This is not something vague. It requires hard work, the effort of thinking through the problem and beginning to look at all beings in a different way.

While many of the obstacles that emerge are the familiar ones, they appear in different forms. One of them provides a clue to the subtle connection between love and asceticism. Shiva represents that strength which results from voluntary self-control carried to its highest point, where it becomes effortless and full of joy. As the paradigm of *yogins,* Shiva is often depicted as besmeared with ashes, carrying a necklace of skulls. This signifies a clarity of vision in which there is no truck with human fantasy, desire or ambition. It represents a courageous recognition of the underground in which most human beings live. This terrible Hades exists owing to the ugliness of human presumption. While there is so much of this everywhere and everyone can see it in themselves, nonetheless, something else that transcends understanding is involved in this perception. A kind of veiling has taken place. One could not see all this ugliness if one were not more than the sum total of all that is repellent, if there were not a seed of Platonic divine discontent moving one constantly towards an ineffable beauty. Shiva stands outside time. He carries in his right hand the drum, which represents the cyclic beat of time, but he himself is beyond time. Even the iconography and mythology of Shiva are amongst the oldest that exist. They precede all known religions and go back five to seven thousand years, to ancient coins and seals. They are part of the prehistoric folk memory of mankind. Shiva always has to do with the truth of the human condition, the truth of human failure, the truth of human persistence, and especially the truth of the possibility of human redemption which can only come with freedom from illusion.

Certainly, the effortless asceticism of Shiva was an ideal beyond all possibility for Parvati. As a young girl, totally devoted to Shiva and feeling totally unworthy of him, she nonetheless wanted to give her whole life to Shiva and to receive his guidance and love. Therefore, Parvati went into a tremendous *tapas* lasting thousands of years. It is quite overwhelming to think of so great a preparation – strengthening, purging, purifying oneself – but people have done these things and done them life after life, thus earning proximity to the great hierophants of the human race. Parvati, propelled by one-pointedness and unconditionality of love, was able to penetrate the veil of Shiva's totally impervious, impartial and cold-seeming impersonality. She was able to touch that in Shiva which knew all along that she had to go through the fire of purgation and trial. Then he could expound to her the most magnificent mystical truths about initiation, reveal to her the magic that is possible in human life, in terms of fundamental philosophical and metaphysical principles, so that she herself came to be revered as a custodian of the Mysteries, invoked like Kwan-Yin for her boundless compassion. She is on everyone's side, and she is immensely resourceful in showing how the door can open for every single being. At the same time, however, she has no illusions, and sees to the core of every human heart.

The essential meaning of the story of Shiva and Parvati involves the hidden heart of the cosmos, the secret heart of humanity and the infinite depths within one's own immortal heart. No education in terms of the imperfect, tortuous and complicating mind has anything to do with true concentration and understanding. Many an athlete learns to concentrate better than a person burdened by words and concepts that have nothing to do with the power of ideation. When the soul's true power of understanding is aroused, it can take wings and remain in a state of deep abstraction for hours, days or even months, visualizing that which must ultimately represent the incarnation of universal Good. Genuine training in this direction can begin with the exercise of thinking outward through a series of concentric and expanding circles. It is not easy to expand one's horizon to include all visible human beings on earth today, much less to include all human beings. Yet to understand the heart of humanity, one must enlarge one's vision to encompass all human souls that are disembodied. This includes all those who died in recent centuries, leaving their shells in *kamaloka*, as well as all those who died earlier and who are in various stages of *devachan*, ranging from hundreds to thousands of years in duration, and who wake up at different times and come as babies onto the earthly scene, becoming involved in different parts of the world, in different families, as puzzled strangers. To think consciously of all human souls in this enigmatic way is to bring one's mind closer to the perspective of Shiva, for Shiva sees all humanity at once.

In principle, it is possible for a perfected being with such an infinite horizon to be an ideal for imperfect human beings only if we presuppose that all souls can free themselves from captivity to images, captivity to the present and, above all, captivity to the froth that surrounds their conceptions of perfected beings. Even though there may be something precious and noble at the root of one's conception of Shamballa, El Dorado or the Golden Age, psychic excitement is generated the moment one materializes it. This excess produces a plethora of escapist tendencies which result in pathetic and irresponsible human beings who cannot do the most elementary things like sitting, reading or writing. Victims of their own fantasy, they want to escape but find there is nowhere to go. The entire delusion is based upon a lie that is fed by popular literature and movies from which a few make a lot of money trafficking in human illusion. It invades the *psyche* of millions of human beings, so that they hardly begin to live or to take any responsibility for their lives. Instead of maturing, they are retarded, pushed towards the doom of nihilism. What provides the pressure behind all this is the toughest peer pressure of all, which comes out of *kamaloka*. One may think that it comes from contemporaries, but in fact it comes from *kamaloka* as the raucous cries of those on the verge of annihilation. They are bitter because they were self-righteous before, and even now have no humility or honesty, but curse and curse with unmitigated fury. With their evil-eyed cocksureness about human weakness, they are convinced that there will be more and more hosts of victims coming out of this world who are going to be taken in, trapped in the sacred name of freedom which is misused, and reduced to a condition that is a prelude to disintegration.

Think, then, of the compassion involved in a being who must know all of this. Looking at the world, Shiva can immediately see its pure potential in the golden embryo of every baby. At the same time, seeing the way so many live and the karma they are creating, he can also see them tortured. This torture is psychological. Though artists may sometimes render it in graphic images or poets like Dante may convey it through metaphors of fire and ice, it is in reality terrible mental self-torture. Once set into motion by one's actions, it is inevitable, because all the life-atoms one has ever misused come back to render one completely coiled, impotent and powerless. No amount of cries for forgiveness can cancel the karma. So much toughness is needed by beings who would take all this into account that one is speaking of a perspective far removed from all but the very greatest of human hearts. Only a Buddha or Shakespeare or Jesus could truly begin to understand the immensity of the human condition, the immensity of the human tragedy and the immensity of the cost of illusion. That is why Shiva is so often shown in a terrible form, dancing in the crematorium, garlanded with skulls. He has seen it all, and he has seen through it all. He has seen all the fake *yogins* and pseudo-*fakirs*, and has also seen the sadder victims, who never learnt how to think for themselves or how to use imagination, speech and self-command to initiate a current for the general good.

As one expands awareness of humanity through ever-increasing concentric circles, in a mythic and mystical sense one is going to enter Hades. One is going to confront the torment of millions of human souls who are snuffed out like candles. This is true whether one considers human beings presently incarnated on the earth – which looked like a necropolis to some in the Victorian Age and is still the same – or whether one begins to be aware of human beings in the invisible realms. The difference between the invisible world and the physical plane is little indeed. To be able to see all this and still believe that there is meaning to it, that everything is totally just and exactly what it is because of long chains of causation going back over hundreds of lives and thousands of years, and yet refuse to condemn a single soul, requires extraordinary courage. No wonder, then, it is impossible to convey such an experience. It requires the wisdom of Hermes to assimilate such a perspective, but that wisdom is not only for the living. It is for the future, when Initiates will come into this world disguised and disseminate the self-regenerating modes of new social structures.

Something of this vast perspective can be glimpsed by looking into the *Puranas*. Even if one reads just a few passages from the many volumes of the *Shiva Purana,* one will be amazed at its scope. The perspective is inclusive of all gods, all *Rishis,* all classes of souls. To begin to get a sense of this is to begin to awaken from the utter absurdity of pseudo-knowledge and gross over-generalization. It takes courage to recognize that one knows too little of the human condition and still less of universal good. Yet one can nonetheless find the strength to enter a series of self-regenerative meditations. That is what Shiva represents and it is what Buddha did archetypally. It is what all great beings have done in the past, and it can be done again at any time by anyone who is ready to go into the deepest series of meditations. If one cannot do it indefinitely and sustain it, one can make small beginnings, using a week or a month, taking advantage of the cycles of the sun and the moon, and especially times such as Shivaratri, the vigil night of Shiva. Such times should be used for spiritual self-regeneration on behalf of the humanity of the future. One may prepare by spending several days living quietly but remaining wide awake, sleeping less than normal and eating less. One could use the time to think about the universal human condition and one's own life in that context. Courage is needed for this kind of extended meditation, because once one has begun it, one cannot get out of it. Yet one is glad at certain times to enter a deeper meditation which is even more detached and in which one can tap an even profounder realm of calmness. Then one can empty out everything that comes out of this conditioned world – touch and taste, the waters, the sky, the fire, the flame, the *aether,* the fire mist, even the most ethereal vesture which is ever invisible behind the cosmos.

At this point, Shiva becomes a link between *Parabrahm* and *Ishvara*. Shiva, indeed, is in another part of himself Vishnu, and in yet another part Brahma. These are all words for a single host under a single, supreme *Logos*. When Shiva has, so to speak, a foot in *Parabrahm*, Shiva has gone to sleep. This is the immovable Shiva, totally indifferent to clime and change, unaffected by earthquakes, cataclysms and geological changes. Untouched by everything, he is the immovable rock, the eternal pillar of light, one with *Parabrahm*, the divine ground in the Divine Darkness. Shiva is also connected to *Ishvara*, the creative *Logos*, but Shiva knows that even something so overwhelmingly glorious as *Ishvara* is only an appearance and a veil. It may last for billions of years, but still that is nothing for Shiva, merely a matter of a few days, according to the old books. What for a human being is a full lifetime is like a moment for Manu, and what is a lifetime for Manu is like a day for Vishnu. But what is like a lifetime for Vishnu is only a day for Shiva. The same immensity of perspective is found in the *Yoga Vasishtha*, panicularly in the discourse of Bhusunda to the Sage Vasishtha. Bhusunda is only another name for the immovable Shiva, the Witness of all cycles and vast epochs of manifestation, myriads of worlds and galaxies. This reaches beyond the solar system and what are called stars and constellations in the myths connecting Shiva with *Dhruva* or *Rohini*.

This level of contemplation is so timeless and boundless, and at the same time so subtle and mobile, that it is often symbolized by Shiva as the dancing wanderer or beggar who travels in rags and who can be in any and every situation. This perspective is so extraordinary that it is no wonder all the old pictures of *Rishis* and *Mahatmas* show them ceaselessly bowing down to Shiva, prostrating before him. They who do so much for humanity over millions of years are in a state of total awe before the immensity of the boundless mental horizon of Shiva. It is mysterious and magical that something so vast and remote is accessible to each and all, and that it can help to regenerate oneself. To earn this help, one must try to burst the boundaries of one's mental and conceptual maps, transcend the luggage picked up along the way through various religions. In talking of Shiva, one is talking of that before which one has to stand speechless because it is so overwhelming. It is like trying daily to look at the sky in order to see one belt of light through all the myriads of stars, and then to go beyond that to an even deeper darkness. This challenge – open only to the mind which is wakeful, courageous and willing to dare – has to do with the ancient Mysteries, which Newton called a pristine science. One cannot go far in learning without recognizing one's place in relation to those who have gone before, those who stand as Teachers and elder brothers. Ultimately, one cannot do this without earning the privilege of entering through meditation into a state of consciousness wherein one can sit and prostrate before the *Ishtaguru*. Only the *Ishtaguru* can light up those centres in human consciousness where one can experience and at the same time accommodate incredible flashes of recognition, seeing one's connection with every being on earth.

There are initiations upon initiations, and Shiva is portrayed as the Initiator of Initiates. As Dakshinamurti, he is depicted in many temples, especially in South India, as a Sage seated cross-legged. He becomes the Teacher, the Initiator of Initiates; the *yogins* he is teaching are the highest human beings in evolution. Yet so great is their overwhelming love for their fellow beings that they sit together like brothers ready to make a new start. Seated in contemplation, Shiva assumes a very specific posture which represents mental and spiritual heroism. This heroism has nothing to do with external conceptions, but involves going into the most arcane recesses of humanity and plumbing to the depths the secret storehouses of all the human race. An extraordinary form of courage is needed for this. Hence, many are called but few are chosen. And of the few that are chosen, few indeed go all the way to complete enlightenment. This is why, as Buddha taught, there can never be more than one such being active in any system.

Shiva encompasses levels upon levels of consciousness which go far beyond everything one has ever learnt or anything one has ever thought. All this is merely a foot-rule too paltry to measure what is so immense. That is why Mount Kailas is an appropriate symbol of the abode of Shiva. It is not the postal address of the hierophants, but rather a sacred representation on earth, amidst the mightiest mountains and snow-capped peaks, of innumerable secrets and hidden storehouses. Behind the pure virgin white snow, all that is good in humanity is preserved, all that is lofty, all that is elevating, all that comes down to the present from the time man became a thinking being through the lighting up of self-consciousness eighteen and three-quarter million years ago. Every noble thought, everything that is inspirational, altruistic and benevolent is recorded. The beautiful flora and fauna of Mount Kailas are such as one can see nowhere else on earth. They are literally beyond the capacity of biologists to understand or analyse. Mount Kailas is a place where the sheer wealth of Nature's material expression mirrors the inexhaustible potentials of the invisible world. But what are inaccessible potentials in the present age were actualities once, and remain so now for those who know. One day they will again become actualities for the humanities of the future. Within so vast a perspective, it can become as natural as breathing to take one's place in the human family, to do that for which one can respect oneself, without props but with the right reminders. One can face past mistakes and be willing to go into the uttermost contrition. One can also release a resolve, in the name of the Guru, with the Grace of Shiva and all the hierophants of humanity, and so move towards a better position at the moment of death, from which one may return to relieve human misery and ignorance, planting seeds for the enlightenment of future humanity.

Hermes, February 1987
Raghavan Iyer

INDEX

B

C

D

E

F

G

H

I

J

K

L

M

N

O

P

Q

R

S

T

U

V

W

Y

Made in the USA
Middletown, DE
28 July 2018